Emanuel Green

The Survey and Rental

of the chantries, colleges and free chapels, guilds, fraternites, lamps, lights and obits in the county of Somerset as returned in the 2nd year of King Edward VI, A. D.

1548

Emanuel Green

The Survey and Rental
of the chantries, colleges and free chapels, guilds, fraternites, lamps, lights and obits in the county of Somerset as returned in the 2nd year of King Edward VI, A. D. 1548

ISBN/EAN: 9783337251918

Printed in Europe, USA, Canada, Australia, Japan

Cover: Foto ©ninafisch / pixelio.de

More available books at **www.hansebooks.com**

Somerset Record Society.

Vol. II.

THE

SURVEY AND RENTAL

OF THE

Chantries, Colleges and Free Chapels
Guilds, Fraternities, Lamps
Lights and Obits

IN THE

COUNTY OF SOMERSET

AS RETURNED IN THE 2ND YEAR OF KING EDWARD VI.

A.D. 1548.

With an Introduction.

BY

EMANUEL GREEN, F.S.A.,
Member of the Council of the Somerset Record Society.

PRINTED FOR SUBSCRIBERS ONLY.

1888.

HARRISON AND SONS,
PRINTERS IN ORDINARY TO HER MAJESTY,
ST. MARTIN'S LANE, LONDON.

Somerset Record Society.

REPORT.

In presenting our second volume I have again the pleasure of reporting favourably of the prospects of our Society.

Since the appearance of the first list of Subscribers we have lost by death and retirement eleven of our number, but we have gained in their place twenty-two new names, with every probability of further additions.

As to future publications I have to report that Kirkby's Quest for Volume III. is in a forward state, and that materials are practically ready for a second volume on Chantries, and also for one on Parish Accounts of the Pre-Reformation period. Steps are also being taken to produce two Glastonbury Custumals and Rentals of the 13th Century, which, taken in connection with that of A.D. 1189 printed by the Roxburghe Club, and Abbot Bere's of the 15th Century, all of them dealing with the same Manors, will supply an unusually complete and instructive series.

These works are in addition to those spoken of in the first Report.

One change has been made. It was found impossible to produce Volume I. in 1886 and Volume II. in 1887. The birth year of the Society, and of the first subscription, has, therefore been post-dated from 1886 to 1887, so that the year of each subscription and the appearance of the volume which depends upon it may coincide, and thereby confusion be avoided.

I may add that we have still in hand some copies of Volume I.

J. A. BENNETT, *Hon. Sec.*

SOUTH CADBURY RECTORY,
BATH.

SOMERSET RECORD SOCIETY.

Account for the Year 1887.

	£	s.	d.		£	s.	d.
To Donations	100	1	0	Harrison, Printing Vol. I. and Circulars	122	13	6
,, Subscriptions...	138	6	0	Fees to Registry at Wells	3	8	6
				Cyclostyle	1	3	6
				Printing, Stationery, and Postages	7	1	0
				Balance in Bank...	104	0	6
	£238	7	0		£238	7	0
,, Balance brought down	£104	0	6				

Examined and found correct,
EDWIN SLOPER, *Auditor.*

List of Subscribers.

ADLAM, W., The Manor House, Chew Magna.
ANTIQUARIES, THE SOCIETY OF, Burlington House.
ARCHÆOLOGICAL SOCIETY, THE SOMERSET, Taunton.

BAILWARD, H., Horsington, Somerset.
BAKER, E. E., Weston-super-Mare.
BATES, E. H., Newton Surmavill, Yeovil.
BATH, THE LITERARY SOCIETY OF, Bath.
BATTEN, J., Aldon, Yeovil.
BENNETT, F. WENTWORTH, Cadbury House.
BENNETT, G., 2, Whitehall Place, London.
BENNETT, REV. J. A., South Cadbury Rectory, Bath.
BIRKBECK, REV. W. J., The Vicarage, Milborne Port.
BLACKER, REV. BEAVER H., 26, Meridien Place, Clifton.
BODLEIAN LIBRARY, THE, Oxford.
BOND, T. TYNEHAM, Wareham.
BOSTON, THE PUBLIC LIBRARY, Boston, U.S.A.
BOURDILLON, E. D., Poundisford Park, Taunton.
BOUVERIE, P. P., Brymore House, Bridgwater.
BRAIKENRIDGE, W. JERDONE, 16, Royal Crescent, Bath.
BRAMBLE, LIEUT.-COL., Cleeve House, Yatton.
BROADMEAD, W. B., Enmore Park, Bridgwater.
BROWNE, THE VEN. ARCHDEACON, Wells.
BUCKLE, EDMUND, 23, Bedford Row, London.
BULLEID, J. G., Glastonbury.
BURBIDGE, REV. E., Backwell Rectory, Bristol.

CARLINGFORD, RIGHT HON. LORD, The Priory, Chewton Mendip, Bath.
CARTWRIGHT, REV. H. A., Whitestaunton, Chard.
CHURCH, THE VERY REV. R. W., DEAN OF ST. PAUL'S, St. Paul's, London.
CHURCH, REV. CANON C. M., Wells.
CLARK, W. S., Street.
CLOETE, W. D., Churchill Court, Congresbury.
COLEMAN, REV. J., Cheddar.

List of Subscribers.

COLBY, REV. R., Ansford Rectory, Castle Cary.
CORK AND ORRERY, THE RIGHT HON. THE EARL OF, Marston, Frome.
COWIE, THE VERY REV. B. M., DEAN OF EXETER, The Deanery.

DANIEL, REV. W. E., Frome.
DAUBENY, W., Stratton House, Park Lane, Bath.
DICKINSON, F. H., Kingweston, Somerton.
DODINGTON, T. MARRIOTT, Horsington, Somerset.
DUCKWORTH, REV. W. A., Orchardleigh Park, Frome.

ELLIS, REV. J. H. 29, Collingham Gardens, South Kensington.
ELWORTHY, F. T., Foxdown, Wellington.
ESDAILE, REV. W., Sandford Orcas Rectory, Sherborne.

FANE, THE HON. SIR SPENCER PONSONBY, Brympton, Yeovil.
FISHER, E., Abbotsbury, Newton Abbot.
FOXCROFT, E. T. D., Hinton Charterhouse, Bath.
FOXCROFT, Mrs., Hinton Charterhouse, Bath.
FREEMAN, E. A., D.C.L., Somerleaze, Wells.
FRY, THE RIGHT HON. LORD JUSTICE, Failand House, Long Aston, Bristol.

GEE, REV. H., St. John's Hall, Highbury.
GEORGE, W., 3, King's Parade, Clifton.
GIBBS, ANTONY, Charlton, Nailsea.
GREEN, EMANUEL, F.S.A., Devonshire Club, St. James's.
GREENFIELD, B. W., 4, Cranbury Terrace, Southampton.
GRESWELL, REV. W., Stowy Court, Bridgwater.

HALLETT, T. P. G., Claverton Lodge, Bath.
HARRIS, R., Wells.
HARVARD COLLEGE LIBRARY, THE, Cambridge, Mass., U.S.A.
HERVEY, THE RIGHT REV. LORD ARTHUR, Bishop of Bath and Wells, Wells.
HERVEY, REV. SYDENHAM, Wedmore Vicarage, Weston-super-Mare.
HIPPISLEY, W. A. COX, 10, High Cross Street, Leicester.
HOBHOUSE, THE RIGHT REV. BISHOP, Wells.
HOBHOUSE, H., Esq., M.P., Hadspen House, Castle Cary.
HOLMES, REV. T. S., Wookey Vicarage, Wells.
HOOPER, HIS HONOUR JUDGE, Thorne, Yeovil.
HORNER, F., Mells Park, Frome.
HORNER, REV. G., Mells Rectory, Frome.

List of Subscribers.

HUNT, REV. W., 27, Glasbury Road, West Kensington.
HUTCHINGS, HUBERT, Sandford Orcas, Sherborne.

JACKSON, REV. CANON, Leigh Delamere Rectory, Chippenham.
JENKYNS, H., Riverside, East Molesey, Surrey.

KNYFTON, MRS., Uphill, Weston-super-Mare.

LEIR, REV. R. L. M., Charlton, Musgrove, Wincanton.
LEIR, REV. W. MARRIOTT, Ditcheat Rectory, Castle Cary.
LONG, COL. W., Congresbury.
LUTTRELL, G. F., Dunster Castle, Dunster.
LYTE, H. MAXWELL, 3, Portman Square, London.

MANNING, R. G., Wells.
MARTIN, A. TRICE, 10, Upper Belgrave Road, Clifton.
MEDLEY, REV. J. B., Lullington Rectory, Frome.
MELLIAR FOSTER-MELLIAR, W. M., North Aston, Deddington, Oxon.
MILDMAY, REV. A. St. JOHN, Hazelgrove House, Sparkford, Bath.
MITCHEL, F., Chard.
MOGG, W. REES, Cholwell House, Temple Cloud, Bristol.
MOYSEY, H. G., Bathealton Court, Wiveliscombe.
MURCH, JEROME, Cranwells, Bath.

NEAL, W., Kingsdon, Somerton.
NORRIS, H., South Petherton.

PAGET, SIR R., BART., M.P., Cranmore Hall, Shepton Mallet.
PERCEVAL, CECIL H. S. J., Henbury, Bristol.
PHELIPS, W., Montacute House, Ilminster.
PIGOTT, C. SMYTH-, Weston-super-Mare.
PINNEY, COL., Somerton Erleigh.
PLUMPTRE, THE VERY REV. E. H., D.D., DEAN OF WELLS, The Deanery.
POYNTON, REV. F. J., Kelston Rectory, Bath.
PRANKERD, S. D., The Knoll, Sneyd Park, Bristol.

ROGERS, REV. E., Odcombe Rectory, Ilminster.
ROGERS, T. L., Yarlington House, Wincanton.

SCARTH, REV. H. M., Wrington Rectory, Bristol.
SINGER, J. W., Frome.

v.

List of Subscribers.

SKRINE, H. D., Claverton Manor, Bath.
SLOPER, E., Taunton.
SOMERVILLE, A. F., Dinder, Wells.
STEPHENSON, REV. J. H., Lympsham Rectory, Taunton.
STRACHEY, SIR E., BART., Sutton Court, Pensford, Bristol.

THOMPSON, REV. ARCHER, Milton, Wells.
THRING, REV. E., Uppingham. (The late.)
THRING, REV. G., Hornblotton Rectory, Castle Cary.
TITE, C., Shutes House, Wellington.
TREVILIAN, E. B. CELY, Midelney Place, Curry Rivel, Taunton.
TYNDALE, J. W. WARRE, Evercreech, Bath.
TYNTE, COL. KEMYS, Cefn Mably, Cardiff.

UNIVERSITY LIBRARY, THE, Cambridge.

WALTERS, G., Somerleaze, Frome.
WARRE, REV. E. D. D., Eton College, Eton.
WAYTE, REV. S., Southampton Villa, Gordon Road, Clifton.
WEAVER, REV. F. W., Milton Vicarage, Evercreech.
WINTERBOTHAM, W. L., Bridgwater.
WINWOOD, REV. H. H., 11, Cavendish Crescent, Bath.
WORDSWORTH, THE RIGHT REV. J., LORD BISHOP OF SALISBURY, The Palace, Salisbury.

YOUNG, REV. E. M., The School House, Sherborne.

Preface.

OF the two documents now printed, the first—the Survey—may be known to those who have had occasion to work among such records. It is given here as a transcript with all abbreviations, a plan considered the best in such cases, as no question can arise as to any changes or alterations or omissions. Being in English the abbreviations can easily be read, but the following explanations will perhaps be an assistance to some. A straight line, —, above a letter means that one letter immediately following has been omitted. A curved line, ⌒, above means that more than one letter has been omitted. A line through p means per or par. A curved line through p means pre or pro; and a comma or special mark, ⁹, between letters in a word means, er, omitted. The termination, ẹ, means es.

The second document—the Rental—the original being in Latin, is entirely unknown, and now appears for the first time. Often mentioned in the Survey its discovery was most fortunate, and we may be especially pleased, as although similar returns must have been made for other counties, this one for Somerset seems to be the only one extant. It is with fair certainty unique; and now by publication safe from accidental destruction.

The question of the purchasing power of money at different times is always a difficult one. Here, as a guide, a difference of twenty times is given: thus a cow, valued in the Survey at ten shillings, or fourteen shillings of the then currency, was in price equal to ten pounds or fourteen pounds in our money of to-day. Some would

Preface.

perhaps think this rather low for the reign of Henry VIII, although good for the time of Elizabeth. The money, it will be noticed, is usually carried out in shillings; sometimes only, to pounds. The pound here, as a coin, had no existence, it was merely an expression on paper meaning a pound of silver. The silver penny of 240 to the lb. was the actual silver legal basis, the shilling being thus only a token. But curiously it may also be noticed the amounts are usually based on the value of thirteen-and-fourpence, or its sub-divisions, six-and-eightpence and three-and-fourpence. This thirteen-and-fourpence was the marc, yet again there was no such coin as this marc, it too was only a paper expression. The sovereign—sufferen as the patent calls it—was first made in the reign of Henry VII, only just before the time of Henry VIII, and so was hardly in use at the time of our valuation. Coined to represent twenty of the then shillings, it now represents twenty of ours, and has become not only the pound of account, but being the gold legal basis, all other coins are only tokens. Its sub-divisions also have ousted the older ones above named, except in some cases where they are still retained for certain fees.

.The Surveys being completed, the next proceeding was the Sale and dispersion of the various properties noted in the Rental, as found recorded in another set of documents known as the "Particulars for Grants." These, with the Foundation Deeds and other annotations, will well make another volume.

Introduction.

AFTER the dissolution of the Monasteries and other larger religious houses and the settlement of the old question of the Supremacy, other questions, also not new, relating to ritual and doctrine, quickly came to the front. As a consequence it was soon foreseen and understood that reform would reach all places however small wherein the old ritual had been used, or where mass had been said. The first public intimation may be discovered in an Act of 1529 (21 Henry VIII,) by which new religious foundations were forbidden, and all gifts to spiritual persons either for their own use, or for life, or for term of years, were declared utterly void. Further, no spiritual person either secular or regular, from the Feast of St. Michael then coming, was to take any particular stipend or salary to sing for any soul; nor take to his use any parsonage or vicarage in farm the lease or grant of any person, upon pain to forfeit forty shillings for every week so doing and to lose ten times the value of any profit received.

Five years later (26 Henry VIII), as "devysed by the advyse of the Counsayle," a survey was made of the true and just yearly value of the ecclesiastical possessions, more particularly, however, of the Cathedrals and parochial churches, and this, as embodied in the return of 27 Henry VIII, is known to us as the *Valor Ecclesiasticus*. The incumbents or patrons of the smaller foundations, foreseeing their impending doom, now began either to sell their lands, or by granting leases to raise fines which they could appropriate, leaving the future to take care of itself.

Introduction.

As the Chantries then were not wholly included, and other like foundations were altogether omitted in the first survey, another Act was passed in November, 1545 (37 Henry VIII), for their especial settlement and to stop the alienations.

The Act sets out that, from time to time there have been divers Colleges, Chantries, and Free Chapels established or founded, some of them by license, some by endowments and wills, and some by other devices. "Sithens which tyme many of the Donors or Founders, and divers others of their avarouse and covetouse myndes and without license have of late entred into the houses and landes, &c., of the same and have expulsed the Prestes, Wardeyns or Incumbentes, and they their heires or assignes doe occupye and enjoye the saide houses and profittes. And some of the Prestes and Wardeyns by covyn betweene them and the Patrons, Donors or Founders, have without license soulde all or part of the landes and belongings. And some of the Prestes and Wardeyns, by assent of the Patrons, and some without such assent, have of late made leases for term of lief or lyffes or yeres, and have not reserved the accustomable rent. And some by covyne have suffered recoveries, levyed fynes, and made other conveyaunces of all or parte of their said possessions, by which some have been clerely dissolved, extincted or determyned, contrary to the wills or intents of the Founders, to the great contempte of the King's auctoritie roiall." It was enacted therefore that all covenants for sale should be void and frustrate, and that all purchase money should be repaid. Finally—and this perhaps was the main intention of the Act—it was decided that as many such chapels were not ruled, nor the profits employed to the intent of the Founders, to reduce and bring them to a decent order the whole of them should be vested in the King.

It will be seen here that the priests or incumbents must have been now very isolated or unsupported, as the high-handed proceeding of a forcible ejectment could be successfully made.

Following this a Commission was issued. (*Pat: 37 Hen. VIII, pt.*

Introduction.

10, m. (1) 36 dors.). This, after reciting the above Act, declared it advisable before proceeding with the same, "to have a true and certain certificate made as well of the nombre and names of the said Chauntries and Colleges, &c., as of the qualities, use, abuses, condicons and necessyties concernyng theym." The Commissioners were consequently instructed to examine, search, and enquire what and how many Chantries or Stipendiaries there were, to what purpose they were founded and how and in what manner the revenues or profits were used. Also how far distant any chapel was from the parish church, that it may be determined whether it should stand and remain or be dissolved or reformed. They were also to repair to the houses of the Chantries and find how many since the 4th February, 1536—xxvij of our reign—had been dissolved or by any other means alienated without license. And to "the intent that the plate, yewelles, ornamentes, goodes and chatalles of the said Chauntries, &c., shall not be wasted or otherwyse imbeslyd, but that the same shall remayne to such godly intentes and purposes as we shall hereafter appoynte, Our Wyll and Pleasure is that you shall make seuerall inventories of the same indented between you and the Masters or Incumbentes of the said Chauntries, &c., and thereupon give charge and commaundment in our name that the same be kept and preserved untyl our further pleasure be knowen." One certificate was to be sent to the Court of Augmentation of Crown Revenue,—a Court established to receive and account for the large additional income arising from these proceedings,—there to remain on record. The Commissioners appointed jointly for Somerset and Dorset were:—William, Bishop of Bath; Paul, Bishop of Bristol; Sir Giles Strangewaye, Knt.; Sir John Horsey, Knt.; Thomas Denam, Esquire; Robert Carye, Gent.; and Roger Kentsey, Gent.

Having gone so far, matters were interfered with and stopped for a time by the death of the King. No action was taken under this Commission.

In the first year of Edward VI, 1547, the Parliament passed another

Introduction.

Act, by which again all Chantries and Colleges, &c., were, as before, given to the Crown. The new Act curiously does not mention property as in any way its basis, as in that of Henry VIII, but makes its base the question rather of doctrine, thus well marking the advance in reform, and reflecting the current opinions. "Consydering," says the Act, "that a greate parte of superstition and errors in Christian Religion hath byn brought into the myndes and estimacon by reasone of the ignoraunce of their verie trewe and perfecte salvacon throughe the deathe of Jesus Christ, and by devising and phantasinge vayne opynions of Purgatorye and Masses satisfactorye to be done for them which be departed, the which doctryne and vayn opynion by nothing more is mayntayned and upholden then by the abuse of Trentalles, Chauntries and other provisions made for the contynuance of the saide blyndness and ignourance; and further considering and understanding that the alteracon, chaunge, and amendement of the same and converting to good and godlie uses, as in erecting of Gramar Scoles to the educacon of youthe in vertewe and godlinesse, the further augmenting of the Universities and better provision for the poore and nedye, can not ne ought to anny other manner parsone be comited then to the King's Highness: It is now ordeyned and enacted that all manner of Colleges, Free Chappelles and Chauntries, having being within five yeres next before the firste day of this present parliament (*i.e.*, 4 Nov., 1547) which were not in actuall and reall possession of the late King, &c., shall, imediately after the feast of Easter next cominge be adjudged and deemed and allso be in the verie actuall and reall possession and seasone (seisin) of the King our Soveraigne Lord and his heirs and successors." Other clauses gave to the King all lands, rents, &c., appointed to be employed wholly to the finding or maintenance of any Obit or Anniversary or other like purpose; or of any Light or Lamp in any church or chapel to have continuance for ever which had been kept or maintained within five years before; and all lands given to any such use for a specified term only were to go to the King for the remainder of such term. It was also enacted that

Introduction.

from the same date all Brotherhoods, Fraternities and Guilds, and all lands belonging to them, and all goods, plate and moveables belonging, "abused of auny of the said coporacons in the abuses aforesaide" should also be vested in the Crown, and power was given to the King at any time to alter the nature or condition of any such Obits, &c., not suppressed, "ne adnichilate," by this Act and to dispose of the same to better uses, such as the relief of poor students in the Universities or otherwise. Any person who had sold away any lands which should have been vested in the Crown under this Act was to repay the purchase money.

Next a Survey was ordered—for the purpose of enquiring into the revenues of such Chantries and Chapels ; to assign lands applicable to Grammar Schools ; to endow vicars ; to assign maintenance for an additional priest in such great towns or parishes where such should be thought necessary ; to assign pensions to priests or poor persons dependent on these dissolved Colleges, &c., such pension not to exceed one annual income ; to enquire as to allowances to the poor and make arrangements for payment thereof; and finally, where necessary, to apply rents towards the maintenance of banks and sea-walls. Certificate was to be made of what was done, to be returned within a year. A Royal Commission duly followed on the 13th February, 1548. (*Pat:* 2 *Ed. VI, pt.* 7, *m.* 32 (13) *dors.*). After setting out the Act, and "myndyng truly, playnly, and certeynly to be enformed of all thynges gevyn vnto us by the saide Acte," Commissioners were appointed, with authority—or any two of them—" to enquyre, survey, and examyn as well by the othes of such persons as you shall thynke convenyent or otherwyse by your wysdomes and discretions what Colleges, Chauntries, Freechappels, Brotherheddes, Fraternities, and Guyldes, Manours, landes, tenementes, hereditamentes and other thynges, ought to come to us by vertue of the saide Acte, and also the foundations, usages, contynuances, vses, qualities, values, condicons, and state, in euery degre of the same and euery of them." All Mayors, Bailiffs, Constables, and other Officers and subjects were

Introduction.

to aid and assist in the execution of the enquiries as the case should require: and finally, of their "doynges and procedynges" the Commissioners, or any two of them, were to certify before the last day of May.

The Commissioners for Somerset and Dorset were:—Thomas Speke, Hugh Poulett, John Rogers, John Seyntlow, and Thomas Dyer, knights; William Moryce, George Lyne, Robert Keylway, and Robert Metcalff, esquires; John Hannan and William Hartegyll, gentlemen. It was through these Commissioners that the Survey and Rental were made and the Certificates of value returned as now herewith printed.

Before proceeding to specially examine these documents, perhaps some notes objective and explanatory may be desirable.

Chantries.

A CHANTRY chapel was usually situate either within a church or in some small, specially built, projecting addition to the building, generally over the vault or near the tomb of the endowing Family; sometimes it was in the churchyard, probably over a burying place of the Founder; sometimes it was at some distance from the church. Chantries were of two kinds, endowed and unendowed, and were established for the maintenance of one or more priests to say a daily mass for the good estate of the founder during life and for the benefit of his soul after death. For the Endowed or Foundation Chantry when endowed with lands, the Crown license was necessary under the Statute of Mortmain, 7 Ed. I; consequently the date of such Foundation can be generally traced. The Chaplain was duly presented by the patron as to an advowson and thus came under the jurisdiction of the Bishop.

The unendowed Chantry was either established for a term of years or existed upon uncertain offerings, these diminishing as the family grief softened until the Chantry disappeared. The priest, called or known as a stipendiary, being nominated by the patron, could be

Introduction.

removed by him; thus the position was lower than in the beneficed or endowed Chantry. Another form of endowment was to pay down a sum of money to a large religious house or monastery, when a deed was exchanged by which a promise was given to celebrate daily or otherwise either for ever or for a fixed term.

Curiously the advowson of a Chantry could be sold, thus a stranger to the family would appoint the priest who would specially represent his patron, the original founder perhaps being forgotten (*Archæologia*, *V*, 38).

Colleges.

COLLEGES originated as large Foundation Chantries, the endowment being sufficient for usually three or more secular priests who resided together, one being chosen chief, alternately officiating for the benefit of the founder, and perhaps adding other duties such as education or assisting in the mother church. Colleges sometimes became Corporations having a common seal as in the case of North Cadbury, where can be detected the beginning of what might have been a much larger institution. The chance, however, seems to have slipped away before the time of the Survey.

Free Chapels.

FREE CHAPELS were as a rule presumably at some time part of a royal demesne, and thus at first were the King's private property, but being built at some distance from the parish church they came into use for the purpose of easing the dwellers near them from a difficult journey. They have been defined as Free, because—unlike the attached Chantry Chapel—they were entirely detached and free from any other structure, but this was not so. They were free as being exempt from all episcopal jurisdiction, the incumbent being appointed by the patron as if he were a private chaplain, the bishop having no power to refuse institution. Nevertheless by some means, in some cases the incumbents became subject to the bishop, and

Introduction.

consequently the exact position of any particular chapel can only be learned from its own special history. They had often the right of burial. The Act of Edward VI provided that nothing therein should extend to any such chapel, nor to any chapel having no more lands than the chapel yard or a little house attached. The first clause refers rather to those larger structures, which built in all respects as churches, were later converted to parochial use, as we see them to-day. The second clause should have saved some small buildings placed in difficult districts or amidst a scattered population. A near case of destruction may be noted under Huish and Langport, where the Surveyor recommends that one of these churches could well be spared and taken down, as they stand within a bird bolt of each other.

Obits.

OBITS were kept yearly to commemorate the death of the Founder, when the office for the dead was performed, alms distributed, and other services held for the soul of the departed. As being rather of a private character the service was usually at a side altar, the cantarist being served by one boy only. An Obit service was held according to the foundation either for a term or for ever, or by request of executors or others of the family for as long as their special payment continued. Monasteries obtained many grants and bequests for the purpose of inscribing the names of the givers on their roll to be thus prayed for annually. Purchase of this privilege was often made during life, when a formal deed or undertaking was exchanged, of which the following may be accepted as the usual form :—To all the childer of our Moder hooly church these present letters indentyd hereafter to see or here . . . Prior, &c., of the House of the Order of . . . sends gretyng and continuacion and augmentacion of hevynly grace. Know your universite, that what grete benyfices and manyfold Almus the which . . . of his grete liberalitie hath hider towarde geven unto us; We, willing and coveting to recompense the said benyfices temporall, as much as in us is with

Introduction.

spirituall gifts as we are bounden, of oon and full consent of all of us and with lisense and consent of our Provincial, newly promysse and upon our good faithe by this writing we graunte for us and our successours for evermore to the said . . . that after the said . . . departe out of this miserable worlde unto the mercy of God, We shall make his Obett at the daie of his decesse to be write in our mortilage and of our convent every Sonday thrugh the yere for ever more to be openly pronounced, folowing after the pronunciacion of the Salme *De Profundis*, with this Colett *Deus Venie largitor*, &c. We shall also make the same Day of his decesse yerely his Obett in our Church, with solempne *Dirige* of our Breder for evermore to be doon; and in the morrow then following with Messe of *Requiem*. Also we bynde us to sing a Trentall of messes yerely by such dayes immediately folowing the said Obett as it may be conveniently doon for ever more. Admittyng the said . . . now as thenne and for evermore to be full and special partaker of all messes, prayers, fastyngs, devocions, and of all other Spiritual suffrages for evermore within our House, God disposing to be doon, &c.

Anniversaries.

ANNIVERSARIES, sometimes called Year Days, were, like Obits yearly commemorations of the death of the Founder but apparently on a larger scale, the payment being heavier, the alms much more liberal, and the assembly consequently much larger. The service might be held at the high altar, if with *Requiem* and *Dirige* the former was sung in the forenoon, the latter in the afternoon. Sometimes as with Obits the legacy was for a limited term, or one or more years.

Trentalls.

TRENTALLS were thirty masses for the dead said daily on thirty consecutive days.

All these endowments for prayers may be considered to include always besides the Founder, his other special friends or near relations alive and dead, and "all the faithful deceased."

Introduction.

Guilds.

GUILDS or Gilds were associations or Fraternities wherein every member paid towards the general charges. Some were religious, others not so; some admitted women, others men only. Their intention was to promote goodwill, and assist the sick much or exactly as do their successors, our village clubs of to-day. Above all other duties they secured masses and prayers for the souls of their Brethren after death, and especially too the attendance of the Members at any funeral, by which means their prayers were then obtained. Except for such a form of combination the poorer class must have gone without any expiatory service; with others who could pay, this difficulty could not exist, and with the wealthy matters were entirely the other way, as it is on record that one founder had seven or eight priests singing in different chapels perpetually for him.

Lights.

LIGHTS were placed before images in the supposition that the saint represented would be pleased with the attention, and so would use his or her intercession for the benefit of the giver.

Lamps.

LAMPS perhaps were rather more important than Lights, and were placed before a principal image or in the chancel. Fortunately the record at Ilminster explains exactly the intention of a Lamp in the chancel there, as burning to the honour and glory of Almighty God and the holy body of Christ.

Of the cows, cattle and sheep given for these Lights there is no further record. They were probably secured by the parochial Vestries. The small rentals were demanded by the collectors at their first audit, and were in some cases paid, as duly entered in the "Minister's Accounts." In some instances the Churchwardens either refused payment or evaded it on some pretence, and in others

Introduction.

these charges were claimed as having passed with the purchase of the land. Where not otherwise accounted for they presumably were allowed to lapse, and so disappeared.

Oratories.

ORATORIES were either chambers within a house licensed for a term in cases of sickness or of age, or small domestic chapels attached to the manor Court when this was distant from the parish church. They were to be used only by the family or the household, it being always carefully provided, as in the case of all Chantries or Free Chapels, that nothing should be done therein to the detriment or loss of the rector or vicar and that at Easter and other great Festivals the parish church should be attended and all dues paid. In 1327 Baldwin Malet, Knt., and his wife were granted the privilege of an Oratory "anywhere" in the diocese until the Feast of St. John Baptist. In such a case the super altar, which was always duly consecrated, was a small stone of portable size and so easily carried from place to place. No priest could officiate without this consecrated stone. An instance of disobedience is met with in 1317, when the rector of Weston in Gordano was excommunicated for so doing (*Drokensford's Register* (Hobhouse), *p.* 128).

As these Oratories had no endowments they are not noticed in the Survey, save an occasional exception where the domestic Chapel had become of more importance than usual.

The Survey.

Glancing now at the Survey for a short analysis, it will be seen that the Rental differs from it somewhat, as the latter notices only land endowments, not gifts in money, cattle, or rent charges, consequently the two together are necessary to show the whole. Even then there were other Foundations omitted by both, these remaining yet to be noticed. The omissions arose from the

Introduction.

properties belonging being concealed from the Surveyors with the intent of being privately appropriated.

During the passing of the before noticed changes, Acts, and Orders, the condition of the Chantries seems to have fallen very low; "slackly" attended, they had been clearly much neglected. Several are found returned as void of incumbent, and others on the recent death of the incumbent remained void. Taking a few others as examples:—

Aileston Sutton.—Chapel was utterly decayed.
Aller.—The money for wax had been withheld three years.
Ashbrittle.—The rent was withheld.
Ashton, Long—in Merriattes Chapel.—From a rental of £4 18s. per annum, twelve pence weekly only was given to the Vicar.
Babcary.—Fodington Chapel had fallen down, clearly decayed.
Batheaston.—The Hermitage Chapel had been occupied for seven years without payment.
Cadbury, North.—The rental retained for seven years.
Charlton Adam.—No mass there for twenty or thirty years. The incumbent however received his salary.
Congresbury.—St. Michael's Chapel in the churchyard was in decay, and used for storing lime and other things. The parishioners offered to buy it.
Hydall in Clevedon.—No incumbent since 26 Henry VIII.
Langford.—No light for ten years.
Longlode.—Stipend withdrawn for seven years.
Milverton.—The inhabitants offered to buy the chapel to use the lead for water pipes.
Pennard, East.—Three years before the Survey the chapel premises were entered and the priest dispossessed.
Poulet.—Money withheld for four years.
Petherton, North.—Rental withheld two years.
Wiveliscombe.—Rent withheld for three years. The chapel used as a store. No mass for eight years.

Introduction.

Wraxall.—The Chantry rent due from the parsonage had been withheld six or seven years.

Winford.—The chapel had been bought by the parishioners nine years before.

Yatton.—The parishioners wished to buy the Old Chapel to make a sluice against the rage of the sea.

Notwithstanding the order against new endowments, bequests for a Stipendiary were made at Bageworth and Wedmore so late as 1 Edward VI, so that on the appearance of the Surveyors only three-quarters of the first year had been received ; the balance was scored down as due to the general account.

The only recorded case of contumacy is at Bath, where the Master of St. John's Hospital would not appear.

The Rental.

The Rental speaks for itself, and is of interest as showing the prices then obtained. That the monastic houses had gathered large manorial estates and lands in almost every parish is well known, although their value and extent are barely realised ; this Return now shows further, for the first time, how firm and deep the grasp was on every class of property.

Plate.

Taking next the plate ; thirty-eight Chantries are returned as having none. In some of these cases there may never have been any, the church chalice, &c., serving the purpose ; and sometimes one set served for more than one endowment. The three Chantries in Frome had but one chalice to all the three, and this one the precentors said was stolen. This is the only record of implied dishonesty. In some cases the patron claimed and kept these things as private property.

Against the thirty-eight vacancies, some being easily accounted for, there are a hundred and eighteen returned with chalices

Introduction.

complete. What became of these is not exactly known, but having been once entered as part of the properties, it must be assumed they were gathered in and sent to London, to disappear in augmentation of the revenue. Unfortunately there seems to be no return extant of the "silver delivered in" from Somerset. The weights were evidently carefully taken, the chalice in Bishop Bubwith's Chantry being entered at $12\frac{1}{4}$ oz. and $\frac{1}{2}$ a quarter, or $12\frac{3}{8}$ oz. The lightest was 5 oz. at North Curry, the heaviest one of the two at Croscombe, 26 oz. all gilt. Mark came near this with one of 23 oz. Martock was content with one of tin; the only example. In Taunton chalices were numerous, four of the Chantries having two each, and the other six having one each. Ilminster takes the lead in value, having three chalices, weight not given ; a silver gilt cross of 120 oz.; a ship with two stones of crystal ; and two cruets and two candlesticks parcel gilt, 89 oz. At Nyned Flory both plate and ornaments were given as a foundation for prayers.

Ornaments.

The ornaments, not generally of much value, were either sold or disappeared locally.

What was included in this term may be seen under Ilminster and Moorlinch and from the following sale, the only one recorded :—

" Parcell of thornamentes belonging to the late colleges and chauntrys, free chapelles, &c., within the Countie of Somerset, viz. :— Five vestmentes of crymson vellat priced and estemed at v*s.* le pece are worth one with another — xxv*s.*

" Fowre deacons and sub-deacons of the same color presed at v*s.* le pece — xx*s.*

" Seven vestmentes of blew and purple veluct preised at iiij*s.* viij*d.* le pece — xxxij*s.* viij*d.*

"One olde cope of clothe of gold flowred with blew veluct — xiij*s.* iiij*d.*

" One cope of crimson vellat with flowers of gold — x*s.*

xvi

Introduction.

"Two other copes, one of blew veluet another of murrey veluet preised at vjs. viijd. le pece — xiijs. iiijd.
Total — cxiiijs. iiijd.

On the 16th February, 3 Ed. VI, these were sold to Robert Freeke, servant of Robert Keilway, Esq., for the sum of cxvs., "to be paid all in hand" (*Chapter House Books*, A $\frac{6}{12}$, *p*. 102).

Lead and Bells.

The lead and bell metal, weighing together 3,647 lbs., were sold 16 March, 3 Ed. VI, to Lawrence Hide, servant to Sir John Thynne, for the sum of £128 10s. (*Chapter House Books*, A $\frac{6}{12}$, *fol*. 162e).

The Chaplains.

The Chaplains were clearly not of the highest merit, yet the general description "of honest conversation but indifferently learned" has a satisfactory sound, reads as being quite genuine, and fairly meets the case. There are two examples of a custom of the time, when at Yatton the incumbent of Clareham is returned as a scholar eighteen years of age; and again at Portbury where the incumbent was a scholar at Oxford. Three—Blackford, Bedminster, and Frome—are returned as gentlemen.

Taking Taunton as being the largest town, its ten Chantries had ten chaplains, the largest income being from St. Nicholas with £16 8s. 4d. No exactness can be absolutely attained, but this sum may for general guidance be said to have been equal to twenty times that amount now, or £320. The total of the ten Chantries—£83 13s. 4d.—would thus be now, say £1,673, this being produced from a hundred and fifty-four small holdings in the best and most frequented parts of the town.

Communicants.

In some places the number of the Communicants—Partakers of the Lord's Supper—is given. In Taunton the number was three

Introduction.

thousand: that is, there were three thousand persons young and old qualified to communicate. Modern surroundings and modern ideas must be forgotten here and it must be remembered, that at this time, as for long afterwards, the old notion of a religious uniformity was retained as a leading imperative idea. There was no option on such a question; no liberty of opinion was allowed; there was no other church or resource for the purpose. These Communicants then were all the inhabitants of all classes above say fourteen years old. Of these three thousand, one-third would be the young and adult, leaving two thousand parents; or one thousand as the entire number of householders. Although not quite pertinent, to make all clearer it may be added that for the purpose of a full census, besides the one child or adult as above over fourteen, there would be on an average to each couple of parents two other children under that age, thus making the population of the parishes of St. Mary and St. James five thousand all told. A large proportion of these would be, as always, of the labouring class or the poorer class below it; the tradesmen too would be but small, not in any way wealthy. Remembering then their surroundings, their very small requirements, their free rental, fixed incomes, and entire absence of anxiety, the position of the Chaplains must have been a very comfortable one. It may be noted that the Communicants are now " Partakers of the Lord's Supper," the mass had ceased, the new order just commenced.

With this change another custom specially connected with the present subject also disappeared. A letter from the Royal Commissioners, now in the Wells MSS., addressed to the Chapter and all Churchwardens, requested them "to abstain from such unmeasurable ringing for ded persons at theire buriall and at the Feast of All Soules. And that from hencefurthe they use to ringe oon bell at such tyme as sicke persones lyeth in extreme daunger of death that they which be haile may be put in remembraunce of theire owne mortalitie and also excited to praie unto God for soche their sicke neighbours, that they may pacientlie suffre death if God send it and the hard

Introduction.

panges thereof for Christes love, who suffred much more for them, and that they may so departe out of this life in true faithe, hope, and charitie, as their sowles may be afterward receaved unto eternale felicitie to raigne with Christ everlastinglie in the Kingdom of Heaven. And when the corps of any such dead person shall be brought to the Church to be buried then to ring also moderatlie in the time of the obsequies thereof and no longer."

At Michaelmas when the Collectors came for the rentals, they found that all had been duly paid on the one side, and received by the other up to Easter, consequently all dues up to that time were "Forgiven." Thus at Easter, 1548, the Chaplains quietly glided out and these Chantries as quietly expired.

Pensions.

The Chaplains received pensions varying in amount according to the original stipend, occasionally almost equalling but never exceeding it. The following list gives the names of the pensioners and the amounts of their pensions, the authorities being Cardinal Pole's Pension Book (*Excheq: Q.R., Miscellaneous Books, No. 32*) and Willis, " History of Abbies " (*V. vij*, 201–203).

			£	s.	d.
Aller	St. Mary's	John Chynne ...	5	0	0
Ailston Sutton	Chantry ...	John Moore ...	1	0	0
Ashton, Long	Chantry ...	Henry Rowe ...	6	0	0
Banwell	Fraternity	John Lloyd ...	3	6	8
Blackford	Free Chapel	John Clerke ...	5	0	0
Bradford	Chantry ...	John Hussey ...	5	0	0
Bridgwater ...	St. George's	John Saunders	5	0	0
—	St. Mary's	John Toller ...	5	0	0
—	Trinity ...	John Juger ...	5	0	0
Cadbury, North	—	Thos. Crybbe ...	3	5	0
—	—	John Teme ...	1	6	0
Cannington...	*see* Ichstoke.				

Introduction.

			£	s.	d.
Catcote	Chantry	Richd. Hodson	3	12	0
Chard	Guild	Wm. Pears	5	0	0
Charlton Makerell...	Chantry	John Drewe	1	4	0
Cheddar	Trinity	John Mattock	4	13	4
Cheriton, South	Free Chapel	Roger Boddell	1	13	4
Coker, East	Chantry	Wm. Slade	5	0	0
Combeflory	Chantry	Robt. Bryce	5	0	0
Compton Pauncfoot	Chantry	Robt. Spyce	3	4	4
Croscombe	Fraternity	Richard Ilonde	5	0	0
—	Horrington Chapel				
Crukerne	Chantry	John Godge	4	3	4
Curry, North	Chantry	John Cribbe	3	5	1
—		John Gent	1	6	0
Dunster	—	Peter Johns	3	6	8
Frome	St. Nicholas	John Lyrpole	5	0	0
—	St. John and St. Andrew	John Burley	5	0	0
—	St. Katherine's	John Frye	5	0	0
Horrington, East	see Croscombe.				
Horsington	see Cheriton, South.				
Ichstoke	Free Chapel	Thos. Shakeley	5	0	0
Ilchester	Trinity	Geo. Carewe	6	13	4
Ilminster	St. Mary's	John Batten	5	0	0
—	St. Mary's	John Poole	5	0	0
—	St. Katherine's	Thos. Mychell	5	0	0
—	Holy Cross	Robt. Olyver	5	0	0
—	St. John Baptist	Math. Broke	4	5	6
Knolle	Free Chapel	John Bradley	3	0	8
Lymington	Chantry	Thos. Raplyn	3	12	0
Monkton, West	Service	Wm. Culverwell	2	8	8
—	—	Wm. Callowe	3	6	8
Moorlinch	see Catcote.				

Introduction.

			£	s.	d.
Nettlecombe	St. John's	John Wetheridge	6	0	0
Newton Placey	Chantry	John Anderson	5	0	0
Norton Hawtfield	Free Chapel	Thos. Ellys	1	6	8
Nunney	Chantry	Robt. Laurence	5	0	0
Petherton, North	Sherston Chapel	John Saunders	3	3	6
—	St. Mary's	Richd. Weaver	5	0	0
Petherton, South	Chantry	Wm. Dyer	5	0	0
Portbury	Free Chapel	Wm. Powell	2	13	4
Shepton Mallet	Church	Wm. Horne	4	0	0
—	—	John Baylie	4	13	4
—	Guild	Robt. Hyll	4	0	0
Sherston	*see* N. Petherton.				
Speckington	Free Chapel	Wm. Hodges	1	18	4
Stavordale	Chantry	Robt. Gane	5	0	0
Taunton	St. Andrew	Hy. Bull	5	0	0
—	Trinity	Robt. Wilkyns	5	0	0
—	St. Etheldred	Wm. Callowe	5	0	0
—	St. Nicholas	John Seyman	4	16	0
—	St. Mary	John Pytte	4	0	0
—	Fraternity	Wm. Trowbridge	4	0	0
—	Swinge's	Alex. Maggott	3	14	4
Trent	Chantry	John Shete	6	0	0
Wedmore	Stipendiary	Robt. Moryce	4	0	0
—	Chantry	John Partridge	4	0	0
Wellington	Service	John Spycer	3	7	5
Wells	St. Cuthberts	John Tanner	3	0	0
—	Hospital	John Dyble	3	6	8
—	La Mountroy	Robt. Derraunt	3	12	8
—	—	John Eringtonne	3	12	8
—	—	John Broke	3	12	8
—	—	Henry Bankes	3	12	8
—	—	Thos. Clerke	3	12	8

Introduction.

			£	s.	d.
Wells	La Mountroy	Robt. Spryte	3	12	8
—	—	John Dible	4	4	8
—	—	Walter Sheppcrde	5	0	0
—	—	John Paule	5	0	0
—	—	William Burgh	5	0	0
—	—	John Shepperde	5	0	0
—	—	John Newes	5	0	0
—	—	Giles Buttal	5	0	0
—	—	Morgan Conye	5	0	0
—	—	Richard Castlyn	5	0	0
Wollavington	St. Katherine's	Robt. Prydell	5	0	0
—	Trinity	Roger Wynbery	5	0	0
Wykeperham	Chantry	John Saunders	3	0	0
Wynscombe	Fraternity	Thos. Suarpone	4	0	0
Yatton	Clarcham	Simon Porter	2	4	4
Yeovil	Trinity	Henry Larbecke	6	13	4
—	—	John Whitewell	6	13	4
—	Holy Cross	Wm. Trevylyan	6	0	0

There appears also in Pole's List William Baylie with a pension of £4 13s. 4d. but without a local habitation. This must be John Baylie, found in Willis's List serving in Shepton Mallet church, who is not otherwise noticed. Of the Chaplains residing in La Mountroy John Dible, as Chaplain to the Hospital and to Martyn's Chantry, seems to have secured a double pension. This return certainly shows a liberal intention, the amounts being high, and even the incumbents at Yatton and Portbury, one a scholar aged 18, the other a scholar at Oxford, receiving their share. Some errors occur in the list. Thus the names Spyce and Bryce are misplaced, Spyce belonging to Combflory, the other to Compton Pauncefoot. Mathew Broke here under Ilminster, should be at South Petherton, and Wm.

Introduction.

Culverwell belongs to West Buckland, not West Monkton. The Incumbents at North Cadbury and Dunster are not named in the Survey. After the pension was granted it appeared that Richard Ilonde was not the right man for East Horrington, and from M'mas 4 Ed. VI, John More was substituted. The document says:—"Memorand: One Richard Eyland was first certefied to be Incumbent there, whereuppon a pencion of *cs.* yerelie was to hym graunted. Butt forasmuche as uppon further examinacon it is proved not to be so, and that the abovenamed John More is trewe Incumbent of the said chapell of Est Horrington, as by a commission certefied into the courte M'mas Term 3 Ed. VI, it may appear, the letters patent made to the said Richard Eyland is surrendered and delyvered into the Courte of Augmentacons. Therefore made a patent for the said John More accordingly." The patent is then set out, dated in February, 5 Ed. VI. (*Miscellaneous Books, Augment. Office, Vol.* 247, *fol.* 6).

Cardinal Pole's List was not made until 1553, so that death may account for some names omitted, as the interval of time may be allowed to account for the other trifling errors.

The Survey

OF THE

COLLEGES, CHANTRIES, FREE CHAPELS, &c.

IN THE

County of Somerset,

AS RETURNED IN THE SECOND YEAR OF KING EDWARD VI.

[*Chantry Certificates (Augmentation Office), No. 42.*]

Decanatus de Crukerne.

1. Ilmynster.

The Chauntrie of Saincte Katerine w'tin the parysshe Churche ther founded by John Wadham, esquier.

Landes tent͠e rent͠e possessions and hereditament͠e in the tenure of sondery p͠sones as more at large pticulerly may appere by the Rentall of the same . . . . xli. iiijs.   **Is yerely worth in**

Whereof in

Rent͠e resolute paid yerely to sondery p͠sones . . . . ixs.

And so

Remainethe clere . . . . ix.'i. xvs.

A Chalice of Silu͠ — xvj oz.   **Plate and ornament͠e.**

Ornament͠e presentyd ther: A suite and a cope of redde velvett, too other copes of the same. A suite and a cope of white damaske moche worne. A cope of blue satten and blue velvett very olde praised at lxvi*s.* viij*d.*

Memord. Thom̅s Michell, clerke of the age of lx yeres Incumbent ther is a man of honest conversacon and indifferently lernyd, and he receyveth yerely for his wages by thandes of the feoffees of the saide Chauntrie — vj*li.*

The same feoffees distributeth yerely out of the premisses to the poore people in tyme of the Annivsarie yerely kept for the founders — viij*s.*

Itm to the poore prisoners remaynyng in the Gaole of Ilchester yerely — iij*s.* iiij*d.*

The Salarie of three priestes celebratynge wtin the sayde parysshe Churche.

Is yerely worthe in Landes tent̅e and hereditant̅e put in feoffment to their use for ev̅ in the tenure of sondery psones as may appere pticulerly more at large by the Rentall of the same — xiiij*li.* xviij*s.* ij*d.*

W^t certeyne other landes and possessions lying in Ilmynster aforesaide dymysed and farme letten by sondery Abbotts and covent of the late monastery of Muchelney in the saide Countie of Somers some tyme lordes of the saide Manor of Ilmynster as may appere by three sev̅all Indentures under their covent seale grantyd to sondery psones to the use of the saide three salaries for terme of certayne yeres in the saide Indentures expressed worthe by the yere ix*li.* viij*s.* vj*d.* . . xxiiij*li.* vj*s.* iiij*d.*

Whereof in

Rente resolute paide yerely to sondery psones for the foresaide landes put in feoffement for ever xviij*s.* And xiij*s.* 1*d.* to

Somerset Chantries.

the righte highe and mightie Prince Edward Duke of Somerset nowe lorde of the foresaide Manor of Ilmynster for the rent and farme of the saide lande graunted for terme of yeres reserved to the foresaide Abbotts and Covent and their successors by the saide Indentures . . . . xxxjs. jd.

And so

Remayneth clere of the saide landes put in feoffemt xiiij*li*. ij*d*. And for the saide landes graunted for terme of yeres viij*li*. xv*s*. v*d*. . . . . xxij*li*. xv*s*. vij*d*.

Three Chalices of Silu; a crosse of silluer gilte cont 120 oz; a shippe of silluer w^t three stones of chrystall, too cruetts, too candlesticke pcell gilte 89 oz. ***Plate and ornamente.***

Ornamente presented ther, twentie paire of olde vestments. A fronte of an aulter clothe of satten of bridges, too curteynes of white sarcenett, ix corporaces w^t their caces, viij aulter clothes of lynen fyve frounte aulter clothes olde and torne, too sacring belle praised at liij*s*. iiij*d*.

Thoms Battyn, clerke, of the age of liiij yeres one of the incubente is of verray honest conversacon and he receyved yerely for his wages by thandes of the feoffees and lessies of the saide landes and possessions w^t iij*s*. iiij*d*. allowed hym yerely for ij lodes of woode — vj*li*. iij*s*. iiij*d*. ***Memord.***

John Poole, clerke of thage of lij yeres a man also of honest conversacon seconde Incubent receyveth yerely for his wages — vj*li*. iij*s*. iiij*d*.

Robte Olyver, clerke, of thage of xl yeres of lyke conversacon thirde Incubent ther receyveth yerely for his wages w^t iij*s*. iiij*d*. allowed hym for the rent of his howse and for the repacons of the same — vj*li*. iij*s*. iiij*d*.

Somerset Chantries.

Ther ys also distributed yerely to the poore people out of the premisses — xxxiijs. iiijd.

Lighte foundyde w'tin the same parysche Churche for terme of certeyne yeres.

Ar yerely worthe in
Landes and possessions dymysed by John Sherborne Abbot of the late monastery of Muchelney aforesaide and the Covent of the same place to sondery psones for terme of 80 yeres. . xls.

Whereof paid

To the saide Duke of Somerset for the yerely rent and farme of the saide landes reserved to the saide Abbot and Covent and their successors . . . . xiiijs. xd.

And so

Remayneth yerely during the saide terme . . . . . xxvs. ijd.

Memord.
The psonage ther is appropriat to the Deane and Chapiture of Bristowe and is worthe by the yere xxiijli. vs.

The Vicarage ther is of the yerely value of xxvli. vs. Wherof Thoms Locke, clerke is incūbent but not resident howbeyt he findeth one priest ther to srve the Cure.

Partakers of the lordes Holy Sooper ther Dcccc persons.

Rcc̄ of luke Walden as money for the last payment pcell of xli. geven for a fyne of certeyne landes apptayninge to the crosse service ther letten by coppie of courte rolle for ij lyves, xxs. Rcc̄ of John Willman as money geven by one Robte Hille als Thresher to be praied for — lxvjs. viijd.

Somerset Chantries.

2. Charde.

The Fraternytie of oure Lady.

Landes, tent͡e, burgages, cotages, and other hereditament͡e now **Is yerely worthe in** in the tenure and occupying of sondery psones as maye appere pticularly more at large by the Rentall of the same xiiij*li*. ix*s*. viij*d*.

    A chalice of Silu̅ gylte, xviij oz.   **Plate and ornament͡e.**
    Ornament͡e praysed at, v*s*.

William Piers, clerke is incu̅bent, and he receyveth yerely for **Memord.** his wages by thandes of the Wardeyns of the saide Fraternitie, vij*li*.

Ther is distributed yerely out of the p̃misses to the poore people of the towne of Charde aforesaide . . . . xiij*s*. iiij*d*.

The Chauntrie of Saincte Katerine.

Landes, tent͡e and other hereditament͡e nowe in the tenure of **Is yerely worthe in** sondery psones as may appere pticulerly more at large by the Rentall of the same . . . . vj*li*. x*s*. viij*d*.

    None.   **Plate and ornamt͡e.**

Robte Slympe clerke is incu̅bent ther, and he receyveth the **Memord.** hole proffect͡e towardes his lyving.

The psonage ther is appropriat to the Provostrie of Wells, and is worthe by the yere — xxviij*li*.

The Vicarage ther is of the yerely value of xxxvij*li*. xvi*s*. whereof John Pilkington clerke is incu̅bent but not resident albeyt he findeth one Curate to minister ther.

Partakers of the lordes holy Sooper ther Dcccclviiij.

3. Crukerne.

The Chauntrie of oure lady w'in the Churche yerde ther.

Is yerely worthe in
Landes tenementẽ and other hereditamentẽ nowe in the tenure of sondery psones as may appere pticulerly more at large by the Rentall of the same .... iiij*li.* xiiij*s.* x*d.*

Plate and ornamentẽ.
A chalice of silũ waying vij oz. ½.
Ornamentes praysed at ij*s.* vi*d.*
Bell mettall vj lb.
Leade I foder ½.

Memord.
John Michell clerke of thage of iiij^{xx} yeres incūbent ther is of honest conversacõn, and he receyveth yerely of the Issues of this chauntrie iiij*li.* v*s.* x*d.* ob.

The Chapell scituate in the churche yarde ther, coṽed w^t leade is praysed worthe vj*li.* xiij*s.* iiij*d.*

The Chauntrie of oure lady w'in the parysshe Church ther.

Is yerely worthe in
Landes teñts and other hereditamentẽ nowe in the tenure of sondery psones as may appere pticulerly more at large by the Rentall of the same .... iiij*li.* xviij*s.* iiij*d.*

Whereof in
Rentẽ resolute payde yerely to sondery psones. . . . . xiiij*d.*
And so
Remaynethe clere .... iiij*li.* xvij*s.* ij*d.*

Plate and ornamentẽ.
Plate none.
Ornamentes praysed at — vi*s.* viij*d.*

Somerset Chauntries.

John Gedge clerke of the age of lx yeres incūbent ther **Memord.** receyveth yerely of thissues of this Chauntrie iiij*li.* vij*s.* iiij*d.*

The ffree Scole ther somtyme callyd the Chauntrie of the Trynitie ther.

Landes tent̄e and other hereditament̄e nowe in the holding and occupying of sondery psones as maye appere more at large by the Rentall of the same . . . . ix*li.* **Is yerely worthe in**

Whereof in

Rent̄e resolute paid yerely to sondery psones . . xviij*s.* ix*d.*

And so

Remaynethe clere . . . . viij*li.* xv*d.*

None. **Plate and ornamt̄e.**

Sir Hughe Paulet, Knighte, and Henry Cricke holden of the **Memord.** Kinges ma^tie certayne customary landes pcell of his graces Manor of Crukerne aforesaide, videlt, too partes of the landes callyd Crafte graunted unto theym by copy of Courte Rolle for terme of their lyves after the custome of the saide Manor to the use of the trynitie and maynteñnce of the saide scole, by the Surveiors of the late attaynted Lorde m̃ques of Exciter, then Lorde of the saide manor, whiche landes be worthe yerely ov̄ and above xl*s.* paide to the Manor of Crukerne aforesaide for the rent and farm of the same landes, — xl*s.*

John Byrde, Scole M^r ther a man of honest conversac̄on well lerned and of goodly judgement, dothe moche good in the countrie in vertuouse bringing uppe, and teaching of Children, having at this present v͞i or v͞ii Scolers, receyved the hole proffecte for his wages. And thenhabitaunt̄e ther be most humble Suters to have the saide ffree scole contynued w^t augmentac̄on of the saide Scole M^r his lyving.

7

Somerset Chantries.

Obitte foundyd wtin the parysshe Churche ther.

Ar yerely worthe in One close of pasture callyd Hannyngs Haye, now in the tenure of John Bevyn — iij*s.* iiij*d.*

Lampes and lightes foundyd wtin the same Churche.

Ar yerely worthe in One annuall rent to be levyed and receyved yerely out of the Issues and Revenues of the landes and tent͡e of Sir Hughe Paulet, Knighte . . . . x*s.*

Lyghte foundyd wtin the Chapell of Misterton annexed to the saydc parysshe Churche.

Ar yerely worthe in One acre of lande ther in the occupying of the Wardens of the same Chapell . . . . viij*d.*

Memord. The psonage ther is devydyd into three porc͡ons—The first porc͡on is worthe by the yere — lv*li.*, graunted to Sir William Herberd, Knighte. The seconde porc͡on is worthe yerely — xx*li.* Whereof Edwarde Horsey is pson. And the thirde porc͡on is worthe yerely — x*li.* Whereof Thom͡s ffreke is pson.

Crukerne is a great market towne and a thoroughe fare betwixt London and Excit͡.

Partakers of the lordes Holy Sooper ther M.

---

4. Southe Petherton.
The ffree Chapell of saincte John.

Is yerely worthe in Landes, tent͡e, and other hereditament͡e nowe in the holdinge and occupyinge of sondery psones, as maye appere by the Rentall of the same . . . . cxij*s.* viij*d.*

Somerset Chantries.

Whereof in
Rent℄ resolute paide yerely to sondery psones . . . . . xvi*s*.
And so
Remaynethe clere . . . . iiij*li*. xvj*s*. viij*d*.

None.
        Bell mettall c lb.   Plate and ornamente.

Matthewe Broke clerk of the age of 1 yeres incūbent ther Memord. receyved clere by the yere. . . . . iiij*li*. v*s*. xj*d*. ob. q.

The Chauntrie wtin the parysh℄ Churche ther founḍyd by Henry late Erle of Brigewater.

Redy money to be levied and receyved at foure terms in the yere by evyn porcons out of the Issues, Revenues, and proffectes of the Manor of South Petherton aforesaid by thandes of the baylyf of the saide Manor for the tyme beinge . . vj*li*. xiij*s*. iiij*d*.   Is yerely worthe in

None but a challice wayinge v oz. ½.   Plate and ornamte.
William Dyer clerke incūbent not resident receyved yerely Memord. of the saide some towards his lyving — vj*li*. 2 *£* 5 . ʋ-ɯ'ɩ xxı.

Lampes and lighte founḍyd wtin the sayde parysh℄ Churche.

ffoure acres of lande gyven to the mayntenñnce of the same in tholding of John Kingeman and others — ij*s*. viij*d*.   Ar yerely worthe in

The Chapell of Lopon wtin the sayde parysh℄.

Landes teñt℄ and hereditamente in thoccupying of Robte Sanford as maye appere by the Rentall of the same . xiij*s*. iiij*d*.   Is yerely worthe in

Somerset Chantries.

Whereof in
Rentꝫ resolute paid yerely to sondery psones ... vijs. viijd.
And so
Remaynethe clere .... vs. viijd.

Memord.   It is not knowen to what intent this lande was gyven to the said Chapell.

This Chapell of Lopon is a Chapell w^t cure annexed to Southe Petherton aforesaide, distaunt from the paryshe churche one myle.

Redy money gyven to the mayntenñce of lyghtꝫ wtin the Chapell of Chelyngton.

Uivert.   Redy money gyven by Robte Holcombe to remayne in stocke to the saide use nowe in the custody of Stevyn graye .... xs.

Memord.   The psonage ther is impropriat to the Deane and Chapiture of Bristowe.

The vicarage ther is of the yerely value of xxiiijli. Whereof Stevyn fforest is Incumbent.

Partakers of the lordes Holy Soop ther cccc$\overset{xx}{}$iiij.

---

5. Curryryuell.

The Chauntrie of Wyke per ham.

Is yerely worthe in   Landes, tentꝫ, and other hereditamentꝫ in the holding of sondery psones as may appere prticulerly more at large by the Rentall of the same. .... lxvjs. viijd.

Somerset Chauntries.

Plate none but a Challice, vj oz. ½.　　　　　　Plate and ornamtẹ.
Ornamentẹ praysed at — viijs. xd.

John Saunders, Clerke, of the age of lvj yeres of honest con- Memorḋ.
versacōn incumbent ther, and receyved yerely towardes his
lyvinge — lxs.

The Chapell belonging to this Chauntrie, distaunt from the
paryshe churche one myle is estemed worthe to be solde —
xiijs. iiijd.

The Chauntrie or ffree Scole foundyd by Margaret late Countisse of Richmond and derby, w'in the late College of Wymborne in the Countie of Dors'.

Landes tēntẹ and other hereditamentẹ lyinge in Curryryvell　Is yerely
aforesaide or els wher w'in the foresaide Countie of Somerset　worthe in
in the holding of John Godybarne al Sheres by Indenture for
terme of yeres.............................xjli. xiiijs.

None.　　　　　　　　　　　　　　　　　　　　Plate and ornamtẹ.
No Incumbent ther.　　　　　　　　　　　　　Memorḋ.

Lyghtẹ foundyd w'in the paryshe Churche ther.

One pcell of arable lande ther contaynyng by estimacōn　Ar yerely
v acres in the holdinge of the parson of the saide towne ... vs.　worthe in

Cattall gyben to the mayntenūnce of lyghtes and obite w'in the same Churche.

Too kyne. One gyven by Johan Woode remaynyng in the　Videlt.
custody of Thoms̄ Pyper praysed at xs. and thother Cowe
remayneth in the custoav of William Beeke praysed at
viijs...................................xviijs.

Somerset Chantries.

Memord. The saide William Becke is a verray poore man and not able to paye for the saide Cowe.

Memord. The psonage ther appropriat to the late Priory of Bysseham is graunted unto Guy Bonvyle by the lres patentę of oure late soūlaigne Lorde Kinge Henry the viijth, datyd the iij^{de} day of August in the xxxviijth yere of his graces reigne.

Ther is w^{t}in the saide paryshe a Chapell, w Cure callyd Bradwey annixed to the saide psonage whereof Nicholas Armstronge is nowe curate founde of the proffects of the saide psonage.

The psonage of Goosebraden, w^{t}in the same paryshe, whereof Ambrose m̃shall is incūbent is worthe yerely . . . . xxvj$s$. viij$d$.

The psonage of Erneshill is worthe yerely xlv$s$.

The Vicarage of Curryryvell aforesaide w^t the Chapell, callyd Weston therunto annixed is worthe yerely — xiiijli.

Whereof William Safferton, clerke, is nowe incūbent not resident, but findeth ij priests, one mynistring at Curryryvell and thother at Weston.

Partakers of the Lordes Holy Soop at Curryryvell cccxvi and Bradwaye aforesaide cxxxv. — cccclj.

Ther is w^{t}in the saide paryshe a house of poore people, callyd the spitle howse, wherin ar iiij pōore people remaynyng, wherunto belongethe too acres of arable lande worthe yerely — ij$s$.

6. Chaffecombe.

Redy money remaynyng in Stocke to the mayntenñce of lighte w'in the p'yshe Churche ther.

Richarde Jane hathe in his occupaçon and kepinge .... xxxiiijs. viijd.	Videlt.
John Colman hathe in his occupaçon and kepinge .... xxxiiijs. viijd.	
	lxixs. iiijd.

7. Swell.

Cattall gyuen to the mayntenñce of lyghte w'in the parysshe Churche ther.

ffoure kyne remaynyng in the custody of sondery psones ther praysed xs. le pece one w^t an other. . . . . xls. — Videlt.

8. Elton.

Cattall gyuen to the mayntenñce of lyghte w'in the parysshe Churche ther.

One Cowe remaynyng in the custody of William Bevyn praysed at — xvjs. — Videlt.

9. Kingesbury.

Obite foundyd wtin the parysshe Churche ther.

Ar yerely worthe in — Certeyne pcells of lande gyven by one John Nabbe to the same use — x*s*.

---

10. Currymallett.

The free Chapell of Sainete James ther.

Is yerely worthe in — Landes teñte and hereditamentẽ in the occupying of John Copston . . . . xlvj*s*. v*d*.

Plate and ornamtẽ. — A Chalice of Silũ waying vj oz.
Ornamentẽ praysed at — ij*d*. Bell mettall — xl lb.

Memord. — No incumbent ther.

Memord. — The psonage ther is worthe yerely — xxiiij*li.* wherof John Welche clerke is nowe incũbent and findeth ij curates ther ministring, viz., Thoms Kytson and Robte Brewer.

Partakers of the lordes Holy Soop there ccxl.

---

11. Whitestaunton.

Redy money reñ in stocke blonging to the Guilde of oure lady ther.

Eidelt. — William ffox and John Ilstone have in their occupacõn and kepinge — xxiij*s*. v*d*. ob.

Somerset Chantries.

Cattall gyuen to the mayntenñce of obite wtin the pyshe Churche yer.

One Cowe remaynyng in the custody of William Podger Videlt. praysed at — xxs.

---

12. ffyffet.

The Chauntrie foundyd by Sr John Speke, Knight wtin the Cathedrall Churche of saincte petre in Exciter in the countie of Deuon.

Landes teñte and other hereditamente lying and beinge w^{t}in Is yerely the paryshe of ffyffet aforesaide in the tenure of sondery psones worthe in by Indenture for terme of their lyves . . . . xj*li*. xvs. x*d*.
                Wherof
Rente resolute paid yerely . . . . ij*s*. vj*d*.
                And so
Remayneth clere . . . . xj*li*. xiij*s*. iiij*d*.

Plate ornamente and incumbent certefied w^{t}in the saide Memord. Cathedrall Churche.

The Deane and Chapiture of Exciter w^{t}in foure yeres last past solde xix acres of woode growing upon the premysses praysed at — ix*li*. xs.

---

13. Knolle.

Redy money remaynyng in stocke to the mayntenaunce of lighte wtin the paryshe Churche ther.

William Morne hathe in his occupaĉon and kepinge — Videlt. xiij*s*. iiij*d*.

Somerset Chantries.

14. Abbotts Ele.

Lighte foundyd w'in the parysshe Churche ther.

Ar perely worthe in — One pcell of medowe lyinge in Ilmore contaynyng half an acre . . . . xij*d.*

Cattall gyuen to the mayntennce of the same lyghtes.

Videlt. — One Cowe gyven by John Gibbes remaynyng in the custody of Thoms Matthewe praysed at . . . . xiij*s.* iiij*d.*

---

15. Shepton Beawchm.

Lyghte foundyd w'in the parysshe Churche ther.

Ar perely worthe in$ — Landes tent̄e and other hereditament̄e nowe in the tenure of sondery psones as maye appere pticulerly more at large by the Rentall of the same . . . . vij*s.*

Cattall gyuen to the mayntennce of the same lyghte.

Videlt. — One Cowe remaynyng in the custody of Roger Paule praysed at . . . . xx*s.*

---

16. Sevyngton.

Redy money gyuen to the mayntennce of a priest ther by the space of one yere.

Videlt. — Henry Tubbe clerke and William Garland have in their occupaćon and keping of the bequest of Thoms Howse, deceased to finde one priest celebrating and singing for the soole of the same Thomas, by the space of one yere . iiij*li.* xvj*s.* viij*d.*

17. Beare Crocombe.

Lyghte foundyd w'in the parysbe Churche ther.

Three closes of pasture callyd Packewere contaynyng fyve acres in the occupying of Richarde Tyse . . . . xiijs. iiijd. *Ar yerely worthe in*

18. Wynsham.

Lyghte foundyd w'in the parysbe Churche ther.

One annuall rent comyng out of one close of pasture ther callyd Vythra—viz., for ij lb. of wex . . . . xijd. *Ar yerely worthe in*

Cattall gyuen to the mayntenñce of the fount taper ther.

William Lappe hathe in his occupying and keping certeyne *Viuelt.* redy money for the price of ij kyne by hym solde . xxvjs. viijd.

19. Donyet.

The Chauntrie w'in the parke ther.

Redy money to be receyued levyed and taken out of the Issues Revenues and proffecte of the Manor of Donyet aforesaide — xxxis. ijd. And out of the Revenues of the Courte of Thaugmentacon of the Kinge maties Crowne, by thandes of his graces Receyvor geñall of the same Revenue w'in the countie of Somerset by vertue of a Decree made in the saide courte in that behalf — lxvjs. viijd. . . . . iiijli. xvijs. xd. *Is yerely worthe in*

Somerset Chantries.

Plate and ornamentȝ. A chalice of Silu̅ gilte — xiiij oz.
Ornamentȝ praysed at — ijs. Bell mettall ½ c.

Memord. Mathewe White clerke of the age of lxx yeres of honest conversacōn althoughe of smalle lernynge incumbent ther.

Decanatus de Taunton.

20. The Towne of Taunton.

The Chauntrie of oure lady wtin the parishe Churche of Mary Magdalene.

Landes, tenṫe and other hereditamenṫe nowe in the tenure of sondery psones as may appere pticulerly more at large by the Rentall of the same . . . . ⸱ x*li.* iij*s.* ij*d.*   Is yerely worthe in

Wherof in
Renṫe resolute paide yerely to sondery psones . . xxiiij*s.* iij*d*

And so
Remaynethe clere . . . . viij*li.* xviij*s.* xj*d.*

A chalice of silū waying — xij oz.   Plate and ornamṫe.
Ornamentes praysed at — v*s.*

John Gully clerke of thage of lxx yeres incūbent ther.   Memord.

The Chauntrie of Saincte Nicholas al Bysshoppes Chauntrie per.

Landes tenṫe and other hereditamenṫe nowe in the tenure of sondery psones as maye appere pticulerly more at large by the Rentall of the same . . . . xviij*li.* ij*d.*   Is yerely worthe in

Wherof in
Renṫe resolute paid yerely to sondery psones . . . xxxj*s.* x*d.*

And so
Remayneth clere . . . . xvj*li.* viij*s* iiij*d.*

Somerset Chantries.

Plate and ornamtẹ. Two challices gilte wainge — xxiij oz.
Ornamentes praysed at — xvijs. vjd.

Memord. John Seman clerke of the age of xxx yeres incūbent ther.

Ther was distributed yerely to xiij almosehowses in Taunton aforesaide wherin do remayne xxvj poore people, according to the foundacōn of this Chauntrie — lvjs. iiijd.

Itm for the repacōns of the same Almoschowses yerely — xxs. And for the repacōns of ij other Almoschowses yerely — vs. Amounting in all to iiijli. xvjd. by the yere.

The Chauntrie of the name of Jesus ther.

Is yerely worthe in Landes teñtẹ and other hereditamentẹ nowe in the tenure of sondery psones as maye appere pticulerly more at large by the Rentall of the same .... viijli. viijs. iiijd.

Wherof in

Rentẹ resolute paid yerely to sondery psones .... ixs. iiijd.

And so

Remayneth clere .... vijli. xixs.

Plate and ornamtẹ. Two Challices wainge — xvj oz. ¼.
Ornamentes praysed at — ixs.

Memord. John Edwardes clerke of the age of l yeres a man of honest conversacōn and indifferently lerned incūbent ther.

The Chauntrie of the Trynitie ther.

Is yerely worthe in Landes teñtẹ and other hereditamentẹ nowe in the tenure of sondery psones as maye appere pticulerly more at large by the Rentall of the same .... vjli. xvjs.

Somerset Chantries.

    Wherof in

Rente resolute paid yerely . . . . xs. xjd.
    And so
Remayneth clere . . . . vjli. vs. jd.

A Challice of silver wainge — xj oz.   Plate and
Ornamentes praysed at — ijs.   ornamte.

Raffe Wylkyns clerke of the age of lij yeres incumbent ther. Memord.

The Chauntrie of Sainete Andrewe.

Landes tente and other hereditamente nowe in the tenure of Es perely
sondery psones as may appere pticulerly more at large by the worthe in
Rentall of the same . . . . vjli. viijs. viijd.
    Wherof in
Rente resolute paid yerely . . . . xiiijs. iijd. ob.
    And so
Remayneth clere . . . . cxiiijs. iiijd. ob.

Two Challice of silver — xij oz.   Plate and
Ornamentes praysed at iijs. iiijd.   ornamte.

Henry Bull clerke of the age of lx yeres incumbent ther.   Memord.

Ther is one voyde pece of grounde, wherupon was sometyme scituate one burgage belonginge to this Chauntrie, and nowe clerely decayed and no proffect or rent receyved for the same, worthe by the yere — iiijd.

The Chauntrie ther callyd Stoynges Chauntrie.

Landes tente and other hereditamte nowe in the tenure of Es perely
sondery psones as maye appere pticulerly more at large by the worthe in
Rentall of the same . . . . iiijli. vijs.

Somerset Chauntries.

Wherof in
Rentẽ resolute paid yerely............. vj*s*. vij*d*. ob.
And so
Remayneth clere .... iiij*li*. iiij*d*. ob.

Plate and ornamtẽ.   A Challice of silver waing — xj oz.

Ornamentes praysed at — iij*s*. iiij*d*.

Memord.   Alexaunder Maget clerke of thage of liiij yeres incumbent ther.

The Chauntrie of Sainete Etheldrede.

Is perely worthe in   Landes tenẽtẽ and other hereditamtẽ nowe in the tenure of sondery psones as may appere pticulerly more at large by the Rentall of the same..................... viij*li*. ij*d*.

Wherof in
Rent resolute paid yerely .... vi*d*.
And so
Remaynethe clere .... vij*li*. xix*s*. viij*d*.

Plate and ornamtẽ.   A Chalice of silṽ waying — viij oz.

Ornamentes praysed at — v*s*. viij*d*.

Memord.   William Callowe Clerke of thage of lvij yeres bachiler of Arte incũbent ther.

The Chapell belonging to the Chauntrie callyd Nethewayes Chapell scituat w^tin the churcheyerde of the late priory of Taunton is praysed worthe to be solde — iiij*li*.

The landes etc. before mencioned, wer presentyd at the first Survey of Collegẽ chauntries etc. and upon this Survey no landes at all presentyd, but a rent charge of vj*li*. ij*s*. vj*d*. to be

Somerset Chantries.

paide yerely by the feoffees of Willm Nethewaye out of the p̃misses, whose heires nowe claymeth the saide lande, howe be yt, they have as yet shewed no sufficient discharge in that behalf, neither by will, feoffem^t or otherwyse.

The fraternytie of the hyghe Crosse ther.

Landes, tentẽ and other hereditamtẽ nowe in the tenure of sondery psones as may appere pticulerly more at large by the Rentall of the same .... viij*li*. x*s*. ij*d*.   *Is yerely worthe in*

Wherof in
Rentẽ resolute paide yerely............... vj*s*.

And so
Remaynethe clere .... viij*li*. iiij*s*. ij*d*.

A Chalice of silṽ waying — xiij oz.   *Plate and ornamt̃e.*
Ornamentes praysed at — x*s*. viij*d*.

Thomas Browne, clerke of the age of lij yeres incũbent ther.   *Memord.*

Ther was distributed yerely to the poore people of the saide towne of Taunton out of the Issues and Revenues of this ffraternitie — xvj*s*.

The fraternytie of the Sepulcre ther.

Landes tentẽ and other hereditamtẽ nowe in the tenure of sondery psones as may appere pticulerly more at large by the Rentall of the same................... viij*li*. xix*s*.   *Is yerely worthe in*

Wherof in
Rentẽ resolute paid yerely.............. ix*s*. iij*d*.

And so
Remayneth clere .... viij*li*. ix*s*. iij*d*.

Somerset Chantries.

Plate and ornamtẹ. Two Challicẹ of silṽ waing xviij oz. ½.
Ornamentẹ praysed at — xvijs.

Memord. William Trowbrigẹ clerke of the age of xlv yeres incumbent ther, who is impotent for that he hathe ꝺved in the kingẹ mat[ies] warres under Sir George Carowẹ, Knight.

Ther was distributed yerely to the poore people of the saide towne out of the Revenues of this fraternitie xlvijs. And for the repacõns of vj almoshouses yerely xiijs. iiijd., amountinge in all to lxs. iiijd. by the yere.

The seruice of oure Lady w'in the parysḥe Churcḥe of Sainctẹ James nere Taunton.

Is yerely worthe in Landes teñtẹ and other hereditamtẹ put in feoffem[t] for eṽ nowe in the tenure of sondery psones as maye appere pticulerly more at large by the rentall of the same vijli xviijd. And also in certeyne customary landes and tentẹ in the tenure of sondery psones as maye lykewyse appere pticulerly more at large by the Rentall of the same — lxvijs. ijd. . . . . xli. viijs. viijd.

Wherof in

Rentẹ resolute paide yerely to sondery psones for the saide landes teñtẹ etc. put in feoffemt for eṽ iiijs. vjd. And to the Bysshop of Winchester for the rent of the saide customary landes xs. vjd. . . . . xvs.

And so

Remayneth clere . . . . ixli. xiijs. viijd.

Plate and ornamtẹ. A Chalice and a pax of silṽ waying — xxv oz.
Ornamentẹ, xs., w[t] certeyne other goodes, xs., belonging to this ꝺvice praysed at — xxs.

24

Somerset Chantries.

John Pytte, clerke of the age of lxiiij yeres, a man of honest Memord. conversacon incumbent ther.

Thenhabitaunte of the towne of Taunton aforesaide the vjth daye of Aprill an° RR E vi^{ti} ij^{do} made humble request unto the comyssionors in man̄ and forme followinge, Wher ther is w^{t}in the saide towne of Tawnton, beinge the greatest, and best m̄ket towne in all that shire in a verray holsome good and plentyfull soyle a faire large and goodly howse newe buylded erected and made for a Scolehowse about xxv yeres nowe past, wherin was a Scole M^r and an ussher founde the space of xij or xiiij yeres, for the vertuouse educacon and teaching of youthe, as well of the saide towne of Taunton, as of the hole contrye to the nombr of vij or viij score Scolers by the Devocon of one Roger Hill of the same towne m̄chaunt nowe deceased. A great Relief also to the same towne of Taunton. And nowe sythe the deathe of the same Roger Hill the saide Scolehowse standyth voyde, w^{t}out either M^r, ussher or Scolers, to the great p̄iudice hurte and discomoditie of the comen welthe of the saide Shire. Whereuppon the saide enhabitaunte make most humble sute unto the Kinge ma^{tie} that yt maye please his highnes to graunte, and assigne suche landes and tent̄e in ppetuytie as shalbe thought mete unto his grace and his most honorable counsaile, to the mayntefince and finding of a Maister and ussher, to teache in the same Scolehowse wch no doubte is most bewtyfull and most necessarie place of all that shire.

The psonage ther is impropriat to the late priory of Taunton.

The Vicarage ther is worthe yerely — xiij*li.* vj*s.* viij*d.*, wherof Robte Reede clerke is nowe incumbent.

Partakers of the lordes holy sooper ther MMM psones.

Somerset Chantries.

21. Northcory.

The Chauntrie ther.

Is yerely worthe in Landes tent̃e and other hereditamt̃e in the tenure of sondery psones, as may appere pticulerly more at large by the Rentall of the same lxixs. id. And in Redy money p^d yerely by the Deane and Chapiture of the Cathedrall churche of Sainctẽ Andrewe in Wells — xls. . . . . cixs. jd.
       Wherof in
Rent̃e resolute paid yerely . . . . iijs. vijd. ob.
       And so
Remayneth clere . . . . cvs. vd. ob.
None but a challice waing — vj oz.

Plate and ornamt̃e. Memord. Leade iij foder ¼.

It is presentyd that xls. pcell of the saide some of cvs. vd. ob, is at the will and pleasure of the Deane and Chapiture of Wellẽ, by them sometyme paide, and sometyme not paide.

The Chapell of the saide Chauntrie, scituate w^tin the churche yerde of Northcory aforesaide is cov̂ed w^t leade presented to be worthe at the uttermost — xvli.

Thom̄s Cribbe clerke of the age of lxvj yeres a man of honest conversac̄on compotently lerned incūbent ther and hathe non other lernyng.

The Salarie of one prieste callyd a brotherhedde priest celebrating w^tin the parysh̃e churche ther.

Is yerely worth in Landes tent̃e and other hereditamt̃e put in feoffement for c̄u to the use aforesaide now in the tenure of sondery psones, as may

Somerset Chantries.

appere pticulerly more at large by the Rentall of the same — xxvjs. And in one Tent w^t thapp̃ tenñce lyinge at Nythe w^tin the paryshe of Northcory aforesaide, dymysed and letten to farme unto Roger Browne *al* Barbor of Netherstowe by the Deane and Chapiture of Welle by Indenture datyd under their comen seale the last daye of Septembr in the yere of o^r Lorde God mdxxxiiij, To have and to holde unto the saide Roger, and his assignes for terme of xl yeres wch Indenture the Wardens of the fraternitie of Northcory p̃chased of the foresaide Roger Browne to the use aforesaide and is wurthe by the yere — iiij*li*. xvs. . . . . vj*li*. xij*d*.

Wherof pd.

To the saide Deane and Chapiture of Welle for the rent and ferme of the foresaide tent w^t the apptenñce at Nythe yerely — xvs.

And so

Remayneth clere . . . . cvjs.

None but a challice — v oz. ½.   **Plate and ornamt̃e.**

John Gent clerke of the age of lxiiij yeres incūbent ther having compotent lernyng, and of good name and reaporte amongest his neighbors.   **Memor̃.**

Memor̃.

The Vicarage ther is of the yerely value of xxj*li*., wherof Richarde Austen clerke is nowe incūbent.

Partakers of the Lordes holy Soop ther, Dccxij.

22. Wellyngton wt Westbuckelande,

a Chapell annex to the parysshe Churche of Wellyngton aforesaide.

The Salary of one prieste celebratynge in Wellyngton aforesaide.

|Is yerely worthe in| Landes tente and other hereditamentẻ in the tenure of sondery psones as may appere pticulerly more at large by the Rentall of the same . . . . lxxvs. xd.

Wherof in

Rentẻ resolute paide yerely . . . . viijs. iijd. ob.

And so

Remayneth clere . . . . lxvijs. vd. ob.

Plate and ornamtẻ. None but a challice waing — vj oz.

Memord. John Spicer clerke of thage of xxxij yeres, a man of honest conversacon well learned, incumbent ther receyved the hole proffects towardes his lyving and hathe a pencon of the Kingẻ ma[tie] of viij mrkẻ by the yere goinge out of the late monastery of Brewton.

Sir Roger Blewet, Knight, hathe w[t]holden one burgage cont one acre and a half comprised in the dede of feoffem[t] the space of vij or viij yeres, and claymethe the same to be his owen enheritaunce not charged in this value.

John Taylor hathe w[t]holden ij burgages contayned in the same feoffem[t] the space of viij or ix yeres claymynge the same to be his owen enheritaunce not charged in this value.

Somerset Chantries.

The Salarye of one prieste, callyd a brotherhed priest celebratyng in westbuckeland.

Landes tēntē and other hereditamentē in the tenure of sondery psones as may appere pticulerly more at large by the rentall of the same. . . . . lviijs. iiijd. **Is yerely worthe in**

Wherof in

Rentē resolute paid yerely. . . . . ixs. viijd.

And so

Remayneth clere . . . . xlviijs. viijd.

None but a challice waing — vj oz. ½. **Plate and ornamte.**

William Culverwell clerke of thage of lvi yeres incumbent ther, a man of honest conversation. **Memord.**

Memord.

The psonage of Wellington aforesaide is impropriate to the Provostrie of Wellē.

The Vicarage ther is of the yerely value of xv*li*. xj*s*., wherof John Elm͡s clerke is nowe incūbent who findeth ij prieste one to mynister at Wellington and thother at west buckelande. P'takers of the Lordes holy Sooper Dcccviij.

---

23. Kyngeston & Cotherston.

The Salarie of one priest ther callyd a Brotherhed priest.

Certeyne Customary landes and possessions in the tenure of sondery psones as maye appere pticulerly more at large by the rentall of the same . . . . xxxixs. **Is yerely worthe in**

Somerset Chantries.

Wherof paide

To the Busshop of Winchester for the rent and farme of the same landes by the yere . . . . vij*s.* j*d.*

And so

Remayneth clere . . . . xxvi*s.* xj*d.*

Plate and ornamtç. None but a challice waing — vj oz. do (½).

Memord. No incubent in this Svice.

Goodes and Cattall remaynyng in stocke for the maytenñce of the same priest.

Videlt. Redy money remaynyng in thandes of John Hammon and Thomas Blauncheflower, iiij*li.* iiij*s.* and six yeowes shepe remaynyng in the custody of the saide John and Thoms praysed at ij*s.* le pece — xij*s.* . . . . iiij*li.* xvj*s.*

---

24. Pytmyster.

The Salarie of one priest ther callyd a Stipendary priest.

Is yerely worth in Certayne customary landes and possessions in the tenure of sondery psones as maye appere pticulerly more at large by the rentall of the same. lvj*s.* viij*d.*

Wherof paid

To the busshoppe of Winchester for the rent and farme of the same landes by the yere . . . . xxj*s.*

And so

Remayneth clere . . . . xxxv*s.* viij*d.*

Somerset Chantries.

None but a challice wainge — vij oz.   **Plate and ornamtę.**

Robte Bayly clerke of the age of l yeres incumbent ther.   **Memord.**

Ther is due to the busshop of Winchester for a fyne ratyd accordinge to the custome of Taunden upon the deathe of one John Parson being teñnte of pcell of the premisses liij*s*. iiij*d*.

Memord.

The Vicarage ther is of the yerely value of xv*li*. x*s*. wherof Thoms Bickam clerke is nowe incūbent.

Partakers of the lordes holy Soop ther ccclx.

---

25. Staplegroue.

Obite foundyd wtin the parysshe churche ther.

One pcell of medowe callyd lowse medowe in the tenure of Robte Knighte . . . . iiij*s*.   **Ar yerely worthe in**

Wherof in

Rentę resolute p^d yerely . . . . vij*d*. ob.

And so

Remayneth clere . . . . iij*s*. iiij*d*. ob.

---

26. Thorne ffawcon.

Lyghte foundyd wtin the parysshe churche ther.

ffoure acres of lande ther nowe in the tenure of Gilbert Bradshawe clerke — iiij*s*.   **Ar yerely worthe in**

Somerset Chantries.

27. Halse.

Cattall gyuen to the mayntenñce of lyghte wtin the parysshe churche ther.

Videlt. Six yeowe shepe remaynyng w^t William Cape and William Blake praysed at ij*s.* le pece . . . . xij*s.*

---

28. Trulle.

The Seruice of oure lady ther.

Memord. Ther is a teñt in Pytmyster holden after the custome of Taunden, the yelding wherof John fforde of Pytmyster solde unto William Voysey of trulle for xij*li.* sterling and after the decease of the foresaide John fforde, the saide William solde the yelding of the saide teñt to the saide S̃vice of oure lady in Trull, ther to remayne.

---

29. Laurence Lydyarde.

Memord.

Ther is a Chapell of stone standing upon the open demayne of Humfray Beymaunt esquier praysed wourthe to be solde — x*s.*

32

Somerset Chantries.

30. Bradford.

The Chauntrie w'tin the p'she ther.

Landes ten̄tꝭ and other hereditam̄ntꝭ nowe in the tenure of sondery psones as may appere pticulerly more at large by the rentall of the same . . . . cxviijs.   *Is yerely worthe in*

     Wherof in

Rentꝭ resolute paide yerely to sondery psones . . . . . . iiijs.

     And so

Remayneth clere. . . . . cxiiijs.

Plate none.   *Plate and ornamtꝭ.*

Ornamentꝭ praysed at — iijs. iiijd.

John Hussey clerke incūbent ther, and is of honest conver-sation indifferently lerned.   *Memord.*

Memord.

The Vicarage ther is of the yerely value of xli. xvjs. viijd. wherof Thom̄s Rousewell is nowe incumbent.

Ꝑtakers of the lordes holy sooper ther ccxxxiij.

---

31. Westemonketon.

The Seruice of oure lady ther.

One halfe acre of medowe lyinge in Bromehaye now in the tenure of John God, jun^r. — xviijd.   *Is yerely worthe in*

Somerset Chantries.

The Salarie of one priest celebratyng in the Chapell belonginge to the hospitall of Sainete Margaret ther.

Is merely worthe in — Redy money to be levied and receyved out of the Issues and Revenues of the late Priorye of Taunton. . . . . lxvjs. viijd.

Plate and ornamte. — A chalice of silu waying — xij oz.
Ornamentꝑ praysed at — xiijs. iiijd. Bell metall xl lb.

Memord. — William Callowe clerke Mr of arte and of verray honest conversation incūbent ther.

The Chapell wherin the same incūbent did mynister coūed wt stones is praysed worthe to be solde — xxs.

Ther be wtin the same hospitall vj poore lazare people havinge for their relief the mansion house of the same hospitall wt a little orcharde adioynyng to the same worthe yerely vs., and also other smalle peellꝑ of lande of the yerely value of xxiijs. xd. and other relief they have none, wherefore they make humble peticōn for augmentacōn of lyving.

---

32. Combflory.

The Chauntrie ther.

Is merely worthe in — Landes teñtꝑ and other hereditamentꝑ in the tenure of sondery psones as maye appere pticulerly more at large by the rentall of the same. . . . . lxxs. iiijd.

Plate and ornamte. — A chalice of Silu gilte — xiij oz. do (½).
Ornamentꝑ none.

Memord. — Robte Sprye clerke of the age of xlviij yeres a man of honest conversacōn indifferently lerned, incūbent ther.

Somerset Chantries.

The Chappell ther.

Three acres and a half of lande in one close in the tenure of Edmunde Turnor clerke psone ther. . . . . vj*s.* viij*d*.   *Is yerely worthe in*

The foresaide iij acres d° (½) of lande was gyven to have one *Memord.* masse in the yere sayde w^tin the same chapell, by the pson of the saide paryshe alwayes for the tyme beinge, videlt, on Mary Magdalyn's daye wheruppon the saide pson claymeth the saide lande.

The saide Chappell did appertayne to the late suppressed Abbey of Athelney, and is scituate on the backesyde of a teñt ther late appertaynyng to the saide Abbey, and nowe pchased by Sir William ffrauncis, knighte, who by purchase of the saide teñt claymeth the saide chapell to be pcell therof.

---

33. Bysshoppes Lydyarde.

The Chapell of oure lady ther callyd Sandylan.

The rent of the saide Chapell and half an acre of lande belonging to the same — xvj*d*.   *Is yerely wurth in*

None.

Bell metall, xxiiij lb.   *Plate and ornamte.*

---

34. Pyned ffory.

Cattall gyuen to the mayntenñce of obite wtin the parysh churche ther.

ffyue yeowe shepe w^t their lambes gyven by Agnes Pery to thuelt. the saide use remaynyng in the custody of John Warre and

Somerset Chantries.

William Wykes, gentilmen praysed at xvjs. ffoure kyne gyven by John Rocle to the same use remaynyng in the custody of the saide John Warre and William Wykes praysed at — iiij*li*. Redy money remaynyng in thands of the same William, warden of the saide store, growen and rysen of the farme of the saide shepe and kyne — xxxijs. iiij*d*. . . . . vj*li*. viijs. iiij*d*.

Plate and ornamentꝭ gyuen by John Rocle to the pyshe churche ther to be prayd for wt̃in the same churche.

Videlt.   A chalice and a pax of silũ waying — xvj oz.
Ornamentꝭ praysed at . . . . xs.

---

35. Cryche.

Cattall gyuen to the mayntẽnce of a lampe wt̃in the paryshe Churche ther.

Videlt.   One kowe gyven by Richarde Hethefeld praysed at xiijs. iiij*d*.

---

36. Langforde Budfelde.

Lightꝭ foundyd wt̃in the parysh churche ther.

Ar yerely wourth in   One teñt w^t certeyne lande therunto belongeing iiijs. vi*d*., and one annuall rent to be rec out of one teñt w^t thapp teñncꝭ in the pysche of Myluton in the tenure of Walter Coram, wch teñt is thenheritaunce of John Sydenham of Dulverton ix*d*. — vs. iij*d*.
                    Wherof in
Rentꝭ resolute paide yerely . . . . xviij*d*.
                    And so
Remayneth clere . . . . iijs. ix*d*.

Somerset Chantries.

The foresaide tent is in decaye, and hathe ben voyde theis **Memor͠d.** ij yeres past, and the lande therunto belonging is a barren and hethie grounde.

Ther hathe ben no lighte kept nor maynteyned w^t the saide annuall rent of ix$d$. w^{t}in the saide churche by the space of x yeres last past.

---

37. Aishebrittell.

The fraternytie of oure lady ther.

Landes — xx$s$., ten͠tρ and annuall rentρ, iiij$s$. xd. ob, as maye **Is perely wurthe in** appere pticulerly more at large by the rentall of the same . . . . xxiiij$s$. xd. ob.

None but a challice — vj. oz.   **Plate and ornamtρ.**

Alexaunder Woode hathe deteyned and w^{t}holden the saide **Memor͠d.** Annuall rent of iiij$s$. xd. ob. by the space of ij yeres nowe last past.

Ther remayneth in thandes of John Mogridge in redy money of stocke belonging to the saide ffraternitie . . . . xj$s$.

Redy money remaynynge in stocke to the use and mayntennce of Lyghte and Lampes w^{t}in the parysshe churche ther.

John Sherland and John Byshoppes have in their handes and **Videt.** safekeping to the use aforesaid . . . . xij$s$.

38. Mpluerton.

The Chauntrie of oure Lady ther.

Is yerely worthe in
Landes tent͡e and other hereditament͡e in the tenure of sondery psones as may appere pticulerly more at large by the Rentall of the same .... viij*li*. vij*s*. vij*d*.

Wherof in
Rent͡e resolute paide yerely to sondery psones .. xxiij*s*. j*d*.

And so
Remaynethe clere . ... vij*li*. iiij*s*. vj*d*.

Plate and ornamt͡e.
Plate none.
Bell metall — xxx lb.
Ornament͡e w^t certayne householde stuffe praysed at — xlij*s*. iiij*d*.
Leade ij foder d° ($\frac{1}{2}$).

Memord.
Elice Salter clerke of thage of $\overset{xx}{\text{iiij}}$ yeres incumbent ther a man of honest conversation verray impotent. The Chapell of the chauntrie standing w^{t}in the churche yerde cou͡led w^t leade is estemed worthe to be sold x*li*. wch thenhabitaunt͡e of the towne of Milu͡lton, beinge the king͡e ma^{ties} tent͡e do desire to bye, for helpe of conveyaunce of water to the towne w^t the saide leade, for lacke wherof they haue nowe great annoyaunce.

Light͡e foundyd for t͡w w^{t}in the parysh͡e church͡e ther.

Ar yerely worthe in
One Annuall rent comyng furthe out of the landes and tent͡s of William Tannor lyinge in Milu͡lton aforesaide. .... v*s*. iiij*d*.

Memord.
The psonage ther is of the yerely value of — xix*li*., wherof Mr. Redman is nowe incūbent.

Somerset Chantries.

The Vicarage ther is wurthe yerely — xxj*li.* xix*s.* xj*d.* Wherof John Dangerde, clerke, is incūbent and resident upon the same.

Ptakers of the lordes holy Sooper ther ccccxl.

Decanatus de Dunster.

39. Kyng Chrimpton.

Goodes and Cattalle gyuen to the mayntenñce of the fraternitie of saincte Katerine ther.

Videlt.   Twentie and foure yeowe shepe remaynyng w^t Thoms Yonge and John Holwaye praysed at ijs. le pece — xlviijs. The same Thoms and John have in their handes in redy money belonging to the same fraternitie — xviijs. . . . . lxvjs.

40. Hawkerygge and Wethypoole.

Lyghte and obitte foundyd wtin the parysshe churche ther.

Ar yerely worthe in   One Annuall rent to be levied and receyued out of the Issues Revenues and proffecte of the landes and teñte of —— Southcote ther . . . . ijs.

41. Selworthy.

Lights and obitte foundyd wtin the parysshe churche ther.

Ar yerely worthe in   Landes teñte and other hereditamente in the tenure of sondery psones as maye appere pticulerly more at large by the rentall of the same . . . . xiiijs.

Somerset Chantries.

Wherof in

Rent℮ resolute pd yerely . . . . ij*d*.

And so

Remaynethe clere . . . . xiij*s*. x*d*.

Alexaunder Popham and William Halley esquiers alleage **Memord.** that the Annuall rent of iij*s*. iiij*d*. pcell of the saide some of xiij*s*. x*d*. cumyng out of certeyne landes and tent℮ pcell of the possessions of the late Dissolued Hospitall or comaundrie of saincte Johans of Buckelande prioris in the saide countie of Somerss was discharged by reason that the saide late Hospitall or comaundrie w^t all the possessions thervnto belonging came unto the handes of oure late soulaigne lorde of famouse memorie Kinge Henry the viijth, by the dissolucon of the late priory of saincte Johans Jerlm in Ingland, wch comaundrye of Buckelande prioris aforesaide, and all the landes and hereditament℮ therto belonging amongst other thing℮ the saide Alexaunder and William did purchace of the saide late Kinge to them and to their heires for eu, and have shewed before the comissionors their lres patent℮ in that behalf, beringe date the xvjth daye of ffebruary in the xxxvjth yere of the saide late kinge his reigne, and thervppon prayen to be discharged of the saide Rent.

Somerset Chantries.

42. Dunster.

The Salarie of one prieste celebratynge w'in the parysshe churche ther.

Is yerely worthe in
Landes tent𝑒 and hereditament𝑒 in the tenure of sondery psones as may appere pticulerly more at large by the rentall of the same .... iiij*li*.

Wherof in
Rent𝑒 resolute pd yerely .... vij*s*.
And so
Remayneth clere .... lxxiij*s*.

Plate and ornament𝑒. Noone.
Memor𝑑. (Nil)

Lyghte foundyd w'in the parysshe churche ther.

Ar yerely worthe in
One half acre of lande lying in wachet gyven to the same use .... xviij*d*.

Wherof in
Rent𝑒 resolute paide yerely .... vj*d*.
And so
Remayneth clere .... xij*d*.

The Chauntrie of Sainte Laurence w'in the parysshe churche ther.

Is yerely worthe in
Landes, tent𝑒 and hereditament𝑒 in the tenure of sondery psones as maye appere pticulerly more at large by the Rentall of the same .... ix*li*. viij*s*. iiij*d*.

Wherof in
Rent𝑒 resolute paide yerely .... xx*s*.
And so
Remaynethe clere .... viij*li*. viij*s*. iiij*d*.

Somerset Chantries.

A Chalice, a pax, ij cruetts and too candelsticke of silv̄ waying — lxxij oz. *Plate and ornamtę.*

Ornamentes praysed at — ixs. iiijd.

John Bayly clerke of the age of lx yeres, a singing man, incumbent ther. *Memord.*

Memord.

The psonage ther was impropriat to the late Celle of Dunster and nowe in the kinge ma^{ties} handes

John Ryse clerke is vicar ther, who receyveth yerely for his salarie of the fermo^r of the foresaide psonage for the tyme beinge —iiijli. and his Diettę.

Ptakers of the Lordes Holy Soop ther — D.

---

43. Wythecombe.

Lyghte foundyd wtin the parysħe Churcħe ther.

Annuall rentę to be levied and receyued of the Issues Revenues and proffectę of the Mano^r of Wythecombe aforesaide . . . . xixd. *Ar yerely worthe in*

---

44. Wyuelescombe.

Obitte foundyd wtin the parysħe Churcħe ther.

Too closes of lande ther callyd Waterlete and Langelande in the tenure of John Conybere . . . . vjs. viijd. *Ar yerely worthe in*

Somerset Chantries.

Memord. The saide John Conybere hathe wtholden the saide rent of vjs. viijd. the space of iij yeres.

Memord.

The presentors have shewed ij dedes of feoffemt, And in one of the same dedes is contayned one burgage wt a garden, letten at the yerely rent of iijs. oũ and above all maner of charge and repris̃, And in the other feoffemt be contayned vj burgages set at the yerely rent of vs. iiijd. aboue all maner charges wch burgages appere to be gyven to the pformaunce of the will of the feoffees and no will therof shewed vnto the com̃yssion's howe be yt the saide presento's do affirme, that the Rent͠e com̃yng of the same have ben alwayes imployed to the repac̃ons of the churche.

Ther is a Chapell wtin the churche yerde ther, wherin hathe ben no masse theis viij yeres past, but vsed to kepe therin suche necessaries as be mete for the repac̃ons of the saide churche and in the same chapell ther is one bell.

Bell metall Do (½) c.

45. Exton.

Cattall gyuen to the mayntenñce of obitts foundyd wtin the parysshe Churche ther.

Videlt. One Kowe and vj shepe remaynyng in the custody of John Piers and John Wether praysed at . . . . xxvjs. viijd.

46. Sampforde Brytte.

Lyghte foundyd wtin the paryshe churche ther.

Annuall rente to be levied and receyued of the Issues and proffecte of sondery landes and tenñte ther as may appere more at large by the rentall of the same. . . . . ijs. iiijd. *Ar yerely worthe in*

---

47. Carehampton.

Lyghte foundyd wtin the paryshe Churche ther.

One Annuall rent to be levied and receyued of the Revenues of the landes and tenñte of —— Safyn ther . . . . iijd. *Ar yerley worthe in*

---

48. Stokegumer cum Capella de Byckenaller.

Lyghte foundyd aswell wtin the paryshe churche ther as wtin the sayde Chapell.

ffyue acres of lande ther in the tenure of Richarde Dodrige and hughe Colys — vijs. ijd. *Ar yerely worthe in*

And one Annuall rent to be levied of the landes and tenñte in Bickenaller belonging to the Deane and Chapiture of Welle — xviijd. . . . . viijs. viijd.

Cattall gyuen to the maynteñnce of lyghte wtin the same Chapell.

Six shepe remaynyng in the custody of Alexandar Jenkyn vielt. praysed at — xijs.

49. Brusheforde.

Lyghte and obitte foundyd w'in the parysshe churche ther.

Ar yerely worthe in — One close of pasture callyd Culverparke *al* Churche close in the tenure of Alice Skynn̅ . . . . v*s*.

---

50. Brympton Raffe.

Certayne Corne or grayne gyuen to the mayntenñce of a lampe w'in the parysshe Churche ther.

Videlt. — Twenty busshelle of Rye, remaynyng in the custody of Roger Webber and Richarde Hyll praysed at v*d*. le bz. . . . viij*s*. iiij*d*.

---

51. Elworthy.

Lyghte foundyd w'in the parysshe churche ther.

Ar yerely worthe in — One ten̅t w̅t a garden theronto belonging, and one acre of arable lande in the cōen feldes ther. . . . . iij*s*. iiij*d*.

---

52. Cutcombe cum Capella de Lowseborowghe annex.

Lyghte and obitte foundyd w'in the parysshe Churche ther.

Ar yerely worthe in — One Annuall rent to be levied and receyved of the Issues and proffecte of certayne landes and ten̅te ther callyd Cresham . . . . iij*s*. viij*d*.

Somerset Chantries.

Cattall gyven to the mayntenānce of Lyghte wtin the sayde Chapell.

Three kyne remaynyng in the custody of Willm Sydernym and Roger Grynslade praysed at — xls. And xvj shepe remaynyng wt the same William and Roger praysed at — xxxijs. . . . lxxijs. *Videlt.*

---

53. Olde Cleue.

Lyghte foundyd wtin the paryshe Churche ther.

Too cotages wt ij gardeyns adioynynge to the same gyven by Adam Warshesade to the vse aforesaide . . . . iiijs. *Ar yerely worthe in*

The Chapell of Iylonde wtin the saide paryshe.

The rent of the sayde Chapell wt a litle howse and certayne arable lande belonging to the same Chapell . . . . xvjd. *Is yerely worthe in*

---

54. Saincte Decomans.

The Chapell of the holy Crosse of Wachet wtin the sayde paryshe.

Landes tenātē and hereditamātē in the tenure of sondery psones as maye appere pticulerly more at large by the Rentall of the same . . . . xxvijs. *Is yerely worthe in*

                Wherof in

Rentē resolute paide yerely . . . . xviijd.

                And so

Remayneth clere . . . . xxvs. vjd.

A Chalice of Silū gilt — viij oz.   Bell metall C lb.   *Plate and Ornamtē.*
Ornamentē praysed at — iijs. iiijd.

55. Netlecombe.

The Chauntrie of saincte John Baptiste wtin the parysh churche ther.

Is yerely worthe in — Landes, tent̃ and hereditament̃ in the tenure of sondery psones as maye appere pticulerly more at large by the Rentall of the same . . . . viij*li.* vj*s.*

Wherof in

Rent̃ resolute paide yerely to sondery psones. . . . xij*s.* ob.

And so

Remayneth clere. . . . . vij*li.* xiij*s.* xj*d.* ob.

Plate and ornament̃. — A Chalice and a pax, w^t ij Cruett̃ of Silũ waying xxxvj oz., And a chalice of silũ and guilte wayinge viij oz. . . . . . xliiij oz.

Ornament̃ praysed at — vj*s.* viij*d.*

Memord. — John Wyther clerke of the age of lx yeres incũbent ther.

The heires of —— Stowey as free suters, owe sute vnto the saide Chauntrie, by homage, fealtie, escuage, and sute of courte, for a mylle, and certayne other landes in Cutcombe.

Ther is growinge about the scite of the premisses ccc trees, oke, ashe, and elme, estemed worthe, ij*d.* le pece — l*s.*

Obitt̃ foundyd wtin the parysh churche ther.

Ar yerely worthe in — One howse in Taunton letten to ferme unto John Darlinge — xviij*s.*

56. Porlocke.

Too Chauntries foundyd w'tin the parysh church ther.

Landes, tenementȩ and hereditamentȩ in the tenure of sondery   Ar yerely
psones, as maye appere pticulerly more at large by the Rentall worthe in
of the same . . . . xxiij*li.* vj*s.* ij*d.*

Wherof in

Rentȩ resolute paide yerely to sondery psones . xvj*s.* ix*d.* ob.

And so

Remayneth clere . . . . xxlj*li.* ix*s.* iiij*d.* ob.

A Chalice of Silu͂ guilte — xiij oz. do (½).   Plate and
Ornamentes praysed at — viij*s.*   Ornamtȩ.

Ther is but one incumbent ther whose name is Robte Lau- Memord. rence, clerke, having no certayne stipend for that he hathe (as he saythe), resigned the saide Chauntrie to the Lorde m̃ques Dorss a yeare past and more.

The underwoodes and copses belonging to the saide Chauntries contayne xx^tie acres, praysed to be wo^rthe cu̅y acre vj*s.* viij*d.* — vj*li.* xiij*s.* iiij*d.*, Wherof was wonte to be solde, and cut downe yerely, ij acres.

Ther was distributed yerely to too poore men remayning ther, by the fundaco͂n of the saide Chauntries, viz., to either of theym by the weke — vij*d.* . . . . lx*s.* viij*d.*

To a clerke S̃ving in the saide ij Chauntries by the fundacio͂n yerely for his stipend or wage — liij*s.* iiij*d.*

To the poore people ther yerely in breade and drinke in the tyme of the Annivsarie kept for the founders — xiiij*s.*

Somerset Chantries.

Lyghte foundyd wtin the same parysbe Churche.

Ar yerely worthe in — One howse ther nowe in the tenure and occupying of John Goulde Junr. — iiij*s*.

Goodes and Cattall gyuen to the mayntenñce of obite wtin the sayde parysbe churche.

Videlt. — Certayne householde stuffe remaynyng in the custody of sondery psones praysed at — xlv*s*. iiij*d*., And one kowe remaynyng in the custody of Petre Torre, praysed at — xiij*s*. iiij*d*. . . . . lviij*s*. viij*d*.

Memord. — The psonage ther is of the yerely value of — xviij*li*., Wherof Robte Broke, clerke, is now incumbent.

Ptakers of the lordes holy Sooper ther cclx psones.

Decanatus de Brydgewater.

57. Gotehurste.

Obitte foundyd w'in ther parysh Churche ther.

Twelue acres and one roode of lande and medowe ther in the tenure of John Rede by Indenture . . . . viijs. *Ar yerely worthe in*

58. Estquantocke Hedde.

Cattall gyuen to the mayntenñce of lyghtes w'in the parysh Churche ther.

ffoure shepe remayninge in the custody of John Bridge and Wiuelt. John Stevyn praysed at — viijs.

59. Coulue cum Strengston annex.

Lyghte foundyd w'in the parysh Churche ther.

One Annuall rent to be levied and receyued of the issues and proffecte of a tent of Sir John Rogers, Knighte, in the tenure of Henry Hastell . . . . vjd. *Ar yerely worthe in*

Somerset Chantries.

60. Stokegurcy cum Capella de Lylstocke annir.
The Guilde of oure lady ther.

Is yerely worth in Too closes of pasture ther callyd Wynkeldons nowe in the tenure and occupying of Elizabeth Walforde.......... ix*s.*
Wherof in
Rent℮ resolute paide yerely................. vj*d.*
And so
Remaynethe clere.................... viij*s.* vj*d.*

Goodes and Cattalles belonging to the same Guilde. Tenne kyne remaynyng in the custody of sondery psones praysed at x*s.* le pece — c*s.*
And redy money remaynyng in thandes of sondery psones — xj*li.* xix*s.* v*d.*.................... xvj*li.* xix*s.* v*d.*

Plate and Ornamt℮. None but a challice — viij oz.

Memord. Richarde ffluet, clerke, of thage of lxxiiij yeres incumbent ther.

Lyghte and obitte foundyd wtin the paryshe churche ther.

Ar yerely worthe in Landes, tent℮ and hereditament℮ in the tenure of sondery psones as maye appere pticulerly more at large by the rentall of the same .... xv*s.* iij*d.*
Wherof in
Rent resolute paid yerely................. v*s.* j*d.*
And so
Remaynethe clere .... x*s.* ij*d.*

Cattall gyuen to the mayntenñce of Lyghtes wtin the sayde Chapell.

Videlt. One kowe remaynyng in the custody of William Taylo*r* of Lyllestocke praysed at— xiij*s.* iiij*d.*

Somerset Chantries.

The psonage ther is of the clere yerely value of lviij*li*. Doctor Aemord. Alroge, Provoste of Eton pson of the same.

The Vicarage is worthe yerely — xxxv*li*. vj*s*. viij*d*., wherof Olyu̅ Stowyng clerke is nowe incūbent, who findeth alwayes ij prieste vnder hym to mynister ther, wherof one sveth at Lyllestocke.

Partakers of the lordes holy Soop ther dcxlvj psones.

61. Lynge.

The ffree Chapell of Sainete michell off Borrowe w̉tin the parysbe ther.

The rent of the same Chapell w^t one close callyd Chapell haye contaynynge one acre w^t the waye leadinge to the same . . . . ij*s*. Is yerely worthe in

A chalice of silu̅ gilte — xiij oz. do. (½). Leade ccc lb. Ornamente praysed at — xvi*d*. Bell metall mdccc lb. Plate and Ornamte.

The iron of the same chapell is thoughte to conteyne one hundreth weighte. Aemord.

62. Bromfelde.

Cattall gyuen to the mayntenānce of lyghte w̉tin the parysbe Churche ther.

One kowe remaynyng in the custody of Thom̅s Hare praysed at — xviij*s*. Worlt.

Somerset Chantries.

63. Spaxton.

Lyghte foundyd w'in the parysche churche ther.

Ar yerely worthe in — Landes and possessions w'in the tenure of sondery psones as by the rentall of the same more at large pticulerly maye appere .... iiijs. xd.

Memord. — Ther are certayne landes w'in the saide paryshe of the yerely value of xs. gyven to the mayntenñce and repare of the churche ther, and always imployed to that vse (as y^t is presentyd) whiche landes ar comprysed in the dede of feoffem^t wherin parte of the premysses charged in Spaxton aforesaide ar specified, but yt is not playnly expressed in the saide Dede to what vse theis landes wer gyven.

64. Cannyngton.

The free Chapell of Echestocke w'in the parysche ther.

Is yerely worthe in — Landes teñte and hereditamente in Cannyngton and Stokegurcy in the tenure of sondery psones as may appere pticulerly more at large by the rentall of the same. .... vjli. xvs. vj$d$.

Plate and Ornamte. — None but a challice — x oz. do. ($\frac{1}{2}$).

Memord. — Thomas Shakle, clerke, of th age of 1 yeres incumbent ther.

Ther be certayne woodes growing upon the landes in Stokegurcy, the value wherof is not presented.

Lyghte foundyd wtin the parysh churche ther.

Tenne acres of lande lyinge in Spaxton, in the tenure of Walter Stone .... viijs. *At yerely worthe in*

Wherof in

Rente resolute paide yerely .... xvd. ob.

And so

Remayneth clere .... vjs. viijd. ob.

---

65. Chedzey.

The Salary of a stipendary priest foundyd wtin the paryshe churche ther for eu͞.

Landes, tente and hereditamte in the tenure of sondery psones as maye appere pticulerly more at large by the rentall of the same .... xxxjs. *Is yerely worthe in*

Wherof in

Rente resolute paid yerely .... iijd.

And so

Remaynethe clere. .... xxxs. ixd.

None. *Plate and Ornamte.*

John Hawkins clerke of the age of xxiiij yeres incumbent ther. *Memord.*

Lyghte foundyd wtin the parysh churche ther.

Landes tenemente and hereditamente in the tenure of sondery psones as may appere pticulerly more at large by the rentall of the same .... viijs. ijd. *At yerely worthe in*

Memord.   The psonage ther is of the clere yerely value of xxxvij*li.* wherof John Newton, clerke, bachelo^r of Divinitie is nowe incūbent, who findeth one priest vnder hym to $ve the cure.

Partakers of the lordes Holy Soop, ccxl psones.

---

66. The towne of Bridgewater.

The Chauntrie of Sainete George w'in the parysbe churche ther.

Is yerely worth in   Landes teñt$ and hereditam^t$ in the tenure of sond^rly psones as may appere pticulerly more at large by the rentall of the same .... vij*li.* iiij*s.* viij*d.*

Wherof in

Rent$ resolute paid yerely .... xxij*s.* ij*d.*

And so

Remayneth clere .... vj*li.* ij*s.* vj*d.*

Plate and Ornamt$.   None but a challice — vij oz. do. (¼).

Memord.   John Saunders, clerke, of thage of l yeres of honest conversacōn incūbent ther.

The Chauntrie of oure lady w'in the same parysbe Churche.

Is yerely worthe in   Landes teñt$ and hereditam^t$ in the tenure of sondery psones as maye appere pticulerly more at large by the rentall of the same .... ix*li.* viij*s.* viij*d.*

Wherof in

Rent$ resolute p^d yerely .... xxviij*s.*

And so

Remayneth clere .... viij*li.* viij*d.*

Plate and Ornamt$.   None but a challice — viij oz.

Memord.   John Tollor clerke of thage of xl yeres incumbent ther.

The Chauntrie of the Trynitie wtin the parysh̄e Churche ther.

Landes teñtē and hereditamentē in the tenure of sondery psones as maye appere pticulerly more at large by the rentall of the same . . . . x*li*. xviij*s*. viij*d*.   Is yerely worthe in

Wherof in

Rentē resolute paid yerely. . . . . xxiiij*s*.

And so

Remaynethe clere . . . . ix*li*. xiiij*s*. viij*d*.

None but a challice — viij oz.   Plate and Ornamtē.

John Jugker clerke of the age of lxiij yeres, compotently lerned incumbent ther.   Memord.

Lyghtē and obittē foundyd wtin the parysh̄e Churche ther.

One Annuall Rent to be levied and receyued of the issues proffectē and revenues of certayne landes, belonginge to the maire baylyffē and Burgesies of Brigewater aforesaide, lyinge in Stower Eston in the countie of Dorss in the tenure of Thomas Boston. . . . . xiiij*s*.   Ar yerely worthe in

The Vicarage ther ys of the yerely value of xij*li*. vj*s*. viij*d*. ob, wherof Thom̄s strete clerke is now incumbent, and findeth one priest under hym to mynister, and helpe to s̃ve the cure ther, wch priest celebrateth eůy sondaye, at a Chapell annixed called horsey distant a myle from the parysh churche.   Memord.

The psonage is impropriat, and is in the kingē maties handes.

Partakers of the lordes holy Soop ther mc psones.

Thenhabitauntē ther make their most humble petic̃on to have a free gram̄er scole erected ther.

67. Northe Petherton.

The free Chapell of Sherston w'in the parysshe ther.

Is perely worth in Landes teñtẻ and hereditamentẻ in the tenure of sondery psones as maye appere pticulerly more at large by the rentall of the same. . . . . lxxs. vijd.

Plate and ornamtẻ. Two challicẻ waing — xiiij oz. do. (½).
Ornamentẻ praysed at — iijs. ixd. Bell metall — xl lb.

Memord. John Saunders, clerke, of the age of l yeres of honest conversacōn incūbent ther.

The Chauntrie of Newtonplacy w'in the sayde parysshe.

Is perely worth in Landes teñtẻ, Tythes and hereditamtẻ in the tenure of sondery psones as may appere pticulerly more at large by the rentall of the same . . . . vijli. vs. iiijd.
      Wherof in
Rentẻ resolute paid yerely . . . . vjs. viijd.
      And so
Remaynethe clere . . . . vjli. xviijs. viijd.

Plate and Ornamtẻ. A chalice of silū pcell guilte waying — xiij oz.
Ornamentes praysed at — viijs. iiijd. Bell metall do. (½) c.

Memord. John Andersey, clerke, of thage of lx yeres incumbent ther.

The Chauntrie of oure lady w'in the parysshe churche ther.

Is perely worth in Landes tenemtẻ and hereditamentẻ in the tenure of sondery psones as maye appere pticulerly more at large by the rentall of the same . . . . vijli. iijs. ixd. ob.

𝕾𝖔𝖒𝖊𝖗𝖘𝖊𝖙 𝕮𝖍𝖆𝖓𝖙𝖗𝖎𝖊𝖘.

Wherof in
Rent℮ resolute, ij*s*. ij*d*. ob. and fees, xvj*s*. viij*d*. paide
yerely .... xviij*s*. x*d*. ob.
And so
Remayneth clere .... vj*li*. iij*s*. xj*d*.
Two challic℮ waing — xij oz. do. (½).   𝕻𝖑𝖆𝖙𝖊 𝖆𝖓𝖉
Ornament℮ — none.   𝕺𝖗𝖓𝖆𝖒𝖙℮.
Richard Versar, clerke, of the age of xlij yeres indifferently 𝕸𝖊𝖒𝖔𝖗𝖉.
lerned incūbent ther.
The ffree rent of x*s*. vj*d*. pcell of the foresaide value, yerely to be levied and paide out of the issues and proffect℮ of the landes of one John Whyting hathe ben w^tholden and detayned theis too yeres past.

𝕷𝖞𝖌𝖍𝖙℮ 𝖋𝖔𝖚𝖓𝖉𝖞𝖉 𝖜^t𝖎𝖓 𝖙𝖍𝖊 𝖕𝖆𝖗𝖞𝖘𝖍𝖊 𝖈𝖍𝖚𝖗𝖈𝖍𝖊 𝖙𝖍𝖊𝖗.
One Annuall rent to be levied and receyued out of the Issues 𝕬𝖗 𝖕𝖊𝖗𝖊𝖑𝖞
and proffect℮ of certayne landes at Rydon w^tin the paryshe of 𝖜𝖔𝖗𝖙𝖍𝖊 𝖎𝖓
Northe Petherton aforesaide sometyme Marmaduke Maun-
sell℮ .... iij*s*. iiij*d*.
Ther was w^tin the saide parysh̄e churche one other Chauntrie, 𝕸𝖊𝖒𝖔𝖗𝖉. whereof one John langdon clerke was incūbent, who died three yeres past and more, whiche receyved yerely for his stipend, vj*li*. xiij*s*. iiij*d*., out of the Revenues of the Courte of the Augmentaçons, and before paide yerely by the late prioresse of Buckeland approprietoresse of the psonage of Northepetherton aforesaide, wch Chauntrie hath ben voyde and in the King℮ mat^ies handes cū sythe the deathe of the saide late incūbent.

The psonage impropriat as before is in the King℮ handes.
The vicarage ther is of the yerely value of xxj*li*. x*s*. v*d*., wherof John Rose *al* Wyllie, clerke, is nowe incūbent.
Ptakers of the lordes holy Soop dcccxj psones.

Decanatus de Pawlet.

68. Hunspyll.

The seruice of oure Lady wtin the parysh churche ther.

Is yerely worthe in
Landes, tentę and hereditamtę in the tenure of sondery psones as maye appere pticulerly more at large by the Rentall of the same . . . . xxxiijs. iijd.

Wherof in

Rentę resolute paid yerely . . . . ijs. xd.

And so

Remayneth clere . . . . xxxs. vd.

Cattall gyben to the mayntennce of the said s'uice.
Thyrtie and three Kyne remaynyng in the custodye of sondery psones praysed at xiiijs. iiijd. le pece . xxiiijli. iiijs. iiijd.

Plate and ornamtę.
A challice of silu waing — ix oz.

Ornamentę — none.

Memord.
Richarde langley clerke of thage of 1 yeres incumbent ther.

The seruice of saincte Nicholas wtin the same Churche.

Is yerely worthe in
Too acres of lande ther in the tenure of John Dūne of Morrewe for terme of his lyffe — ijs.

Cattall gyben to the saide seruice.
Sixe Kyne remaynyng in the custody of sondery psones praysed at xiijs. iiijd. le pece . . . . iiijli.

Plate and Ornamtę.
A challice of silu waing — ix oz.

Ornamentes — none.

Somerset Chantries.

Incumbent none. *Memord.*

It is presented that the foresaide ij acres of lande wer gyven by one Agnes Keneryge towardes the mayntefince of the saide ꝑuice to contynue so longe as the saide lande shoulde reste unclaymed by the next righte heires whiche nowe is claymed by Agnes the wyffe of William sterte, as the presento's do saye.

The psonage ther is of the yerely value of iiij^{xx}*li.*, wherof *Memord.* Doctor Creton is nowe incumbent and findeth one priest to mynister and ꝑve the cure ther.

Ꝑtakers of the lordes holy Sooper ther—dvj psones.

---

69. Wullavington.

The Chauntrie of saincte John Baptiste wtin the Churche yarde ther.

Landes tenemtꝭ and hereditamtꝭ in the tenure of sondery psones as may appere pticulerly more at large by the rentall of the same — xlviij*s.* ij*d.* And in Redy money paide yerely out of the Revenues of the Courte of the Augmentacons by vertue of a Decre ther made — iiij*li.* xvij*s.* iiij*d.*. . . . . . vj*li.* v*s.* vj*d.* *Is yerely worthe in*

Wherof in

Rentꝭ resolute paid yerely . . . . iiij*d.*

And so

Remayneth clere . . . . vj*li.* v*s.* ij*d.*

A Chalice of silu̅ pcell gilt waying — xij oz. *Plate and Ornamtꝭ.*
Ornamentꝭ praysed at . . . . vj*s.* viij*d.*

Bell metall lx lb.

Somerset Chantries.

Memord. Robte Stone clerke incumbent ther.

The Chapell is scituate w^tin the Churche yarde of Wullavington.

The Chauntrie of the Trinytie ther.

Is yerely worthe in Landes tenemt͠e and hereditamt͠e in the tenure of sondery psones as may appere pticulerly more at large by the rentall of the same — xlviijs. ijd. And in Redy money p^d yerely out the Revenues of the Courte of the Augmentac̄ons, by vertue of Decre ther made — lxxiijs. iiijd. . . . . vj/li. xviijd.

Wherof in

Rent͠e resolute p^d yerely . . . . iiijd.

And so

Remayneth clere . . . . vj/li. xiiijd.

Plate and Ornamt͠e. A Chalice of silu̅ pcell gilte waying — xviij oz.

Ornament͠e praysed at . . . . vjs. viijd.

Memord. Roger Wymbery clerke incumbent ther.

The Chauntrie of Saincte Kateryne ther.

Is yerely worthe in Landes tenementes and hereditamt͠e in the tenure of sondery psones as may appere pticulerly more at large by the Rentall of the same — xlviijs. ijd. And in Redy money paide yerely out of the Revenues of the Courte of Thaugmentac̄ons by vertue of Decree made in the same co^rte, — lxxiijs. iiijd. . . . vj/li. xviijd.

Wherof in

Rent͠e resolut paid yerely . . . . iiijd.

And so

Remayneth clere . . . . vj/li. xiiijd.

Somerset Chantries.

A chalice of silū all gilte in the custody of William Hody **Plate and** esquier, waying —. (*Not recorded*.) **Ornamṫe.**

Ornamentes praysed at — vjs. viijd.

Robte Prydyll clerke incumbent ther. **Memord.**

---

70. Greyngton.

Goodes and Cattall gyuen to the mayntenūnce of lyghte wt̕in the parysbe Churche ther.

One kowe remaynyng in the custody of John Bridge praysed **Widelt.** at xxs. And in redy money remaynyng in the handes of John Loveney — xjs. . . . . xxxjs.

On good ffrydaye yerely was distributed to the poore people **Memord.** of the proffecte of the p̃misses, ijd. ob.

---

71. Polett.

Lyghte foundyd wt̕in the parysbe Churche ther.

One Annuall rent to be levied and receyued of the Issues **Ar yerely** and Revenues of certayne landes in Hunspill late in the tenure **worthe in** of Richarde white for ij lb. of wex by the yere . . . . xiiijd.

The saide ij lb. of wex or xiiijd. for the same yerely hathe **Memord.** ben wtholden by the foresaide Richarde White the space of iiij yeres last past.

Somerset Chantries.

72. Cosyngton.

Lyghte foundyd w'in the parysshe Churche ther.

At yerely worthe in Cattall gyven to the mayntennce of the saide lyghte.
One acre of lande in the tenure of Roger Joyce ..... vj*d.*
Three Kyne remaynyng in the custody of sondery parsones praysed at — xvj*s.* le pece .... xlviij*s.*

73. Bawdrybe.

The ffree Chapell of fforde.

Is yerely worthe in
One teñt or Burgage in Stowell w'in the parysshe of Murlynche letten to Richarde Brent and others for terme of their lyves .... xxvj*s.* viij*d.*

Plate and Ornamt̃ẹ. None.

Memord. John Popwell clerke of thage of lxv yeres incūbent ther.

The parsonage ther is of the yerely value of — xvj*li.*, Wherof the saide John Popwell is incumbent who findeth one priest vnder hym to ?ve the cure.

Partakers of the lordes Holy Sooper ther iiij^{xx} psones.

Jurisdictio Glaston.

74. Budleyghe cum Capella de Baltesboroughe annex̃.

Obite foundyd w'tin the parysbe Churche ther.

One Annuall rent gyven by John Camell to be levied and receyued of the Issues and Revenues of certayne landes in Budleighe aforesaide . . . . iiij*s*.   Ar yerely worthe in

Goodes and Cattall gyuen to the mayntenñce of Lyghte as well w'tin the sayde parysbe churche as w'tin the sayde Chapell.

One Kowe remaynynge in the custody of Mathewe   Udelt.
   gregory praysed at . . . . xvj*s*.
And redy money remaynyng in thandes of sondery
   psones ther . . . . lix*s*. v*d*.

                                                          lxxv*s*. v*d*.

75. Mydlesoye.

The fraternitie of the name of Jesus ther.

A Chalice of silũ waying — ix ounc℮.   Plate and Ornamt℮.
Ornament℮ praysed at — xij*s*.

Ther be neither landes teñt℮ nor hereditam't℮ belonging to Memord. the saide fraternitie for the same was alwayes mayntayned only of the Devocõn of the people.

76. Weston.

The Seruice of oure lady ther.

Is perely worthe in ffoure acres and a half of lande lyinge in the feldes of Mydlesoye in the tenure of William Godfrey . . . . . . viij*s.* vj*d.*

Plate and Ornamt͡ę. Two challic͡ę waing — xij oz.
Ornament͡ę praysed at — xlij*s.*

---

77. Murlynche.

The Chauntrie of Catcote w'in the parysh͡e ther.

Is perely worthe in Landes tent͡ę and hereditam'͡ę in the occupying of Richarde Hodson clerke incumbent ther — xiij*s.* iiij*d.* And in all the Tythes of Catcote the tythe corne only except, and res͠ued to the pson of Murlynche aforesaide — lxvj*s.* viij*d.* . . . . . . iiij*li.*

Plate and Ornamt͡ę. A Chalice of sil͠u pcell gilte waying — xvj ounc͡ę.
Ornament͡ę praysed at . . . . lxxiij*s.* iiij*d.*

Bell Metall DCC wayght by estima͠c, vidlt, thre bell͡ę in the steple, a sancte bell: too leche bell͡ę in the chardge of William Cooke.

Memord. Richarde Hodshon clerke of the age of xlvij yeres incūbent ther.

The pticulers pcell of ye saide ornamt͡ę. A cope of blue taffata; vestment͡ę v paire, one of grene vellvett verraye olde, too of olde rotten taffita and too others of olde ragged Silke torne, a table, a cheste, too crock͡ę, too paxes, and an olde crosse of latten and an hollye water pott͡ę. An albe. A Surplesse. An olde palme clothe of canvas. An olde shete. A towell, and an alter clothe.

Somerset Chantries.

78. Strete cum Capella de Walton annex.

Obite foundyd w'in the parysh Churche ther.

One Annuall rent to be levied and recyved of the Issues and Revenues of foure acres of lande in Glastonbury, whiche landes belonge and were gyven to the pyshe churche of Strete for the Repa̅cons of the same churche . . . . xvjd.   Ar yerely worthe in

79. Glaston.

The Chauntrie ther.

Redy money to be levied and receyued of the Issues and Revenues of the late attaynted Monastery of Glaston, by thandes of the generall Receyvo^r of the saide Revenue, by vertue of Decree made by the gẽnall Surveyo^rs of the Kinge ma^{ties} landes in the Prince Counsell Chamber as maye appere by the same Decree . . . . vj$li.$ iij$s.$ iiij$d.$ Is yerely worthe in

A Chalice of silu̅ pcell gilte waying — ix oz.   Plate and Ornamtc.
Ornamentc praysed at . . . . xvij$s.$ iij$d.$
Bell Metall c lb.

Thomas Wellyswo'thie al ffletcher clerke incu̅bent ther.   Memard.

Ther be w'in the sayde paryshe of Glaston, Too Almoschouses, thone callyd Mawdelyns havinge ix poore people therin who receyve yerely of the Kinge ma^{tie} by thandes of his grace Receyvo^r of the saide countie after the rate of xd. le pece, eu̅y weke. The other callyd the newe Almosehouse, havinge x

Somerset Chantries.

poore people, paide in lyke maner after the rate of cũy of them vij*d*. le weke.

The personage ther is impropriat, and is in the Kinges ma^(tie) handes of the yerely value of lxxij*li*. Ptakers of the lordes Holy Sooper ther, DCC psones.

80. Westpennarde.

A Stocke of money gyuen to the mayntennce of lyghte wtin the parysshe churche per.

Item.	Redy money remaynyng in thandes of Thom̅s Wilkyns and Willm̅ Maple . . . . xlvj*s*. viij*d*.

Decanatus de Axbrige.

81. Wedmour.

The Chauntrie of oure lady ther.

Landes Teñtẽ and hereditamentẽ in the tenure of sondery **Is yerely worthe in** psones as maye appere pticulerly more at large by the Rentall of the same . . . . viij*li*. xvij*s*. vj*d*.
Whereof in
Rentẽ resolute paid yerely to sondery psones . . xxix*s*. viij*d*.
And so
Remayneth clere . . . . vij*li*. vij*s*. x*d*.

Two challicẽ waing — xij oz. **Plate and Ornamente.**
Ornamentẽ praysed at — vj*s*. viij*d*.
Bell Metall do (½) c.

William London clerke of the age of lx yeres incumbent ther. **Memord.**

It is presented, that parte of the premisses ben fee simple landes and parte graunted by lease for terme of yeres by sondery Deanes of Wellẽ, lordes of the Manoʳ of Wedmoʳ, and that thone is not knowen from thother, ne can presently be devyded.

The Seruice of Sainctẽ Anne w'tin the parysh̃e Churche ther foundyd for terme of yeres.

Landes, teñtẽ and hereditamentẽ w'in the Manoʳ of Wedmoʳ **Is yerely worthe in** aforesaide, dymysed and letten to farme by William Cosyn some-tyme Deane of the Cathedrall Churche of Saincte Andrewe in

Somerset Chantries.

Wellẹ then lorde of the saide Manoʳ unto sondery psones inhabitauntẹ of Wedmoʳ aforesaide for terme of iiij^{xx}xix yeres to the vse and mayntenñnce of the saide ȝuice, as by the Indenture of the same vnder the seale of the same Deane, datyde the first daye of September in the yere of oure Lorde God MDIX at large more playnly yᵗ maye appere . . . . ix*li.* vj*s.* ij*d.*

Wherof in

Rents reȝued upon the same Indenture yerely during all the saide terme, to the foresaide Deane and his successours for the Rent and farme of the premysses . . . . lxj*s.* x*d.* ob.

And so

Remayneth clere duryng the said terme . . vj*li.* iiij*s.* iij*d.* ob.

Plate and Ornamtẹ.   Two Challicẹ waing — xiij oz.

Ornamentẹ — none.

Memord.   John Partridge clerke of the age of lx yeres incumbent ther.

The ffree Chapell of Blackeforde.

Is yerely worthe in   The Rent of the foresaide Chapell· wᵗ the Tythes of corne and haye of Blackeforde aforesaide . . . . vj*li.*

Plate and ornamtẹ.   Two challicẹ waing — xj oz.

Ornamentẹ — none.

Memord.   John Clerke, gentilman, incumbent ther.

The saide Chapell is distant from the paryshe churche one myle and a half, and thenhabitauntẹ ther be xxiiij housecholdes.

The Quantytie or value of the lede Iron and Bellẹ, belonging to the saide Chapell be not presented.

Somerset Chantries.

The Salarye of one priest celebratynge w'in the parysh churche ther foundyd for terme of yeres.

Redy money gyuen by Walter Stone clerke by his last Will and testam^t, to the vse and mayntenance of the salarie of one priest celebratinge w'in the paryshe churche ther for terme of vij yeres begynnynge at the feast of saincte John Baptiste in the furst yere of the reigne of oure most drade soueraigne Lorde the Kinge ma^{tie} that nowe is, to be paide yerely by th'executo^{rs} of the last will and testam^t of the foresaid Walter Stone duringe the terme aforesaide . . . . vj*li*. *Is yerely worthe in*

Two Challice waing — xij oz.   *Plate and Ornamnte.*
Ornamente — none.

Robert Morice clerke incumbent ther hathe receyued iiij*li*.xs. *Memord.*
for iij quarters of a yere, endyd at Thanunciacon of oure lady an° ij^{do} E vj^{li} after the rate aforesaide.

One masse callyd Jesus masse foundyd w'in the sayde parysh churche.

One Annuall rent to be levyed and receyued of the Issues and Revenues of one pece of lande w'in the saide paryshe callyd Chaterly in the tenure of Thomas Broke . . . . ij*s*. *Is yerely worthe in*

The moytie of this Annuall rent was yerely gyuen and *Memord.*
bestowed upon a poore woman w'in the paryshe ther. . . . xij*d*.

The vicarage ther is of the yerely value of — xx*li*. viij*s*., *Memord.*
Wherof John fitz James clerke is now incumbent.

Partakers of the lordes Holy Sooper ther — M psones.

Ther be w'in the saide paryshe xij seuall villages, wherin

the saide nombȝ of people dothe dwell, having sondery chapells annexed, for their ease of Dyvine Suice, some three myles from the parysche churche.

---

82. Chedder.

The Chauntrie of the Trynytie w'in the parysche churche ther.

Is yerely worthe in
Landes teñtes and hereditamtᵉ in the tenure of sondery psones as may appere pticulerly more at large by the Rentall of the same .... cxij*s*.

Wherof in
Rentᵉ resolute paid yerely to sondery psones ..... v*s*. v*d*.
And so
Remayneth clere .... cvj*s*. vij*d*.

Plate and Ornamtᵉ.
A Challice waing — xij oz.
Ornamentᵉ — none.

Memord.
John Mattocke clerke incumbent ther.

The premisses eữy thirde yere stande charged wᵗ — xvj*d*., towardes the mayntenñce of the frythe or fense of Westbury parke pteynyng to the Busshoppe of Bathe.

The Chauntrie of oure lady w'in the parysche churche ther.

Is yerely worthe in
Redy money to be levied and receyued of the Issues, Revenues and proffectᵉ of the late monastery of Wytham, w'in the countie of Somerss, by thandes of the geñall receyvoʳ of oure souaigne Lorde the Kinge, of the Revenues of his gracᵉ court of Augmentacõns w'in the saide countie, by vertue of Decre made in the saide co'te in that behalf ... vj*li*. xiij*s*. iiij*d*.

A Chalice of Silv̄ waing — xj oz.   **Plate and Ornamtẹ.**
Ornamentes praysed at — viijs.

John Hawkyns clerke late incūbent ther, dyed the xvjth daye **Memord.**
of January anno primo E. vi^{ti} and nowe no incūbent ther.

Obite foundyd w^tin the sayde paryshe churche.

Landes and teñtes put in feoffm^t to the saide vse in the   **Ar yerely**
tenure of sond^r)y psones as may appere pticulerly more at large **worth in**
by the rentall of the same . . . . xxjs. iiijd.
Wherof in
Rentẹ resolute paid yerely . . . . vs.
And so
Reymaneth clere . . . . xvjs. iiijd.

The vicarage ther is of the yerely value of — xxiijli. xvjs. **Memord.**
viijd., Wherof Thom̄s Whyte clerke is nowe incumbent.

Ptakers of the lordes Holy Sooper ther — dxx psones.

---

83. Banwell.

The fraternitie ther.

Landes teñtẹ and hereditam^tẹ in the tenure of sondery **Is yerely**
psones as may appere pticulerly more at large by the Rentall **worthe in**
of the same . . . . lxxjs.
Wherof in
Rentẹ resolute paid yerely . . . . iijd.
And so
Remaynethe clere . . . . lxxs. ixd.

Somerset Chantries.

Plate and Ornamtẽ.   A challice of silũ waing — vj oz.
Ornamentes — none.

John lloyde clerke of thage of xlvij yeres incũbent ther.

The Chapell of Sainete George ther.

Is yerely worthe in   The Rent of the saide Chapell w^t one litle pece of grounde contaynyng one roode wherin the same Chapell is scituate — vj*d.*

Plate and Ornamtẽ.   A Chalice of silũ waing — vj oz.   Bell ⎫
Ornamentẽ praysed at — ij*s.* vj*d.*   Metall ⎬ xllb.

Memord.   ' The vicarage ther is of the yerely value of xxx*li.*, wherof William Nobbe clerke is nowe incũbent, who findethe one priest to helpe to mynister and s̃ve the cure ther.

Partakers of the lordes holy Sooper — cccc psones.

---

84. Estbrent.

Goodes and Cattall gyuen to the mayntẽnnce of a priest w^tin the parysbe churche ther.

Videlt.   Six kyne remaynyng in the custody of sondery psones, praysed at x*s.* le pece — lx*s.* and redy money remaynyng in thandes of Petre Jennet and John Gryffythe — ix*li.* . . . . . xij*li.*

85. Congresbury, wt the Chapell of Laurence Wyke annexed.

Cattall given to the mayntennce of obitte and lighte w'in the sayde Chapell.

Too kyne remaynyng in the custody of William Tyrrell and *videlt.* John Kinge praysed at — xviijs.

The Chapell of saincte Michell scituate w'in the churche *Memord.* yarde ther nowe in decaye and unkevered wherin lyme is stecked, leade molton, and suche other necessarie busynes don at the tyme of the reparinge of the paryshe churche ther is praysed wo^rthe to be solde — xxs.

The pyshono^rs be humble suters to bye the same chapell to the foresaide vse.

86. Southbrent.

Obitte foundyd w'in the paryshe churche ther.

One annuall rent to be levied and recyued of the Issues and Revenues of the landes and tente of John Gilling, lyinge in the boroughe of Axbrige — xiijd. *Ar yerely worthe in*

Redy money given to the vse and maytenaunce of a priest celebratynge w'in the paryshe Churche ther.

Redy money remaynyng in thandes of Richarde Tille, xiiijs. *videlt.* Willm Syme, xs., Nicholas Bybbyll, xs. Thoms Bonnche, xiiijs., Johane Palwebbe, xs. and William Watkyns, xiiijs.,—lxxijs.

                And in thandes of John Burton, Executo^r of the last will and testam^t of the late pson of Bryan of the bequest of the saide pson to the vse aforesaide — xx*li*. . . . . xxiij*li.* xij*s*

Memord.   The saide some of lxxij*s.* is thoughte desperate, forasmoche as the occupio^{r}s of the same be verray poore psones.

Memord.   The foresaide John Burton alleageth, that he hathe paide out of the foresaide some of xx*li.* for the debte of the saide Testato^r, x*li.* xj*s.* viij*d.* And further that he standeth in sute w^t the nowe incūbent of the saide benefice of Bryan for delapidacōns of the same. And so moche of the said money as shall remayne (the foresaide delapidacōns discharged), the saide John Burton is content to aunswer vnto the Kinge ma^{tie} at all tymes.

87. Lymplesham.

Goodes and Cattall gyuen to the mayntenānce of a priest w^{t}in the paryshe Churche ther.

Videlt.   Too kyne remaynyng in the custody of Thoms Banwell and William Lyone, praysed at — xxiiij*s.* And redy money remaynyng in thandes of the same Thomas and William — xxiiij*s.* . . . . xlviij*s.*

88. Marke.

The Seruice of oure lady w^{t}in the paryshe Churche ther foundyd for terme of yeres.

Is yerely worthe in   Landes tēnte and hereditam^{te} w^{t}in the Mano^{r}s of More, Southyoke and Marke in the countie of Somerss dymysed and

Somerset Chantries.

letten to farme by John Gunthorpe sometyme Deane of the Cathedral Churche of saincte Andrewe in Wellę then lorde of the saide Manoͬs, unto sondery psones pyshenoͬs and enhabitũntę of Marke aforesaide for terme of iiij^{xx}xix yeres to the use and maynteñnce of the saide Ꝗuice, as by the Indenture of the the same vnder the seale of the same Deane datyd the xxvth daye of Octobͬ) in the yere of oͬ lorde God MCCCCLXXIX at large more playnly maye appere . . . . viij*li.* xvj*s.* vj*d.*

Wherof in
Rent reꝺued upon the same Indenture yerely duringe all the saide terme, to the saide Deane and his successoͬs for the rent and farme of the p̃misses . . . . lx*s.* vij*d.* ob.

And so
Remaynethe clere duryng the sayde terme . . . cxv*s.* x*d.* ob.

Eighte kyne and a half remaynyng in the custody of sondery persons, praysed at seuall rates, amounting in all to — iiij*li.*viij*s.* And redy money remaynyng in stocke in thandes of sondery prsones — xviij*li.* xxij*li.* viij*s.*	Goodes and Caitall gyuen to the mayntenaunce of the saide Seruice.
Two challices waing — xxiij oz. Ornamentes praysed at — xxvj*s.* viij*d.*	Plate and Ornamtę.
George Kendall clerke incũbent ther.	Memord.
The psonage ther is in the lorde Protectoͬs gracę handes.	Memord.

Ther is one priest founde of the Devocõn of the people, besydes the foresayde Ꝗuice and besydes the curate of the same paryshe.

Ꝑtakers of the lordes holy Soop ther cccl psones.

Somerset Chantries.

89. Querwere.

The free Chapell of Ayleston Sutton w^tin the parysbe ther.

Is perely worthe in   The Tythe corne and haye of sondery acres of lande in Aileston aforesaide letten to Thomas Bocher . . . . xxiijs. iiijd.

Plate and Ornamte.   None.

Memord.   John More clerke incūbent ther.

The Chapell is vtterly decayed.

---

90. Blagdon.

Lyghte foundyd w^tin the parysbe churche ther.

Is perely worthe in   Landes tēntē and hereditan^{te} in the tenure of sondery psones as may appere particulerly more at large by the rentall of the same . . . . xs.

---

91. Bledon.

Cattall gyuen to the mayntenaunce of the Salarie of a priest celebratynge w^tin the pysbe churche ner.

Vidett.   Seven kyne remaynyng in the custody of sondery psones praysed at viijs. le pece — lvjs.

Somerset Chantries.

92. Crysten.

Obite foundyd w'in the pyshe churche ther.

Too acres of lande lying upon the comen hill ther in the occupying of John Payne — xvj*d.*   Ar yerely worthe in

---

93. Loxton.

Lyghte and obite foundyd w'in the paryshe churche ther.

Six acres of lande medowe and pasture in the occupying of sondery psones — vj*s.*   Ar yerely worthe in

---

94. Bageworth.

Obite foundyd w'in the pyshe churche ther.

Too acres of pasture lyinge in Hartefelde gyven to the sayde vse — iij*s.* iiij*d.*   Ar yerely worthe in

Redy money gyuen for the Salarie of a priest to celebrate w'in ye pyshe churche ther for terme of one yere.

Phylyp Saye deceased by his last will and testam^t bequethed vj*li.* for the salarie of one priest celebrating w^t the saide paryshe churche, by the space of one yere, to be paide by his executo^rs. Who according to the teno^r of the same will found one priest by the space of iij qrters of a yere endyd at Thannūciaĉon of oure lady an° ij^{do} E. vj^{ti} and paide vnto the saide priest for his wages iiij*li.* x*s.* And so yitt remayneth in thandes of the sayde executo^rs, as pcell of the foresaide some of vj*li.* bequethed as before . . . . xxx*s.*   Vixelt.

95. 𝔚𝔢𝔰𝔱𝔟𝔲𝔯𝔶.

𝔒𝔟𝔦𝔱𝔢 𝔣𝔬𝔲𝔫𝔡𝔶𝔡 𝔴𝔱𝔦𝔫 𝔱𝔥𝔢 𝔭𝔞𝔯𝔶𝔰𝔥𝔢 𝔠𝔥𝔲𝔯𝔠𝔥𝔢 𝔱𝔥𝔢𝔯.

Ar yerely worthe in   Landes teñte and hereditamte in the tenure of sondery psones as may appere pticulerly more at large by the Rentall of the same . . . . xiijs. viijd.

Wherof in

Rents resolute paid yerely . . . . xiijd.

And so

Remaynethe clere . . . . xijs. vijd.

---

96. 𝔅𝔲𝔯𝔫𝔢𝔥𝔞𝔪.

𝔗𝔥𝔢 𝔬𝔩𔡑𝔢 ℭ𝔥𝔞𝔭𔢫𔢲 𝔱𝔥𝔢𝔯.

Is yerely worthe in   The rent of the sayde Chapell w^t one acre of lande wherin the same Chapell is scituate . . . . xxd.

Cattall gyuen to the mayntenñce of the ffraternytie of oure lady ther.

Videlt.   Nyne Kyne remaynynge in the custody of sondery psones, praysed at xs. le pece —iiijli. xs. And for the rent and farme of the same kyne beinge behinde vnpaide the space of one yere — ixs. And redy money remaynyng in thandes of sondery psones — lxiijs. iiijd. } viijli. ijs. iiijd.

Memord.   Ther be no landes teñte nor hereditamente belonginge to this fraternitie.

Cattall gyuen to the mayntefince of lyghte and obite w'tin the parysh churche ther.

Eyghte kyne remaynyng in the custody of sondery **Widell.** psones praysed at seu̅all rates, amounting in all to the so̅me of . . . . lxxiiijs.

97. Axbrygge.

Obite foundyd w'tin the parysh churche ther.

Landes teñtẹ and hereditamentẹ in the tenure of sondery **Ar yerely** psones as maye appere pticulerly more at large by the Rentall **worthe in** of the same . . . . xxxvijs.

The Stewarde and Burgesies of the guildehall in the Boroughe **Memord.** of Axbrige aforesaide, claymeth the foresaide landes etc of the gifte of the Donors, wch they saye, was graunted vnto the saide Stewarde and burgesies for eu̅. And that they and their successors, shoulde bestowe yerely, for the mayntefince of eu̅y the saide donors seu̅all obitẹ, seu̅all so̅mes of money, amounting in all to the yerely value of — xxvijs. Howebeyt, they can shewe as yit, no good mattier of manyfest proffe herof.

98. Wynscombe.

The fraternitye of oure lady ther.

Landes teñtẹ and hereditamentẹ in the tenure of sondery **Is yerely** psones as may appere particulerly more at large by the Rentall **worthe in** of the same . . . . iiij*li.*

Somerset Chantries.

Plate and Ornamtę.
None but a Challice waing — ix oz.

Memord.
Thomas Snarpon clerke of the age of xl yeres incumbent ther.

The Chapell of Sampford wtin the parysbe ther.

Is yerely worthe in
The rent of the saide Chapell w^t a certeyne pcell of lande contaynyng by estimacōn one Roode wherin the same Chapell is scituate . . . . xij$d$.

Plate and Ornamtę.
A challice waing — ix oz.

Ornamentę praysed at — ij$s$. xd.

Cattall gyuen to the mayntefince of a priest celebratyng wtin the parysbe Churche ther.

Cattell.
Three kyne remaynyng in the custody of Richarde wocar and willm̃ vrche praysed at viij$s$. le pece . . . . , xxiiij$s$.

Decanatus de Bedmyster.

99. Clyvedon cum Hydall.

The ffree Chapell of Hydall.

One messuage callyd Hydall beinge w'tin the Towne of Clyvedon aforesaide w't all and singuler, landes, medowes, pastures and fedinge thervnto belonging, letten to farme to John Bulbecke for terme of lxiij yeres, by Indenture datyd the xijth daye of m̄che in the xxvjth yere of the reigne of oure late soūaigne lorde, Kinge Henry the viijth . . . . iiij/*li.*   *Is yerely worthe ut*

None.   *Plate and Ornamte.*

Ther hathe ben neyther incumbent, nor other mynister resident upon the saide ffree Chapell, syns the date of the foresaide Indenture, but the lessie receyveth the proffecte of the same to his owen vse as may appere by the first booke of Survey of College Chauntries etc. And ther is nothing presented concernyng this ffree Chapell at the last Survey, howesoeū the mattier goeth.   *Memord.*

---

100. Lyttelton.

Lyghte foundyd w'tin the parysshe churche ther.

The moytie of the rent of one acre of pasture in fframboroughe in the tenure of John Hodges . . . . xij*d.*   *Ar yerely worthe in*

Somerset Chantries.

Memord.   The other moytie of the rent of the saide acre of pasture is gyven and appoynted, to the finding, making, and repayringe of a gate betwixt the Manor of lytleton and framboroughe aforesaide.

---

101. Wrexall.

Obite foundyd w'in the paryshe Churche ther.

Ar yerely worthe in   Too teñtẹ w' their gardeyns scituate in Templestrete w'in the Citie of Bristowe. . . . . xiij*s*. iiij*d*.

---

102. Morton Hawtefelde.

The ffree Chapell ther.

Is yerely worthe in   Landes, teñtẹ, tythes, hereditamtẹ and other proffectẹ letten to farme vnto Arthure Payton for terme of the Incumbentẹ lyffe . . . . xxvj*s*. viij*d*.

Plate and Ornamtẹ.   A chalice of silũ waying — xix oz. do ($\frac{1}{2}$).
Ornamentẹ praysed at — xviij*d*.
Leade do ($\frac{1}{2}$) fooder.
Bell metall c lb.

Memord.   Thoms Elys clerke incũbent ther.
The Chapell is partely coũed w' leade.

103. Eston in Gordano.

Obite foundyd w'in the paryshe Churche of sainct George ther.

One howse ther callyd the Churche house put in feoſem' for eū for the mayntenñce of the same . . . . ·. . . iijs. iiijd.   Ar yerely worthe in

---

104. Clutton.

Lyghte foundyd w'in the paryshe churche ther.

ffoure acres of lande in the tenure of Thoms lokey. . . . . ijs.   Ar yerely worthe in

---

105. Porteshede in Gordano.

The chapell of oure lady Caponer al Capianer.

The rent of the saide Chapell . . . . viijd.   Is yerely worthe in

---

106. Chelworthe.

Lyghte and obite foundyd w'in the paryshe churche ther.

One acre & iij roodes of lande ther in the tenure of Robte Elme and Richarde Parsones — xiijd.   Ar yerely worthe in

107. Pryston.

Lyghte foundyd w'in the paryshe churche ther.

Ar yerely worthe in — One acre of lande ther gyven by Roger ffraunce . . . . . . ij*s*.

---

108. Henton Blewet.

Foure masses foundyd w'in the paryshe churche ther.

Ar yerely worthe in — One pece of grounde ther callyd Kentecrofte . . . . ij*s*.

---

109. Wynforde.

The Chapell of oure lady ther.

Is yerely worthe in — The rent of the saide Chapell w't a pece of grounde wherin the same chapell is scituate . . . . vj*d*.

Redy money gyven to the mayntenance of the saide Chapell. Memord. — Redy money rec left in thandes of sondery psones of the said paryshe — xvj*s*. viij*d*.

The parysheno'rs (saye) that they boughte this chapell ix yeres nowe past of one Mr. Vaughan sūnte to Sir Thoms Arundell knighte, then Survcio' of the suppressed landes w'in the saide countie.

Lyghte foundyd w'in the sayde Chapell.

Ar yerely worthe in — One acre and a halfe of lande in the tenure of Thoms Amysbury — viij*d*.

110. Walketon.

Lyghte foundyd w'in the paryshe churche ther.

One Annuall rent to be levied and receyued of the Issues and Revenues of one teñt w^t thapp'teñnce ther, nowe in the tenure of Richard Burret, for 1 lb. of wex . . . . vj*d*.   *Ar yerely worthe in*

---

111. Backwell.

Obite foundyd w'in the paryshe churche ther.

One Annuall rent to be levied, and receyued of the Issues and Revenues of the landes and teñte of —— Trystram ther. . . vj*d*.   *Ar yerely worthe in*

---

112. Chewe Magna cum Capella de Dundrey annex[?].

Obite foundyd w'in the paryshe churche ther.

One Annuall rent to be levied and receyued of the Issues and Revenues of the landes and teñte of John Horsington ther . . . . xiij*s*. iiij*d*.   *Ar yerely worthe in*

There was yerely distributed to the poore people in tyme of the obit in breade, iij*s*. iiij*d*. out of the p̃misses according to the teno^r of the last will and testam^t of the foresaide John horsington.   *Memord.*

Lyghte foundyd w'in the paryshe churche ther.

ffoure acres of lande ther gyven to that intent. . . . . . .xvj*d*.   *Ar yerely worthe in*

Somerset Chantries.

113. Compton Martyn.

Cattall gyuen to the mayntenũce of obite w'in the parysshe churche ther.

Videlt. One kowe remaynyng in the custody of William Myller praysed at — xvj*d*.

114. Yatton.

The ffree Chapell of Clareham.

Is yerely worthe in Landes tente, tythes and other hereditamente and proffecte, in the tenure of sondery psones as maye appere pticulerly more at large by the Rentall of the same . . . . lviij*s*. vij*d*. ob.

Wherof in

Rent resolute or penc̄on paide to the Vicar of yatton yerely . . . . x*s*.

And so

Remaynethe clere. . . . . xlviij*s*. vij*d*. ob.

Plate and Ornamtẽ. Noone but a challice guilt — vij. oz.

Memorđ. Symon Porter a scoler of the age of xviij yeres incumbent ther.

An olde Chapell ther.

Memorđ. The saide chapell scituate w'in the churche yarde of Yatton is ptely coũyd w' leade, — ij food'] do (½).

Thenhabitaunte of yatton aforesaide, make humble sute to bye the same Chapell to make therw' a slluse against the rage of the See, for the safegarde of the countrye.

Somerset Chantries.

Memord.

The psonage ther is of the yereley value of xlij*li*., wherof fraunce Mallet, Docto^r is nowe incūbent, not resident ne findeth eny priest ther.

The vicarage is of the yerely value of — xxxvj*li*. wherof Willm Lyson doctor is incūbent, who findeth ij priese to ṽe the paryshe.

Partakers of the lordes holy Soop ther — D psones.

---

115. Compton Dando.

Lyghte foundyd wtin the paryshe churche ther.

One Annuall rent to be levied and receyued of the Issues and Revenues of one house ther callyd Tuckershouse in the tenure of Alice Tucker widowe . . . . vj*s*.

Ar yerely worthe in

---

116. Portbury the paryshe of oure lady.

The Chauntrie or free Chapell of o^r lady ther.

Landes tent̄e and hereditam^{te} in the tenure of sondery psones as maye appere pticulerly more at large by the Rentall of the same . . . . xxvij*s*.

Is yerely worthe in

None.

Plate and Ornamte.

William Powell a Scoler in Oxforde incūbent ther.

Memord.

It is thoughte that a tent̄ w^t thapptennce in the tenure of William Russell of the yerely rent of xxx*s*. oũ and above the premysses, dothe belonge to this Chauntrie or ffree chapell, whiche teñt one —— Shipman claymeth and possesseth. enquire quo jure.

Jerome Grene wolde be examyned, who know^t moche herin.

The Chapell of Saincte Katerine ther.

Is yerely worthe in   The rent of the saide Chapell, w^t a pece of grounde wherin the same Chapell is scituate. . . . . xvj*d*.

Plate and Ornamt̃ẽ.   Too chalice waying — xviij oz. do (½).
Ornamentes praysed at — ij*s*. v*d*.
Leade iij fooder.
Bell metall (½) C.

Memord.   Ther be non other landes teñtẽ or hereditamtẽ belonging to this Chapell.

Obite and Trentalles foundyd w'in the pyshe churche yer.

Ar yerely worthe in   Three teñtẽ w'in the Citie of Bristowe scituate in the streate ther callyd, Balan streate . . . . xlv*s*.

Memord.   The vicarage ther is of the yerely value of — xij*li*., wherof Roger Sandforde clerke is nowe incumbent.

Ꝑtakers of the lordes holy Sooper ther, ccc psones.

---

117. Bedmyster.

The ffree Chapell or hospitall of saincte Katerine ther.

Is yerely worthe in   Landes teñtẽ and hereditamtẽ in the tenure of sondery psones as maye appere pticulerly more at large by the Rentall of the same . . . . xxj*li*. xv*s*. iiij*d*.

Somerset Chantries.

Wherof in
Rentȩ resolute paid yerly . . . . vs. iiijd.
And so
Remayneth clere . . . . xxjli. xs.

A chalice of silṽ waying — viij oz. do (½).   **Plate and Ornamtȩ.**
Bell metall C lb.
Ornamentes praysed at — iiijs. vjd.

William Clerke gent (as yt is saide) Maister of the same **Memord.**
hospitall by the Kingȩ lřes patentȩ, not yit shewed.

Ther be no poore people mayteyned or releved wᵗ the premisses, saving that the saide Mr. Clerke assigneth iij cotages pcell of the same hospitall woʳthe yerely — xxs. not charged in this value, for the poore men to dwell in, and other relief, they have non but as God sendeth.

The priest alwayes incūbent before hym was bounde to saye masse there thryse eṽy weke.

No fundaͨon shewed.

The ffree Chapell of knolle.

Landes, teñtȩ, tythes, hereditamᵗȩ and other proffectȩ in the **Is yerely worthe in**
tenure of sondery psones, as may appere pticulerly more at large
by the Rentall of the same . . . . lxvjs. viijd.

None but a challice — ix oz.   **Plate and Ornamtȩ.**
Bell metall — do (½) C.

John Bradley clerke incumbent ther.   **Memord.**
The Chapell is distant from the paryshe churche a quarter of a myle.

The Chapell scituate w'tin the paryshe churche yerde ther.

Is yerely worthe in
The rent of the same Chapell in thoccupying of the parysheno's ther — xij*d*.

The Chapell of sainete petre of Bysporte.

Is yerely worthe in
The rent of the saide Chapell w^t a pece of grounde inclosed, wherin the same Chapell is scituate — xx*d*.

Plate and Ornamt̃e.
A chalice of Silṽ waying — xix oz. do (¼).
Ornament̃e praysed at — vj*s.* ij*d.*
Bell metall do (½) C.

Lyghte foundyd w'tin the paryshe Churche ther.

Ar yerely worthe in
One Annuall rent to be levied and receyued of the Issues and Revenues of the landes and tenement̃e of John Kemys of Knolle — vj*d.*

Memord.

The psonage ther is of the yerely value of xxviij*li.*, wherof Henry willm̃s, clerke is nowe incumbent.

The vicarage ther is of the yerely value of x*li.*, wherof Nicholas Sampforde clerke is nowe incũbent, who findeth one priest to helpe to mynister ther.

Ptakers of the lordes holy Soop ther, cccxx psones.

118. Longaisheton.

The Chauntrie w'in the paryshe churche ther foundyd by Syr Richarde Chocke knyght.

Landes teñte and hereditam'e in the tenure of sondery psones, as maye appere pticulerly more at large by the Rentall of the same.................. viij*li*. vijs. viij*d*.   *Is yerely worthe in*

     Wherof in

Rente resolute paid yerely.................... xjs.

     And so

Remayneth clere............... vij*li*. xvjs. viij*d*.

A challice of silu̅ waing — ix oz.   *Plate and Ornam'te.*
Ornam'ente praysed at — iijs.

Henry Houghe clerke incumbent ther.   *Memord.*

The Salarie of a priest celebratyng w'in the Chapell of oure lady callyd merygate chapell foundyd by Niclas Chocke and Henry Chocke.

Landes tente and hereditamente put in feoffement, in the tenure of sondery psones as maye appere pticulerly more at large by the Rentall of the same............. cviijs. vj*d*.   *Is yerely worthe in*

     Wherof in

Rente resolute paide yerely............... xs. vj*d*.

     And so

Remayneth clere.................. iiij*li*. xviijs.

None but a challice — ix oz.   *Plate and Ornam'te.*
Leade — vij fooder.

Somerset Chantries.

Memord. No incumbent in this ꝑvice saving that the feoffees in the p̃misses beinge bounden to finde a priest w^t the proffectꝭ of the same, dyd gyve wekely to the Vicar ther, xij$d$., and the residue of the proffectꝭ converted to their owen vses.

The same Chapell is coũd w^t lede.

Obite foundyd w̃tin the parysh churche ther.

Ar yerely worthe in   Landes tentꝭ and hereditamentꝭ in the tenure of sondery psones as may appere pticulerly more at large by the Rentall of the same . . . . vij$s$. viij$d$.

Wherof in

Rent resolute paid yerely. . . . . vs.

And so

Remayneth clere . . . . ij$s$. viij$d$.

Lyghte foundyd aswell w̃tin the parysh churche ther as w̃tin the foresayde chapell of o^r lady callyd Mergate Chapell.

Ar yerely worthe in   Annuall Rentꝭ to be levied and receyued of the Issues Revenues and proffectꝭ of the landes and tentꝭ of sondery psones ther . . . . vs. viij$d$.

Cattall gyuen to the mayntenance of the same lyghte.   One kowe remaynyng in the custody of Thom̃s Everede praysed at — xs.

Memord.

The vicarage ther is of the yerely value of xli. xs., wherof John Roughe clerke is nowe incumbent.

Partakers of the lordes holy Sooper ther, cclx psones.

Decanatus de Froome.

119. Farley Hungerforde.

The Chauntrie of Saincte Leonarde w'in the Castell ther.

          ^{lxiijs. iiijd.}
One capitall messuage or farme w^t thapp'tenñce lyinge and beinge in Tellysforde in the tenure of Anthony Besye, and other   ^{cxviijs. iiijd.} landes teñte and hereditamentę in the tenure of sondery psones, as maye appere pticulerly more at large by the Rentall of the same . . . . ix*li*. xx*d*.   *Is yerely worthe in*

    Two challicę waing — xviij oz.   *Plate and Ornamtę.*
    Ornamentę — none.

    The Incumbent departed this lyffe in ffebruary anno ij^{do} E. vj^{ti}.   *Memord.*

    The Chapell is scituate w^tin the Kingę ma^{ties} Castle of ffarley aforesaide.

    The Kingę ma^{tie} is patrone of the paryshe churche of Tellysforde aforesaide, by reason of the foresaide Capitall Messuage.

Lyghtę foundyd w'in the parysbe churche ther.

    Too acres of arable lande ther in thoccupyinge of the wardeyns of the same paryshe churche — xx*d*.   *Ar yerely worthe in*

    The psonage ther is of the yerely value of — viij*li*., wherof hughe woodes clerke is nowe incumbent.   *Memord.*

    Partakers of the lordes holy Sooper ther iiij ij^{xx} psones.

120. Phylyppes Norton.

Lyghte foundyd wtin the parysh churche ther.

Ar perely worthe in

Annuall rente to be levied and receyued of the Issues and Revenues of the lande and tente of Henry Clerke, xij*d*., and John vigar vj*d*.. . . . . xviij*d*.

Cattall gyuen to the mayntenñce of obite wtin the same churche.

Uiuelt.

Too kyne remaynyng in the custody of Richarde Smythe and Richarde Parsons praysed at xvj*s*. le pece . . . . . . xxxij*s*.

121. Camerton.

Lyghte foundyd wtin the parysh churche ther.

Ar perely worthe in

One Annuall rent to be levied and receyued of the Issues and Revenues of the lande and tente of Richarde Bawne for Do. (½) lb. of wex. . . . . iij*d*.

122. Lauerton.

Lyghte foundyd wtin the parysh churche ther.

Ar perely worthe in

One Annuall rent to be levied and receyued of the Issues and Revenues of one tent ther, belonginge to the hospitall of Mary Magdalene in Bathe . . . . xij*d*.

123. Holcombe.

Obite foundyd w'in the paryshe churche ther.

Certayne landes ther in the tenure of William Protant .... xiijs. iiijd. — Ar yerely worthe in

---

124. Wulverton.

Lyghte foundyd w'in the paryshe churche ther.

One Annuall rent to be levied and receyued of thissues and Revenues of the pasture grounde of Mr. Horton callyd Hawkyns Hame lyinge in Rode. .... vjd. — Ar yerely worthe in

---

125. Merston.

Lyghte foundyd w'in the paryshe churche ther.

One Annuall rent to be levied and receyued of thissues and Revenues of the lorde Stourton's Medowe ther callyd Bynhill in the occupying of Johan Smythwike, vid. .... ijs. — Ar yerely worthe in

---

126. Kylmersdon.

Lyghte foundyd w'in the paryshe churche ther.

Landes teñte and hereditamente in the tenure of sondery psones, as maye appere pticulerly more at large by the Rentall of the same. .... viijs. viijd. — Ar yerely worthe in

Somerset Chantries.

127. Radstocke.

Lyghte foundyd w'in the parysbe churche ther.

Ar perely worthe in   One Annuall rent to be levied and receyued of thissues and Revenues of the landes and teñtȩ ther sometyme the Lorde M⁾neys and nowe the Lorde Thom͞s Howardes. . . . . vj*d*.

---

128. Chuton.

w⁺ the Chapelle of Eston maior, Eston minor, Palton, Enborowe and Faringdon annex⁹.

Lyghte foundyd w'in the parysbe churche ther.

Ar perely worthe in   One howse ther callyd Barrowe howse in the tenure of John Elys — xx*d*.

Cattall gyuen to the mayntefiñce of lyghte w'in the Chapell of Eston maior.

Cidelt.   One kowe remaynyng in the custody of John Hipsley praysed at — viij*s*.

Cattall gyuen to the mayntefiñce of lyghte w'in the chapell of Palton.

Cidelt.   One kowe remaynyng in the custody of Thom͞s Dando praysed at — x*s*.

The Chapell of Eston minor.

Plate and Ornamtȩ.   A challice of silū waying — xij oz.   Leade — ij fooder.
Ornamentȩ praysed at — ij*s*. x*d*.   Bell metall — xvij c.

Memord.   This Chapell maye welbe spared, for that Eston maior standeth w'in ij furlonge, and nerer the towne.

Somerset Chantries.

The Chapell of Enborowe.

The saide Chapell is couled wt leade, and so that the same Memord. may be tyled, thenhabitaunte ther ar content that the kinge matie have the leade.

Memord.

The vicarage ther is of the yerely value of xxxj*li.*, wherof John Gye clerke is nowe incūbent, who findeth in cūy of the saide chapelle one priest to mynister.

Partakers of the Lordes holy Soop ther — ccccxix psones.

129. Rode.

Lyghte foundyd w'in the parysh churche ther.

One annuall rent to be levied and receyued of the Issues and Revenues of the landes and teñte of John Sturgyes, gent .... xviij*d*. Ar yerely worthe in

130. Barkeley.

Lyghte and obite foundyd w'in the paryshe churche ther.

Landes teñte and hereditamte in the tenure of sondery psones as maye appere pticulerly more at large by the Rentall of the same .... xj*s.* iiij*d*. Ar yerely worthe in

Wherof in
Rente resolute paid yerely .... x*d*.
And so
Remayneth clere .... x*s.* vj*d*.

Somerset Chantries.

Memord. It is presented that an annuall rent of vijs. pcell of the p̃misses was gyven in this wyse, viz., for the pascall lyght, iiij lb. of wex; for obitẽ ijs. vjd. and the rest to remayne to the churche of Froome.

131. Dunney.

The Chauntrie ther.

Is yerely worthe in
Landes teñtẽ and hereditamentẽ in the tenure of sondery psones as maye appere pticulerly more at large by the Rentall of the same................................ vij*li*. xs. iiijd.

Wherof in
Rentẽ resolute paide yerely.............. iiijs. vjd.
And so
Remayneth clere.................... vij*li*. vs. xd.

Plate and Ornamtẽ.
A chalice of silũ waying — xiij oz.
Ornamentes praysed at — lxixs.

Memord. Richarde laurence clerke of thage of lx yeres incũbent ther.

It is presentyd that ij teñtẽ or cotages w*t* their app'tenncẽ of the yerely value of xvjs. pcell of the premisses wer graunted and dymysed towardes the mayñteñnce of this chauntrie for terme of cxx*tie* yeres, in the viij*th* yere of the reigne of Kinge Henry the vj*th*, and yt is not yitt knowen in whome the enheritaunce of the same dothe remayne.

Ther remayneth in the Chapell of this Chauntrie ccc lb. of iron in barres inclosinge the founders Tombe, wo'the xxs.

𝕾omerset 𝕮hantries.

Lyghte foundyd w'in the parysh churche ther.

Landes and hereditamt̃e in the tenure of sondery psones as maye appere pticulerly more at large by the Rentall of the same . . . . xij*d*.   **Ar yerely worthe in**

Memor̃d.

The psonage ther is of the yerely value of xv*li*., wherof Richarde Basinge is nowe incumbent. Partakers of the lordes holy Sooper ther, ccxxviij psones.

---

132. Mydsomer Norton.

The Salarye of one priest celebratynge in the Chapell of the guilde of oure lady w'in the parysh churche ther.

Certaine pcell̃e of aireable lande lying in Halowtro w'in the paryshe of lytleton letten to John Dando and others for terme of their lyves . . . . x*s*.   **Is yerely worthe in**

Cattall gyuen to the mayntenaunce of the same Salarye.

Foure kyne verray olde remaynyng in the custody of sondery psones praysed at seũall rates amounting in all to . . . . . . lxj*s*.

Two challice waing — xviij oz.   **Plate and Ornam̃te.**

Ornament̃e praysed at v*s*. iiij*d*.

Leade iiij food⁊).

Bell metall — vij lb.

The Chapell wherin the priest did celebrate standeth ioynyng   **Memor̃d.**

Somerset Chantries.

to the northesyde of the paryshe churche ther and is coū̇ed w*t* leade. And yf the saide Chapell shoulde be taken downe, the foresaide northesyde of the churche wolde lye open.

---

133. 𝔉𝔯𝔬𝔬𝔪𝔢 𝔖𝔢𝔩𝔴𝔬𝔬𝔡𝔢.

𝔗𝔥𝔢 𝔣𝔯𝔢𝔢 𝔠𝔥𝔞𝔭𝔢𝔩𝔩 𝔬𝔣 𝔖𝔞𝔦𝔫𝔠𝔱𝔢 𝔎𝔞𝔱𝔢𝔯𝔦𝔫𝔢 𝔱𝔥𝔢𝔯.

Is yerely worthe in — Landes teñtℯ and hereditamtℯ in the tenure of sondery psones as may appere pticulerly more at large by the rentall of the same .... vj*li.* xij*d.*

Plate and Ornamtℯ. — None but a challice — ix oz.

Memord. — John ffrye, gentilman, incumbent ther.

𝔗𝔥𝔢 ℭ𝔥𝔞𝔲𝔫𝔱𝔯𝔦𝔢 𝔬𝔣 𝔖𝔞𝔦𝔫𝔠𝔱𝔢 𝔄𝔫𝔡𝔯𝔢𝔴 *al* 𝔰𝔞𝔦𝔫𝔠𝔱𝔢 𝔍𝔬𝔥𝔫 𝔅𝔞𝔭𝔱𝔶𝔰𝔱𝔢 𝔱𝔥𝔢𝔯.

Is yerely worthe in — Landes teñtℯ and hereditamtℯ in the tenure of sondery psones as maye appere pticulerly more at large by the rentall of the same .... vij*li.* xviij*s.* x*d.* ob.

Wherof in

Rentℯ resolute p^d yerely .... vj*s.* viij*d.*

And so

Remayneth clere .. .. vij*li.* xij*s.* ij*d.* ob.

Plate and Ornamtℯ. — A challice waing — ix oz.

Ornamentes praysed at — x*s.* vj*d.*

Memord. — George Burley clerke incumbent ther.

Somerset Chantries.

The Chauntrie of Sainctè Nicholas wtin the paryshe churche ther.

Landes tentẹ and hereditamentẹ in the tenure of sondery psones as maye appere pticulerly more at large by the rentall of the same . . . . vij*li*. xvj*s*. iiij*d*.   Is yerely worthe in

             Wherof in

Rentẹ resolute paide yerely . . . . iiij*s*. viij*d*.

             And so

Remayneth clere . . . . vij*li*. xj*s*. viij*d*.

Plate none.   Plate and ornamtẹ.

Ornamentẹ praysed at — viij*s*.

John Lurpoole clerke incumbent ther.   Memord.

The Chauntrie of oure lady wtin the same churche.

Landes tentẹ and hereditamtẹ in the tenure of sondery psones as maye appere pticulerly more at large by the rentall of the same . . . . vij*li*. ix*s*. viij*d*.   Is yerely worthe in

             Wherof in

Rentẹ resolute paid yerely . . . . v*s*.

             And so

Remaynethe clere . . . . vij*li*. iiij*s*. viij*d*.

Plate none.   Plate and ornamtẹ.

Ornamentes praysed at — viij*s*.

Robert Graye clerke incumbent ther.   .   Memord.

Ther was but one chalice belonging to all the saide iij Chauntries wch the presento's saye was stollen.

Somerset Chantries.

Obitte foundyd w'in the parysshe churche ther.

Ar yerely worthe in — One annuall rent gyven by Margaret Osbo'ne to be levied and receyved of the Churche wardeyns of Trowbrige for the tyme beinge... x*s*.

Lyghte foundyd w'in the same churche.

Ar yerely worthe in — Too teñtẽ ther gyven by the Prior and Convent of the late priory of Bradleyghe nowe in thooccupying of Andrewe Gadbury and Raffe Cooper......... .... xvj*s*.

Memord.

The Vicarage ther is of the yerely value of xxij*li*. wherof Walter Collyns clerke is nowe incūbent.

Partakers of the Lordes Holy Sooper there DCCCXL psones.

Froome Selwoode aforesaide is a great m̃ket Towne.

Decanatus de Ilchester.

134. Mountague.

Lyghte foundyd w'in the parysshe churche ther.

One annuall rent to be levied and receyved of the issues revenues and pffecte of the landes and tente of Thom's Philippes esquier ther . . . . xij*d*. *Ar yerely worthe in*

---

135. Northperote.

Lyghte foundyd w'in the parysshe churche ther.

Annuall rente to be levied and receyued of the issues and revenues of the landes and tente of sondery psones ther . xj*s*. iij*d*. *Ar yerely worthe in*

---

136. Aller.

The Chauntrie of oure lady ther.

Landes tente and hereditamente letten to farme by Indenture vnto Thom's Clerke for terme of his lyffe . . . . vj*li*. ij*s*. *Is yerely worthe in*

A chalice of silu pcell gilte wayinge — xix oz.   *Plate and ornamte.*

Ornamente praysed at — xiiij*d*.   Bell metall — xl lb.

Somerset Chantries.

Memord. John Chynne clerke of thage of lx yeres incūbent ther.

The Chapell is scituate in the base co'te of the Mano' place ther foundyd by thaunceto's of therle c.f Huntington wch chapell is coūed w' stone wo'the to be solde — xxvjs. viijd.

Lyghte foundyd w'in the paryshe churche ther.

Ar yerely worthe in One annuall rente to be levied and receyued of the issues and revenues of the Mano' of Bere w'in the saide pyshe nowe the heires of Courteney for x lb. of wex. . . . . vs.

Memord. Neither the saide wex nor money for the same hathe ben paide the space of iij yeres last past, but hathe ben w'holden by the saide heires of Courteney.

Memord.

The psonage ther is wo'the yerely xxxvjli. xiiijs. xd., wherof John Chambo', Docto' of phisicke is now incumbent who findeth one priest to mynister ther.

Partakers of the lordes holy Soop ther cxxiiij psones.

---

137. Northouer.

Lyghte foundyd w'in the paryshe churche ther.

Ar yerely worthe in One halfe acre of medowe in thoccupying of the churche-wardeyns ther — xiiijd.

138. Ilchester Burrowe.

The free Chapell of the holy Trynytie of Whyteball ther.

The rent of the same Chapell wᵗ all the landes, teñtẹ, and hereditamentẹ belonging to the same letten to farme to Thomˢ Duporte for terme of xl yeres by Indenture datyd the xxviijᵗʰ daye of June in the xxxvijᵗʰ yere of the reigne of oure late soũaigne lorde of famouse memory Kinge Henry the viijᵗʰ, as in the same Indenture more playnly maye appere . . . . . xvj*li.* x*s.*   **Is yerely worthe in**

None.   **Plate and ornamtẹ.**

George Carrowe clerke incũbent ther.   **Memord.**

The Chapell is scituate wᵗ in the towne of Ilchester.

No fundac̄on shewed.

The Chapell callyd Mychelle at Bowe.

The rent of the same chapell wᵗ one roode of lande and one olde Dovehouse ther — iiij*d.*   **Is yerely worthe in**

Memord.

The psonage ther is wurthe yerely — ix*li.* ij*s.* vj*d.*, wherof Gycles Hylling clerke is nowe incumbent.

Partakers of the lordes holy Soop ther iiijˣˣxv psones.

139. Lympngton.

The Chauntrie of oure lady w'in the parysshe churche ther.

Is yerely worthe in
The Mansion house of the same Chauntrie and certeyne landes thervnto belonginge . . . . viij*s*.

And in redy money to be levied and receyued yerely of thissues and revenues of the Manor of Lymyngton aforesaide nowe the lorde m̄ques Dorsett*e*. . . . . . lxxij*s*.

iiij*li*

Plate and ornam'te.
A Chalice of Silu̅ waying — xj oz.
Ornament*e* praysed at . . . . xvj*d*.

Memord.
Thomas Raplyn clerke incūbent ther.

Lyghte foundyd w'in the parysshe Churche ther.

Ar yerely worthe in
Too acres of arable lande in the tenure of John Eston ther, vj*d*. And one annual rent, iiij*d*., to be levied and receyued of thyssues and revenues of the landes of John Lye in Lymyngton aforesaide . . . . x*d*.

Memord.

The psonage ther is wo'the yerely — xxj*li*. vj*s*. v*d*. ob., wherof the foresaide Thom's Raplyn is nowe incūbent.

Partakers of the Lordes Holy Sooper ther, ciiij psones.

140. Martocke.

The Chauntrie w'in the paryshe churche ther.

Landes teñte and hereditamte in the tenure of sondery psones as maye appere pticulerly more at large by the rentall of the same — xiiij*li.* v*s.* iiij*d.*   *Is yerely worthe in*

Whereof in

Rente resolute, v*s.*; fees xxiij*s.* iiij*d.*; and annuyties paide yerely to sondery psones, vj*li.* xiij*s.* iiij*d.* — viij*li.* xx*d.*

And so

Remayneth clere — vj*li.* iij*s.* viij*d.*

A Chalice of Tynne.   *Plate and Ornamte.*
Ornamentes praysed at — ij*s.*

John Skute clerke incūbent ther.   *Memord.*

The Salarie of one priest to celebrate w'in the paryshe churche ther foundyd for terme of yeres.

Certayne landes medowes and pastures lyinge w'in the paryshe of Martocke aforesaide dymysed and letten to farme by Thom's Harrys sometyme Treasore' of the Cathedrall church of saincte Andrewe in Welle and proprietarie of the paryshe churche of Martocke aforesaide to the same Treasorie vnyted and annexed vnto sondery psones inhabitaunte of Martocke aforesaide for terme of iiij^{xx}xix yeres, to the vse and mayteñnce of the saide Salarie, as by thindenture therof made under the seale of the foresaide Treasoro' datyd in the feast of saincte m)tyn the bysshop, in the vth yere of the reigne of Kinge Henry the vijth at large more playnly may appere . . . . . . lx*s.*   *Is yerely worthe in*

Somerset Chantries.

     Wherof in
Rent res)ued upon the same Indenture yerely during all the saide terme to the foresaide Treasoro^r and his successours for the rent and farme of the p̃misses............vj*s*. viij*d*.
     And so
Remaynethe clere durynge the sayde terme..... liij*s*. iiij*d*.

Plate and ornam͡te. None.

Memo͡rd. No incumbent in this ſvice.

The premysses after thexspiracõn of the saide lease shall reu͂te holy vnto the Treasoro^r of the saide Cathedrall Churche for the tyme beinge.

The Chapell of Longelode.

Is perely worthe in The rent℮ of the sayde chapell w^t one pece of grounde callyd chapell haye and one litle cotage w^t one acre of arable lande....................... xvj*d*.

Plate and ornam͡te. A chalice of silu͡ waying — xiij oz.
Ornament℮ praysed at — v*s*. iiijd.

The Salarie of a Stipendarye priest ther.

Is perely worthe in Redy money to be levied and receyued of the Issues and Revenues of the Mano^r of Martocke nowe the Duke of Suffolk℮, by thandes of the baylyff of the saide mano^r for the tyme beinge — xl*s*.

Plate and ornam͡te. None.

Memo͡rd. Stevyn Nurse clerke incumbent ther.
The Salarie of the saide Incumbent hathe ben alwayes viij

Somerset Chantries.

m̄rkẹ by the yere untill the Duke of Suffolke that dede ys, about vij yeres nowe past, and eůsythe, hathe wᵗdrawen the saide Salarie saving the foresaide sōme of xls.

The chapell wherin the saide incūbent was wont to celebrate, callyd oʳ ladyes chapell scituate nere vnto the mansion place of the saide Manoʳ was plucked downe and solde by the saide Duke, vij yeres past.

Thenhabitauntẹ ther did of olde tyme gyve to the lorde of the saide Manoʳ certeyne busshellẹ of wheate callyd churche yerde wheate towardes the finding of the saide priest, whiche wheate is paid at this daye, but the salarie wᵗdrawen as before.

Lyghte foundyd wᵗin the parysshe churche ther.

One annuall rent to be levied and receyued of the issues and Revenues of a teñt wᵗ thapprteñnces in Pykesaishe. . . . . . viijd.   Ar yerely worthe in

Lyghte foundyd wᵗin the chapell of Stapleton wᵗin yᵉ same parysshe.

One annuall rent to be levied and receyued of thissues and Revenues of an acre of medowẹ belonging to a teñt in thamlet of Stapleton in thoccupying of John Borowe. . . . . xijd.   Ar yerely worthe in

Memorᵈ.

The psonage of Martocke is impropriat to the Treasurie of the Cathedrall churche of Wellẹ.

The Vicarage ther is woʳthe yerely — xv*li* ixs. xd.   The incūbent wherof findeth ij priestẹ to mynister, one in the paryshe churche and thother in the chapell of Stapleton aforesaide.

Partakers of the lordes holy Soͨop ther ixiij psones.

141. Charlton Adam.

The Chauntrie or free Chapell sometyme callyd the Chapell of the Holy Gost.

Is yerely worthe in The rent of the saide chapell w^t all the landes medowes pastures and hereditamentes belonginge to the same letten to farme vnto John Larder esquier for terme of xxj yere by Indenture dated vnder the seale of Thom's Russell clerke late incūbent ther the last daye of mche in the xxxvjth yere of the reigne of o^r late souaigne lorde Kinge Henry the viijth. xxvj*s.* viij*d*.

Plate and ornamte. None.

Memord. The chapell is adioynyng to the howse of the saide Mr. larder, wherin was no masse theis xx or xxx yeres howbeyt he paide the saide rent to the incūbent for the tyme being.

No incūbent ther.

Obite foundyd w^tin the paryshe churche ther.

Memord. Ther is a howse w^tin the same paryshe comonly callyd the churche house gyven to the mayntenñce of the saide obitte, as maye appere by the feoffemte therof; wch howse is praysed wo'the to be solde — lx*s.*

William Hodges hathe p'chased of the Kinge ma^{tie} the Mano^r of Charlton Adam aforesaide as maye appeare by his lres patente of the same, who vnder colo^r of the saide p'chace claymeth the foresaide house to be pcell of the saide mano^r.

Somerset Chantries.

142. Charleton Makerell.

The Chauntrie ther.

Eyghte acres of medowe and xxx acres of arable lande lying in the comon medowes and feldes ther in thoccupyinge of John Drewe. . . . . xxvjs. viijd.   **Is yerely worthe in**

None.   **Plate and ornamtẹ.**

John Drewe jun^r incūbent ther.   **Memord.**

---

143. Longe Sutton.

The Chapell of Upton.

The rente of the same Chapell. . . . . iiijd.   **Is yerely worthe in**

A chalice of silū waying — xviij oz.   **Plate and ornamtẹ.**

Ornamentẹ praysed at — xxd.

The chapell is half a myle from the paryshe churche and maye well be spared.   **Memord.**

Ther be no landes belonging to this chapell.

The Chapell of Knolle.

The rente of the same Chapell . . . . iiijd.   **Is yerely worthe in**

A chalice of silū waying — xviij oz.   **Plate and ornamtẹ.**

Ornamentes praysed at — xxd.

This Chapell is a quarter of a myle from the paryshe churche and maye well be spared.   **Memord.**

Ther be no landes apperteynyng to this chapell.

144. Evylton.

The ffree Chapell of Evylton w'in the lordeshyp of Spekyngton.

Is yerely worthe in

The rent and farme of lv acres of arable lande medowe and pasture w^t their app'tenñces letten to farme vnto william hodges the yonger for terme of xl yeres by Indenture datyd the seconde daye of Aprill in the first yere of the reigne of oure soūaigne Lorde the Kinge ma^tie that nowe is,—xxxiijs.iiijd. And in sondery Tythes payable yerely by sondery psones, viijs. iiijd. . . xljs. viijd.

Plate and ornamt̃e.

None.

Memord.

William Hodges clerke incūbent ther.

The chapell standing w'in the paryshe of Spekington is the verray ffree chapell or chauntrie self, as farre as the presento^rs can saye.

The foresaide william Hodges about ij yeres nowe past, solde of the saide grounde xxxij elmes estemed at xljs. iiijd.

Memord.

The psonage ther is of the yerely value of xxxij*li*. wherof Thom^s Daye is nowe incumbent

Partakers of the lordes Holy Soop ther cxlj psones.

---

145. The Borough of Langporte *al* Lamporte.

The Chauntrie of John Heron foundyd w'in the paryshe churche ther.

Is yerely worthe in

Landes tent̃e and hereditamt̃e in the tenure of sondery psones as maye appere pticulerly more at large by the Rentall of the same. . . . . viij*li*. ijs. xjd.

Somerset Chantries.

Wherof in
Rente resolute paide yerely to sondery psones ... xxs. xd.
And so
Remayneth clere .... vijli. ijs. jd.

A chalice of silu waying — xij oz.   Plate and ornamte.
Ornamente praysed at — vs.

John Benet clerke incumbent ther, who hathe also a yerely Memord. penĉon out of the house of Glaston of iiijli.

The Salarie of too prieste ther callyd fraternitie prieste.

Redy money to be levied and receyued of thissues Revenues and proffecte of the landes tente and hereditamte belonginge to the Porte Ryve and comynaltie of the saide Borrowe by thandes of the Receyvo^r of the same Revenues, viz. for the stipened or Salarie of either of the saide prieste cvjs. viijd. .... xli. xiijs. iiijd.   Is yerely worthe in

None.   Plate and ornamte.

Walter Hancocke clerke incumbent in one of the foresaide Memord. Suices, and thother Suice is voyde and hathe ben by the space of a yere and a quarter.

It is presentyd that theis ij Suices have had contynuaunce only at the will and pleasure of the porteryve and comynaltie of of the saide Borowe w'out eny fundaĉon, wherfore the same porteryve and comynaltie make humble Peticon That they maye be suffered and licenced, to converte the saide stipendes to the repaĉons and maynteññce of the Bridge ther whiche is a great bridge of stone w^t xxx arches beinge the great staye of that Towne and all the contrye theraboute.

Memord.

The churches of Huyshe and Lamporte ar all one benefice, the psonage wherof is impropriat, to the Archedeaconrie of Welle and is yerely wo'the — xxviij*li*.

The vicarage ther is wo'the yerely xiiij*li*. x*s*., wherof Thomƒ Rosyter is nowe incūbent.

One of theis ij churches maye well be spared and taken downe, for they stande w'in a burdebolte shote together.

Ptakers of the lordes holy Soop ther ccccxx psones.

The Burrowe of Lamporte *al* Langporte aforesaide is a m̃ket Towne sore in decaye.

146. Stoke subtus Hambden.

The free Chapell of Sainete Nicholas ther.

Is yerely worthe in
Landes tentę tythes and hereditamtę in the tenure of sondery psones as maye appere pticulerly more at large by the Rentall of thē same.................. xj*li*. ix*s*. v*d*.

Wherof in

Rentę resolute paide yerely .... vj*s*. vij*d*.

And so

Remayneth clere .... xj*li*. ij*s*. x*d*.

Plate and ornamtę.
A chalice of silũ remaynyng in thandes of the incūbent waying—(*not stated*). Leade iiij foder.

Ornamentę praysed at — iij*s*. iiij*d*.

Bell metall, ccc lb.

Somerset Chantries.

Thoṁs Canner clerke incūbent ther.   **Memord.**

The saide Chapell is distaunt from the paryshe churche one myle and more and thenhabitauntꝭ dwellers about the same moost humbly besechen to have the saide Chapell stande for their ease of Dyvyne ꝯuice and mynistracōn and that the pson ther may have the tythes, lxvjs. viijd., due to the saide ffree chapell pcell of the foresaide value, allowed towardes the salarie of the mynister ther.

Memord.

The psonage ther is of the yerely value of xxxiijli., wherof the foresaide Thoṁs Canner is nowe incūbent, and resident in saincte Stevyns at Westmͬ, who findeth one Curate to mynyster in the pyshe churche of Stoke aforesaide, and also one priest singing in the foresaide free chapell, removable at the pleasure of the saide pson.

Partakers of the Lordes Holy Sooper ther clx psones.

Somerset Chantries.

Decanatus de Cary.

147. Doultynge w^t the Chapelles of West Cranmer, Est Craum?, Downed, and Stoke Saincte Michell annexed.

Cattall gyuen to the mayntenñce of a priest wtin the paryshe churche ther.

Videlt. Six kyne remaynynge in the custody of sondery psones praysed at scuall rates amounting in all to lviijs. and xl.^{tie} shepe remaynyng also in the custody of sondery psones praysed at — xxxiijs. iiijd. iiijli. xjs. iiijd.

Cattall gyuen to the mayntenñce of Lyghtes wtin the same churche.

Videlt. One kowe remaynyng in the custody of Amye Kynman praysed at . . . . viijs.

Redy money putt in stocke to the mayntenñce of a priest wtin the Chapell of Weste Cranmer.

Videlt. Redy money remaynynge in thandes of Thom^s Davys — xxvjs. viijd.

Cattall gyuen to the mayntenñce of lyghte wtin the same Chapell.

Videlt. One kowe remaynyng in the custody of thexecuto^{rs} of John Haryes p'ysed at — viijs.

Somerset Chantries.

Redy money putt in stocke to the mayntenñce of lyghte w'in the Chapell of Downed.

Redy money remaynynge in thandes of George Warre — Udelt. vijs.

The Guylde of Stokelane al Michell Stoke w'in the parysh of Doultyng.

Landes, teñtẹ and heriditamtẹ in the tenure of sondery psones as maye appere pticulerly more at large by the Rentall of the same .... iiij*li*. iijs. iiij*d*.   *Is yerely worthe in*

Wherof in

Rentẹ resolute paid yerely .... iiijs. vj*d*.

And so

Remayneth clere .... lxxviijs. x*d*.

One teñt and a house callyd the bakehouse w' their app'teñncẹ in Stoke aforesaide, dymysed and letten to farme by Henry Erle of Northūberland, vnto sondery psones inhabitauntẹ of Stoke, wardeyns of the saide Guilde, for terme of iiijxx xix yeres to the use and maynteñnce of the Salarie of a p̃est celebrating w'in the said chapell of Stoke, by Indenture datyd the xxj'th daye of July in the yere of o' lorde God mdxxij as by the same Indenture at large more playnly maye appere .... xls.

Wherof in

Rent resued upon the saide Indenture yerely duringe all the saide terme to the foresaide Erle and his heires for the rent and farme of the p̃mysses .... xiijs. x*d*.

And so

Remayneth clere during the sayd terme ...... xxvjs. ij*d*.

Plate and ornamtℯ.	A challice waing — xvj oz.
	Ornamentes praysed at — vijs. iiijd.
Memord.	Thoms Horte *al* Yetton of thage of lxvj yeres an impotent and lame man incūbent ther.

Thenhabitauntℯ of Stoke aforesaide being distaunt from their paryshe churche ij myles p̃chased the landes teñtℯ and hereditamtℯ before specyfied wᵗ their owen money, to thentent to have a priest to celebrate in the Chapell ther, for their ease of Dyvine ℈uice.

Thenheritaunce of the saide lease remayneth in the heires of therle of Northumb̃ᵉland aforesaide.

Memord.

The vicarage ther is of the yerely value of xxjli., wherof Willm Burman clerke is nowe incumbent, who findeth iij priestℯ, one to ℈ve the cure ther, one at Westcranm̃ and Estcranm̃, and one at Downed and Stoke saincte Michell.

Partakers of the lordes Holy Soop wᵗin the saide paryshe dclxxv p̃sones.

148. Castell Cary.

Obite foundyd wᵗin the paryshe churche ther for terme of certeyne yeres.

At yerely worthe in	One annuall rent to be levied and receyued of the Issues and proffectℯ of certayne landes callyd Hayes lyinge wᵗin the Lordeship of Bratton late in the tenure of Henry Riesse for terme of xxxiij yeres yit to cū . . . . xs.

Somerset Chantries.

149. Pulton wt the Chapell of Wotton annexed.

Cattall gyuen to the mayntenñce of lyghte wtin the parysshe churche ther.

Three kyne remaynyng in the custody of sondery psones **Videlt.** pysed at xs. le pece — xxxs.

Lyghte foundyd wtin the sayde chapell.

Six acres of lande ther in thoccupyinge of John Alforde and others — xs. **Ar yerely worthe in**

---

150. Parlyngton.

Lyghte foundyd wtin the parysshe churche ther.

Too acres of lande lyinge in the feldes of Galhampton wtin the paryshe of Northe Cadbury — xvjd. **Ar yerely worthe in**

---

151. Awmesforde.

Redy money gyuen to the mayntenñce of a priest ther by the space of one qrter of a yere.

Redy money gyven by Richard Cooper remaynyng in **Videlt.** thande of Henry Cary — xxvjs. viijd.

Somerset Chantries.

152. Kyngton Manfelde.

Cattall gyuen to the mayntenance of lyghte wtin the parysshe churche ther.

Videlt. One kowe remaynyng in the custody of Richarde Barnes of Estchaledon praysed at — xvs.

153. Horneblougbton.

Lyghte foundyd wtin the parysshe churche ther.

Ar yerely worthe in One annuall rent to be levied and receyued of the Issues and Revenues of a certayne pasture ther callyd the Softclose, nowe Richard M'shalle esquier. . . . . xiid.

154. West Lydforde.

Cattall gyuen to the mayntenance of obitte wtin the parysshe churche ther.

Videlt. Foure kyne remaynyng in the custody of diuse psones ther paysed at xs. le pece — xls.

155. Bratton.

Redy money putte in stocke to the mayntenance of lyghte wtin ye parysshe churche ther.

Videlt. Redy money remaynyng in thandes of Augustine Barons and Thom's Satchet — xvjs. viijd.

Somerset Chantries.

156. Babcary.

The ffree Chapell of ffodyngton.

Landes medowes pastures tythes and hereditamt̩ in the tenure of sondery psones as may appere pticulerly more at large by the Rentall of the same . . . . xls. iiijd. — *Is yerely worthe in*

None. — *Plate and ornamt̩.*
John Dwale clerke incumbent ther. — *Memord.*

The chapell is fallen downe and clerely decayed.

---

157. Maperton.

Redy money putte in stocke to the mayntenñce of lyghte wtin the parysshe churche ther.

Redy money remaynyng in thandes of Anthony Letforde xvs. *Videlt.*

---

158. Lampet.

Cattall gyuen to the mayntenñce of lyghte wtin the parysshe churche ther.

One kowe remaynyng in the custody of William Catcote *Videlt.* praysed at — xijs.

Somerset Chantries.

159. Charleton Musgrove.

Redy money put in stocke to the mayntenñce of lyghte ther.

Eldelt.   Redy money remaynynge in thandes of John Whites .. xx*s*.

---

160. Estpenmarde wt the Chapell of Westbradlye annex'd.

The Chapell callyd Stone Chapell.

Is perely worthe in   The rent of the saide Chapell scytuate in a pcell of grounde of George Milbo'ne, gent wt one teñt and an orcharde adioynyng, contaynyng half an acre wherin the priest ther ʒving did dwell . . . . iij*s*.

Memord.   The saide George Milbo'ne about iij yeres past enteryd into the foresaid teñt and orcharde and dispossessyd the priest.

    The ʒest was founde of the devocõn of thenhabitaunt(e) ther, who gave to hym and his successo's the foresaide teñt.

Redy money put in stocke to the mayntenñce of one masse and lyghte wtin the parysshe churche ther.

Eldelt.   Redy money remaynyng in thandes of sondery psones ther — xlij*s*.

Redy money put in stocke to the mayntenñce of lyghte wtin the Chapell of Westbradley.

Eldelt.   Redy money remaynyng in thandes of John Lockeston . . .
                                                   vj*s*. viij*d*.

161. Stoketristor.

Redy money put in stocke to the mayntenñce of lyghte wtin the parysshe church ther.

Redy money remaynyng in thandes of Richarde Thicke . . Videlt.
vs. xd.

---

162. Pulle.

Cattall gyuen to ye maynteñnce of lyghte and obite wtin the parysshe churche ther.

Fyue kyne remaynyng in the custody of sondery psones Videlt. y^{er} pysed at seuall rates . . . . lviijs. iiijd.

---

163. Sparkeforde.

Goodes & Cattall gyuen to the maynteñnce of lyghte wtin the parysshe churche ther.

One kowe remaynyng in the custody of John Martyn the Videlt. yonger of Weston Bampfelde praysed at — xxs. And redy money remaynyng in thandes of John Hardyng sen xxs. — xls.

---

164. Penselwoode.

Redy money put in stocke to the maynteñnce of obite wtin ye parysshe churche ther.

Redy money remaynyng in thandes of Illyn . . . . . . xxd. Videlt.

165. Compton Paunsforde alias Paunsfoote.

The Chauntrie w^tin the parysh churche ther.

Is yerely worthe in
Landes teñtẹ and hereditamtẹ in the tenure of sondery psones as may appere pticulerly more at large by the Rentall of the same .... vj*li.* vij*s.* viij*d.*

Wherof in
Rentẹ resolute paid yerely .... v*s.* ix*d.*
And so
Remayneth clere .... vi*li.* xxiij*d.*

Plate and ornamtẹ.
A chalice of Silṽ pcell gilte remaynynge in the custody of Humfraye Keyns gent wayinge — xvij oz.
Ornamentẹ praysed at .... vj*s.* viij*d.*

Memord.
Robte Bryce clerke of thage of liiij yeres incumbent ther.

The same Robte presenteth that Sir Walter Pauncfoote knyghte gave x*li.* in money to p'chase lande to make out x mrkẹ yerely to the priestẹ salarie ther wch was delyṽede to Bartilmewe Husy of Wiltshire besydes Salysbury by thandes of his wyffe executrix to Henry Paunsfote her former husbande.

The fundacõn and parte of the other evidences of this Chauntrie remayneth in the custody of the Mr. of the Almosehouse of Sherbo'ne and thother parte of the evidence rem w^t the foresaide Humfray Keynes.

Redy money put in stocke to the mayntenñnce of lyghte & obite w^tin the parysh churche ther.

Videlt.
Redy money remaynyng in thandes of Agnes Pierce vj*d.* and Agnes Wysse, xxiiij*s.* viij*d.*

Memord.

The p̃sonage ther is wo͛the yerely — viij*li*. xv*s*. wherof James Dole clerke is nowe incumbent.

Partakers of the lordes Holy Sooper ther iiijiiij p̃sones.

---

166. Mylton.

Cattall gyuen to the mayntenñce of lyghte w͞tin the parysℏe churcℏe ther.

Three kyne remaynyng in the custody of sondery p̃sones Vĩelt. praysed at seũall rates amountyng in all to. . . . . lv*s*.

---

167. Wyncaulton w͏ᵗ Stau͡lŏell.

Too Chauntries foundyd by the lorde Zouche for the mayntenñce of too prieste celebratyng in the chapell of y͏ᵉ name of Jesus at Stau͡lŏell aforesaide.

Redy money to be levied and receyued of the Issues **Is yerely worthe in** Revenues and profecte of the Mano͛s of Pytcombe and Colle in the countie of Somer͛ss nowe in the possession of Richarde Zouche sonne and heire of the Lorde Zouche by thandes of the baylyf of the saide Mano͛s yerely to be paide, viz., to either chauntrie priest — vj*li*. xiij*s*. iiij*d*. . . . . xiij*li*. vj*s*. viij*d*.

A challice waing — xviij oz.   **Plate and ornamt̃e.**

Ornamentẽ none.

Somerset Chantries.

Memord. Robte Gane clerke and Morgan Cony clerke incumbentᵉ ther.

The chapell wherin the saide ij chauntrie priestᵉ did celebrate callyd the chapell of Jesus is scituate wtin the saide lorde Zouches howse at Staūdell aforesaide.

Obitte foundyd w'in the parysshe churche ther.

Ar yerely worthe in One annuall rent to be levied and receyued of the Issues and Revenues of one teñt wt thapp'teññces ther late in the tenure of John Balhed . . . . iijs. iiijd.

Memord.

The psonage and vicarage ther wer impropriat to the late priorye of Staūdell and after the dissoluc̃on of the same p'chased by the foresaide lorde Zouche of the Kinges Maᵗⁱᵉ, who findeth a curate to mynyster ther having for his yerely salarie — vjli.

Partakers of the lordes Holy Soop ther — cciiij psones.

---

168. Batcombe.

Cattall gyuen to yᵉ mayntenñnce of yᵉ fraternytie ther.

Videlt. Nyne kyne remaynynge in the custody of sondery psones pysed at viijs. le pece —lxxijs.

169. Dycheat.

Cattall gyuen to the maynteñnce of a priest celebratynge w̅tin the parysshe churche ther.

XXI^{tie} kyne remaynyng in the custody of John Owkye, and William Darvall praysed at seu̅all rates amounting in all to . . . . xvij*li.* xij*s.* iiij*d.* Videlt.

Cattall gyuen to the maynteñnce of lyghte w̅tin ye same churche.

One kowe remaynyng in the custody of Johanne Kinge praysed at . . . . xvij*s.* Videlt.

170. Cokelyngton.

Goodes and cattalles gyuen to the maynteñnce of lyghte w̅tin the parysshe churche ther.

Too kyne remaynyng in the custody of Henry Serser and Thom̅s Collys praysed at seu̅all rates amounting to xxj*s.* And redy money remaynynge in thandes of Thom̅s Duñe, vij*s.* xxviij*s.* Videlt.

171. Northcadbury.

The Salarye of one prieste foundyd by Thomas Clare w̅tin ye parysshe churche ther.

Landes teñt^e and hereditam^{te} lying in North Cadbury and Kylm̅sdon in the tenure of sondery persones . . . . lx*s.* Is yerely worthe in

Somerset Chantries.

Plate and ornamt̄e. None.

Memord. Walton White clerke some tyme incumbent in this service, and now voyde.

Therle of Huntington entered into the saide landes ij yeres past, and claymeth the same by waye of exchete being lorde of the Manoʳ of Northcadbury aforesaide.

It appereth further that John Wotes, Thoṁs Rendall and other copteno'rs do clayme all the saide landes havinge entered into the same for vij yeres past and have taken pte of the rentẹ and p'ffectẹ yerely hetherto, and some parte of the saide rentẹ have stayed in thandes of the teñntẹ upon the clayme of the pson of the saide paryshe.

Lyghte foundyd wtin the same churche.

Ar yerely worthe in Six acres of lande wᵗin the saide paryshe in thoccupying of Nicholas Walker clerke, person ther . . . . iiij*s.*

Memord.

The psonage ther ys of the yerely value of — xxviij*li.* xiij*s.* iij*d.* ob. Wherof Nicholas Walker clerke is nowe incumbent.

Ptakers of the lordes Holy Sooper ther — ccxlij psones.

Robte Baron of Northcadbury sayithe that this benefice is a College and no psonage because yt is comōnly callyd a College and hathe ben tyme out of mynde and in all spirituall courtes they vse to call the incūbent, the Rector of Northcadbury and not pson as they call others.

The same saithe yᵗ is wrytten in the churche bookẹ ther **Obitus Wiłłmi Botrax fundatoris huius Collegii,** and in some place Ecclie.

Somerset Chantries.

Ther be also incident and apperteynyng to the same benefice sondery porc̄ons of tythes and lande comyng out of other smalle beneficꝫ and Mano͞rs.

172. Brewton.

Memord.

Thenhabitauntꝫ of the towne of Brewton aforesaide the xxith daye of Aprill año R. Rs. E. vj^{u} ij^{do} made humble request vnto the com̄yssiono͞rs in mañ and forme following. Wher ther was w^{t}in the foresaide towne a faire Scolehouse for a free gram̄ Scole, newly buylded erected and made in the xjth yere of the reigne of oure late soũaigne lorde of famouse memory Kinge Henry the viijth by Richarde, busshop of London, John Fitz James, and John Edmondꝫ Docto͞r of Dyvinitie, who did gyve and assigne to the maynteñnce of the same Scole, landes and teñtꝫ to the yerely value of xij*li.* for the vertuouse educac̄on and teaching of the yewthe as well of the saide towne of Brewton, as of the hole contrie, nowe decayed by reason that Heughe Sherwoode late Scolem͞r ther surrendered the saide landes into the Kingꝫ Maties handes vj or vij yeres nowe past, who indevoring hym self rather to lyve licentiously at will then to travaile in good educac̄on of yewthe according to the godly fundac̄on of the saide Scole, founde the meanes by his saide surrender to obtayne by Decre out of the courte of augmentac̄ons of the Revenues of the Kingꝫ Maties Crowne for terme of his lyffe one Annuytie or penc̄on of C^s, and the foresaide Scolehowse, w^t a gardeyn, and a close of lande thervnto adioynyng, contaynyng by estimac̄on iiij acres lyinge in Brewton aforesaide, discharged

Somerset Chantries.

also therby of eny further ffree teaching or keping of Scole ther, to the great Decaye as well of vertuouse bringing uppe of yewthe of the saide shire in all good lernyng, as also of thenhabitaunt℮ of the King℮ saide towne of Brewton of great relief that cam therby. Wherfore the saide inhabitaunt℮ made moost humble sute vnto the King℮ Matie that yt may please his highnes of his bounteouse libᵉalitie to restore the saide Scolehowse, landes and tent℮, to the vse godly purpose and intent of the fundaēon of the foresaide Bysshop, John fitz James and John Edmond℮.

173. Shepton Mallett.

The Salarye of one priest celebratyng wtin ye parysshe churche ther foundyd for terme of yeres.

Is perely worthe in   Certayne pcell℮ of lande and pasture callyd Smaldon lyinge w^tin the lordeship of Eucryche dymysed and letten to farme unto one Richarde Renyon nowe deceased, by Adriane late busshop of Bathe and Well℮ by Indenture datyd vnder his seale in the yere of our lorde God MDV for terme of lxi yeres wch Richarde Renyon by his last will and testam^t gaue the foresaide Indenture and his terme of yeres in the same conteyned of and in the premysses then not expyred to the vse and mayntennce of the said Salarie during the said terme . xv*li.* vj*s.* viij*d.*
Wherof in
Rent resued upon the saide Indenture yerely duringe all the saide terme to the saide busshoppe and his successo's for the rente and farme of the premisses . . . . ix*li.*
And so
Remaynethe clere duryng all the sayde terme. vj*li.* vj*s.* viij*d.*

None but a challice — vj oz.   **Plate and ornamtẽ.**

William Hurne clerke incūbent ther.   **Memord.**

Thenheritaunce of the p̃misses is nowe in the lorde protecto's grace.

The Guylde or fraternptie of the Trynytie and Saincte John Baptyste win the paryshe churche ther foundyd for the mayntenñce of too priestẽ.

Landes teñtẽ and hereditamentẽ in the tenure of sondery psones, as maye appere pticulerly more at large by the Rentall of the same .... xv*li*. xiiij*s*. vj*d*.   **Is yerely worthe in**

Wherof in

Rentẽ resolute pd yerely to sondery psones .... xvij*s*. ij*d*.

And so

Remayneth clere .... xiiij*li*. xvij*s*. iiij*d*.

Plate none.   **Plate and ornamtẽ.**

Ornamtẽ praysed at — xl*s*.

Robte Hill clerke one of the saide brotherhed priestẽ receyued yerely for his salarie — cxiiij*s*. viij*d*.   **Memord.**

The other s̃vice is voyde.

Ther is a comõn woode apperteynyng to the sayde Guilde cont iiij^{xx} acres callyd Haridge in the paryshe of Kylm̃sdon, wherin grow^t ccxl okes praysed at ij*d*. le pece — lx*s*. ; and iiij^{xx} asshes p^{r}ysed at 1*d*. le pece — vj*s*. viij*d*.

The soyle and herbage of the saide woode is comẽn to div̄se lordes teññtẽ and therfore is not charged in this value.

Somerset Chantries.

Redy money remaynyng in stocke belonging to the saide fraternitie.

Ther remayneth in thandes of Richarde Joyse and Thoṁs Campion wardeyns of the saide fraternitie wᵗ xls. for the rent of Smaldon letten to Mr. Horner my lorde protectoʳs sũnte, as maye appere by their bookes of accompte therof made and remaynyng.................... x*li*. xiijs. vjd.

Lyghte and obitte foundyd wᵗin the parysbe churche ther.

At yerely worthe in

Landes teñtᵉ and hereditamᵗᵉ in the tenure of sondery psones as maye appere pticulerly more at large by the rentall of the same........................... lxxjs. viijd.

Wherof in

Rentᵉ resolute paide yerely.................. ijd.

And so

Remayneth clere.................... lxxjs. vjd.

Memord.

Ther was distributed yerely as well out of the Revenues belonginge to the foresaide guilde, as also out of the saide landes and teñtᵉ graunted for the mayntenñce of lightes and obitᵉ, to the poore people ther xxxs. viijd. paide by thandes of the Wardeyns of the same as appereth by their accomptes.

The towne of Shepton Mallet aforesaide is a great m̃ket towne.

The psonage is of the yerely value of xl m̃rkᵉ wherof John Pollarde clerke is nowe incũbent, who findeth one priest to mynyster ther.

Partakers of the lordes Holy Sooper ther (*number omitted*).

174. Corsecombe.

The Guylde or fraternytie of Corsecombe wt the ffree chapell of Esthorryngton to the same Guylde or fraternytie unytyd and annexyd.

Landes tentꝭ and hereditam'ꭇ in the tenure of sondery psones as maye appere pticulerly more at large by the Rentall of the same .... xxviij*li*. vij*s*. ij*d*. **Is yerely worthe in**

Wherof in

Rentꭇ resolute paide yerely to sondery psones ... iiij*s*. iiij*d*.

And so

Remayneth clere .... xxviij*li*. ij*s*. x*d*.

A chalice of silṽ all gilte waying — xxvj oz. **Plate and ornamtꭇ.**
A chalice of silṽ pcell gilte waying xvj oz.
Ornamentꭇ praysed at .... xxxviij*s*. iiij*d*.
Leade cccc lb.

This guilde or fraternytie was foundyd and erected for the **Memord.** findinge and mayntenñnce of iiij priestꭇ, wherof one to mynyster in the foresaide ffree chapell of Esthorrington.

The advousion of the same free chapell dothe belonge to the foresaide guilde or fraternytie.

The saide ffree chapell is ptely coũed wt leade, and is praysed wo'the to be solde — xxvj*s*. viij*d*.

Ther is a woode belonging to the foresaide guilde, callyd Esthorrington woode, cont x acres, wherin doth growe lvij okes callyd scrobes, wherof xvi be praysed at viij*d*. le pece and xlj at iiij*d*. le pece — xxiiij*s*. iiij*d*. Itm the vnderwoode or copies of

Somerset Chantries.

the saide x acres is praysed at vij*s*. le acre — lxx*s*., amounting in all to the some of — iiij*li*. xiiij*s*. iiij*d*.

Richarde Castlyn clerke one incūbent ther, who receyved yerely for his salarie or wages — vj*li*.

Richarde Ayland clerke one other incūbent ther, who receyved yerely for his wage — vj*li*.

Too ſuices voyde.

Redy money remaynyng in stocke belonging to ye said guilde.

Ther remayneth in thandes of the wardeyns of the saide Guilde or fraternytie as appereth by their accomtes. . . . . . c*s*.

Lyghte and obite foundyd w'in the parysshe churche ther.

Ar yerely worthe in Landes teñtℯ and hereditamtℯ in the tenur of sondery psones as maye appere pticulerly more at large by the Rentall of the same . . . . xxx*s*. viij*d*.

Wherof in

Rentℯ resolute pd yerely . . . . x*s*. iiij*d*.

And so

Remayneth clere . . . . xx*s*. iiij*d*.

Memard. Ther is gyuen by the dede of feoffem^t wherin the saide landes be graunted to the maynteñnce of the ringing of Curfewe nightly w'in the paryshe churche of Corsecombe aforesaide iiij*s*., by the yere to be levied of the value of the p̃mysses.

Ther is gyven yerely by the same feoffem^t out of the foresaide yerely value, towardes the repac̃ons of the Almoshouse in Corsecombe aforesaide — viij*d*., and towardes the relief of the poore inhabitauntℯ of the same paryshe — vij*d*.

Somerset Chantries.

Memord.

The psonage ther is wo'the yerely — xij*li.*, wherof is no incumbent at this present.

Partakers of the lordes Holy Sooper ther — ccxx psones.

Ther be ij Almoshowses w'in the saide towne, whiche have great nede of relief.

Decanatus de Marston.

175. Peupll.

The Chauntrie of the Trynytie foundyd w'tin the parysshe churche ther.

Is yerely worthe in   Landes teñte and hereditamte in the tenure of sondery psones as maye appere pticulerly more at large by the rentall of the same .... xj*li*. xj*s*.

Wherof in
Rente resolute paide yerely to sondery psones ...... vj*s*.
And so
Remaynethe clere .... xj*li*. v*s*.

Plate and ornamte.   Plate none.
Ornamente praysed at — xv*s*. viij*d*.

Memord.   Henry Lyrbecke clerke of the age of l yeres incumbent ther, of honest conversation, and a good singinge man.

The Chauntrie of oure lady foundyd w'tin the same churche.

Is yerely worthe in   Landes teñte and hereditamte in the tenure of sondery psones as maye appere pticulerly more at large by the rentall of the same .... xij*li*. xj*s*. ij*d*.

Wherof in
Rente resolute paide yerely to sondery psones ... xj*s*. iiij*d*.
And so
Remaynethe clere .... xj*li*. xix*s*. x*d*.

Somerset Chantries.

A chalice of silũ gilte wayinge — xv oz.   Plate and ornamtẽ.
Ornamentes praysed at — xxvij*s.* iiij*d.*

John Whitewell clerke of thage of xlvij yeres incũbent Memorð. ther.

One burgage scituate in the Highestrete in the tenure of Gyles Hacker at the yerely rent of xiij*s.* iiij*d.*, pcell of this value aforesaide is graunted to this chauntrie, but for terme of iiij^{xx} yeres begynnyng at michelm̃s año R. Rs. E. iiij^{ti} octavo, as appereth by a dede therof seen and remaynyng.

The Chauntrie of the name of Jesus foundyd wtin the sayde Churche.

Landes teñtẽ and hereditamtẽ in the tenure of sondery psones as maye appere pticulerly more at large by the rentall of the same . . . . viij*li.* vij*s.* vj*d.*   Is yerely worthe in

Wherof in

Rentẽ resolute paide yerely to sondery psones . . . . . . iij*s.*

And so

Remaynethe clere . . . . ∴ viij*li.* iiij*s.* vj*d.*

Plate none.   Plate and ornamtẽ.

Ornamentes praysed at — xxij*s.* v*d.* ob.

William Harvy clerke of the age of lvj yeres incũbent Memorð. ther.

The Chauntrie of the Holy Crosse foundyd wtin the sayde parysh Churche.

Landes teñtẽ and hereditam^{t}ẽ in the tenure of sondery psones as may appere pticulerly more at large by the rentall of the same . . . . viij*li.* xv*s.* viij*d.*   Is yerely worthe in

Somerset Chantries.

                Wherof in
        Rentẹ resolute payde yerely . . . . xiij*s*. vj*d*.
                   And so
        Remayneth clere . . . . viij*li*. ij*s*. ij*d*.

Plate and ornamtẹ.   A chalice of silu̅ p̱cell gilte waying — xiij. oz.
Ornamentẹ praysed at — xix*s*. ij*d*.

Memord.   William Trevylyan clerke of thage of lx yeres incumbent ther.

The Chapell or personage of Pytney *al* Mershe or Kyngton.

Is yerely worthe in :   All the tythes as well great as small to the saide chapell or psonage belonging, one yere w^t an other . . . . vj*li*.

Plate and ornamtẹ.   None.

Memord.   Laurence Orcharde clerke incu̅bent ther, who receyveth the hole proffectẹ of the same, as his psonage.

P̱takers of the Lordes Holy Soop̱ ther xxx psones.

The chapell is vtterly decayde and fallen downe longe ago and the saide inhabitauntẹ resorte alwayes to the paryshe churche of Yevill aforesaide for dyvine s̃uice and other mynistraco̅n to be had, for the wch the foresaide incu̅bent alwayes from tyme to tyme compoundeth and agreyth w^t the vicar or curat of Yevill for the tyme being.

Memord.

The psonage ther is in the Kingẹ gracẹ handes.

The vicarage is of the yerely value of xviij*li*. wherof John Symmes clerke is nowe incu̅bent, who findeth one priest besydes hymself to helpe to mynister.

Somerset Chantries.

Partakers of the Lordes Holy Soop ther Dcccxxij psones.

Ther is a poore Almoshouse wch hathe great nede of relief and augmentaĉon of lyving.

Ther is a chapell scituate w^tin the churche yarde of Yevill keŭed w^t leade contaynying by estimaĉon nighe one fooder praysed wo^rthe to be solde — iiij*li*., wch thenhabitaunt℈ ther desire to have for a scolehouse.

The towne is a great market Towne, and a thoroughe faire. ·Leade j food⁊].

---

176. Milborne Porte.

The fraternytie of sainete John the Euangelyste ther.

The rent of one close of pasture ther in the tenure of William Sampson.................................. ij*s*. **Is yerely worthe in**

Too kyne remayning in the custody of John Elys and John Holewaye praysed at xxix*s*. iiij*d*. Certayne householde stuffe remaynyng in the custody of the wardens of the saide fraternitie praysed at viij*s*. and redy money remaynyng in thands of William Meire, ix*s*............................ xlvj*s*. iiij*d*. **Goode and Cattalle remaynyng in stocke belonging to the said fraternitie.**

Lyghte foundyd wtin the parysbe churche ther.

Annual rent℈ to be levied and receyved of the Issues and Revenues of the landes and teñt℈ belonginge to the commaltie of the saide towne of Mylbo^rneporte, xij*d*., and of the land℈ and teñt℈ of William Hannam and Robte Longe ther, vj*d*. .. xviij*d*. **Ar yerely worthe in**

Memord.

The vicarage ther is of the yerely value of xx*li*. wherof Robte Hale clerke is nowe incūbent, who findeth one Sr William to ǵve the cure ther, who is insufficient for that purpose.

Ptakers of the Lordes Holy Soop ther—ccxx psones.

---

177. Estcoker.

The Chauntrie wtin the parysbe churche ther.

Is yerely worthe in   Landes, teñtę and hereditamentę in the tenure of sondery psones as maye appere pticulerly more at large by the Rentall of the same . . . . vj*li*. xvij*s*. vj*d*.

Plate and ornamtę.   None.

Memord.   William Slade clerke of the age of l yeres incūbent ther.

The Chapell of oure lady of Burton.

Is yerely worthe in   The rent of the saide Chapell w^t a pece of grounde wherin the same Chapell is scituate in thoccupying of Gyles Harryson and others . . . . xx*d*.

Plate and ornamtę.   None.

Leade—ccc lb.

Bell metall—xl lb.

Memord.   The vicarage ther is of the yerely value of xiij*li*. x*s*., wherof Robte Philipson clerke is nowe incūbent.

Ptakers of the lordes Holy Soop ther—cclx psones.

178. Westcoker.

Memord.

Ther be XX^{tie} acres of lande w'in the paryshe ther, in thoccupying of the p'son ther, wo'the yerely x*s*., whiche is thoughte to be gyven to the thentent that Curfewe shoulde be nightly ronge w'in the paryshe churche ther betwixt daye and nighte wch is contynued untill this present daye, to thentent that all travello's by the waye (the same village being a thoroughe fare betwene London and Exciter) might thereby cū into their p'fect waye, or to the saide village of Westcoker.

---

179. Northcherpton.

Lyghte foundyd w'in the paryshe churche ther.

One rode of grounde ther in the tenure of Richarde Saunders—vj*d*. *Ar yerely worthe in*

Cattall gyven to the mayntenance of obitte w'in the same paryshe Churche.

One kowe remaynyng in the custody of William Jennys praysed at viij*s*. *Witelt.*

180. Abbas Combe.

Redy money put in stocke to the mayntenñce of lyghte w'in the parysshe Churche ther.

Videlt.   Redy money remaining in thandes of Roberte Hobbes—xij$s$.

181. Stowell.

Redy money put in stocke to the mayntenñce of lyghte w'in the parysshe Churche ther.

Videlt.   Redy money remayning in thandes of Edwarde Clenche of Gotehill—ij$s$.

182. Corton.

Obitte foundyd w'in the parysshe churche ther.

Ar perely worthe in   One annuall rent to be levied and receyued of the Issues Revenues and proffecte of the landes and teñte of Tristram Storke in thoccupying of William Googe of Holwaye . vj$s$. viij$d$.

183. Horsyngton.

The free chapell off Sowthe Cheryton w'in w'in (sic) the parysshe of Horsyngton.

Is perely worthe in   The rent of the saide Chapell w^t half an acre of lande wherin the same Chapell is scituate w^t all the landes teñte and

Somerset Chantries.

hereditam^{t}ȝ whatsoev̄ to the same ffree chapell belonging or appteynyng, dimysed and letten to farme, to Elizabeth fitz James of Temple Combe widowe for terme of xx^{tie} yeres by Indenture dated vnder the seale of Roger Boydell clerke incūbent ther, the vth daye of maye ano R. R. E. vi^{ti} p'mo as in the same Indenture more at large may appere . . . . xxvj$s$. viij$d$.

None.   **Plate and ornamtȝ.**

Bell mettall xl lb.

Roger Boydell clerke incumbent ther.   **Memord.**

Redy money put in stocke to the maynteñnce of lyghte wtin the paryshe Churche ther.

Redy money remaynynge in thandes of William Oram, xs., **Videlt.** William Downton ij$s$. iiij$d$. and dyūse others of the same paryshe, lxiiij$s$. viij$d$. . . . . lxxvij$s$.

---

184. Hengstryge.

Cattall gyuen to the maynteñnce of lyghte wtin the paryshe churche ther.

One kowe remaynyng in the custody of Hughe Royall **Videlt.** praysed at xs.

---

185. Trent wythe the Chapell of Abdere.

The Chauntrie w'in the paryshe churche ther.

Is yerly worthe in

The rent of the mansion house of the saide chauntrie w^t a stable and a gardene adioynyng to the same—ij*s*. And in redy money to be levied and receyved of the Issues Revenues and proffectȩ of the College in Oxforde called Oryell College w^t xiij*s*. iiij*d*. yerely for thobbite of John ffrancke—viij*li*.—viij*li*. ij*s*.

Plate and ornamtȩ.

A chalice of silū waying—xx oz.

Ornamentes praysed at iiij*li*. j*d*.

Memord.

John Shete clerke of thage of lvj yeres incūbent ther.

Ther hathe ben yerely distributed emongest the poore people of the paryshe ther, x*s*. viij*d*., pcell of the saide sōme of xiij*s*. iiij*d*. graunted for the mayntefince of the said obit.

Memord.

The psonage ther is worth yerely, xxiij*li*. iij*s*. iiij*d*., wherof Amere Tuckefeld clerke incumbent, who findeth ij priestȩ to mynister, one in the paryshe churche ther, and thother in the foreside Chapell of Abdere. Partakers of the lordes Holy Soop ther ciiij^{xx} psones.

186. Marston Magna.

The Salary of one priest foundyd w'tin the parysshe churche ther for terme of certayne yeres.

One annuall rent to be levied and receyued of the Issues and Revenues of the landes and tenementę of Robte Kelwaye for terme of xxij yeres yit to come . . . . vj*s.* viij*d.* — *Is yerely worthe in*

Redy money remaynynge in thandes of Thoms Goodson, lxvj*s.* viij*d.*, and Nicholas Shude lxvj*s.* viij*d.* and William Barber lxvj*s.* viij*d.* . . . . x*li.* — *Redy money put in stocke to the mayntenūnce of the saide salarie.*

None. — *Plate and Ornamtę.*

Leade j food'. — *Memord.*

No incūbent at this present in the saide sŭice.

The incūbent was maynteyned further by the devocōn of the people; and had non other lyving in certeyntie.

The Chapell wherein the saide priest dyd mynister, wynynge to an Ile of the pyshe churche ther is couered w*t* leade contaynyng as before.

Memord.

The vicarage ther is wo'the yerely x*li.*, wherof Robte Elyat clerke is nowe incūbent.

Partakers of the Lordes Holy Suoper ther cxl psones.

Decanatus de Bathe.

187. The Paryshe of Saincte Michell by the Bathe w'in the Citie of Bathe.

Lyghte foundyd w'in the paryshe churche ther.

Ar yerely worthe in
 One annuall rent to be levied and receyued of the Issues and Revenues of a tent w^t thappteñnc̛ scituate in Walcote strete w'in the saide Citie nowe in the tenure of William Abyam . . vj*d.*

Memord.

Ther is an hospitall callyd Saincte Johans Hospitall w'in the saide paryshe, having landes, teñt̛ and hereditam^t̛ thervnto belonging of the clere yerely value of xxv*li.* xiij*s.* viij*d.* ob.

The hospitall was erected (as y^t is saide) for the relief of vj poore men, and one priest or maister to g̃ve them, havinge their contynuall lyving upon the same.

This hospitall is annexed to the paryshe churche of saincte Michelle̛ aforesaide and the pson of the saide churche is maister of the same Hospitall.

The residue of the p̃ffect̛ ar imployed and receyved by the saide Maister.

The ornament̛ of the Hospitall ar estemyd wo'the, — xv*s.* ij*d.*

No fundac̄on shewed, neither wolde the Maister appere.

188. The Parysbe of oure Lady w'in the Gate off Bathe.

Obitte foundyd w'in the parysbe churche ther.

Certayne landes, teñte, burgage and cotages ther in the tenure of sondery psones wherof as yit is no pticuler rentall delyu̅ed .... iiij*li*. ij*d*.   *Ar yerely worthe in*

---

189. The Parysbe of Saincte Michell w'out the Southe gate of Bathe.

Obitte foundyd w'in the parysbe churche ther.

Certayne landes, teñte, burgage and cotagies ther, in the tenure and occupying of sondery psones, the rentall wherof, as yit is not delyu̅ed .... xlj*s*. iij*d*.   *Ar yerely worthe in*

Ther was distributed yerely to the poore people resorting to the saide obite, out of the revenues of the p̃misses, xx*s*. ix*d*.   *Memord.*

---

190. The Parysbe of Stalles w'in the saide Citie.

Obite foundyd w'in the parysbe churche ther.

Annuall rente to be levied and receyued of the Issues Revenues and proffecte of the landes and teñte of sondery psones ther .... l*s*. ij*d*. ob.   *Ar yerely worthe in*

Ther was distributed yerely out of the saide some, to the poore people resorting to the saide obite, — vj*s*. viij*d*.   *Memord.*

Somerset Chantries.

Lyghte foundyd w'in the same churche.

Ar yerely worthe in — Annual rente to be levied and recevued of the Issues Revenues and proffecte of the landes and tent͠e of sondery psones ther . . . . vj*s.* ij*d.*

---

191. The Paryshe of Saincte James w'in the saide Citie.

Obite foundyd w'in the paryshe churche ther.

Ar yerely worthe in — Annuall rente to be levied and recevued of the Issues, Revenues and proffecte of the landes and tent͠e of sondery psones ther . . . . iij*s.* vij*d.*

---

192. Fresshesorde.

Lyghte foundyd w'in the paryshe churche ther.

Ar yerely worthe in — One pece of lande ther callyd Churche mede contaynying one roode. . . . . vj*d.*

---

193. Weston juxta Bathe.

Obite foundyd w'in the paryshe churche ther.

Ar yerely worthe in — One tent͠ w^t a gardeyne ther callyd the churchehouse in thoccupying of the wardeyns of the same churche . . . . . . ij*s.*

194. Bathforde.

The chapell scituate in the comen strete of Shokerwyke w'in the sayde parysh.

The rent of the saide Chapell wherin oblacons wer wont to be made, now in the occupying of Robte Tyler . . . . iijs. iiijd. *Is yerely worthe in*

Redy money put in stocke to the maynteñnce of lyghte w'in the paryshe churche ther.

Redy money remaynyng in thandes of John Lynage, xxs. Videlt. and Willm Gamage, xs. xxxs.

195. Newton Sayntloo.

Lyghte foundyd w'in the paryshe churche ther.

Seven acres of arable lande lying in the comen felde ther in thoccupying of John Grevys clerke pson ther . . . . iiijs. *Is yerely worthe in*

It is presented that this rent groweth but euy seconde Memord. yere.

196. Bathe Eston w' the Chapell of Caterne annexed.

The Chapel scituate in Horteley w'in the sayde parysh.

The rent of the same Chapell wherin an Armyte sometyme dwelled and nowe in the occupying of William Lewys, — ijs. viijd. *Is yerely worthe in*

Somerset Chantries.

Memord. The same William Lewys hathe occupyed the saide Chapell or Armitage by the space of xij yeres last past w^tout eny thinge paying therfore.

Cattall gyuen to the mayntenaunce of lyghte w^tin the sayde Chapell of Caterne annexed.

Videlt. Foure shepe remaynyng in the custody of Thom̄s Woodwarde praysed at ij*s.* le pece — viij*s.*

The Citie of Welles w̔ᵗ the Cathedrall Churche of Sayncte Andrewe ther.

197. The Parysshe of saincte Cutberte w'tin the Citie of Wellẹ.

The Chauntrie foundyd wtin the parysshe churche ther callyd Tanners Chauntrie.

Redy money to be levied and receyued of the Issues Revenues and proffectẹ of the landes teñtẹ and hereditamentẹ belonging to the Maister and comm̄altie of the saide Citie of Wellẹ.................................. lxvjs. viijd.   **Is yerely worthe in**

None.   **Plate and Ornamtẹ.**

John Turnoʳ clerke incūbent ther.   **Memord.**

The Salarye of too stipendary Priestes celebratynge wtin the saydẹ Churche.

Redy money to be levied and receyued of the Issues, Revenues and proffectẹ of the landes and teñtẹ belonging to the saide Maister and comm̄altie, vīz., to either prieste for his salarie yerely cxiijs. iiijd., to be paide by thandes of the Receyvoʳ of the Revenues of the saide landẹ............ xjli. vjs. viijd.   **Is yerely worthe in**

None.   **Plate and ornamtẹ.**

Somerset Chantries.

Memord. The incũbentẹ names be not presented.

It is presented that ther is no fundacõn of theis ij priestẹ, but they have been kept from tyme to tyme of the Dovocõn of the saide M^r and comynaltie to mynister in the saide churche for that the cure is verray great.

Obite foundyd w'in the paryshe churche ther.

Ar yerely worthe in Annuall rentẹ to be levied and receyued aswell of the Issues and Revenues of the landes and teñtẹ belonging to the foresaide maister and comynaltie, iiij*li*., as also of the Revenues of one teñt in Chambleyns strete w'in the saide Citie, belonging to the vicar of the saide paryshe for the tyme beinge . . . . iiij*li*. xvj*d*.

Memord. Ther was yerely distributed to the poore people ther, out of the premisses, — xiij*s*. iiij*d*.

The Salarie or stipend of one priest celebratyng in the chapell scituate w'in the Almoschouse of Welles aforesayde w'in the sayde paryshe.

Is yerely worthe in Redy money to be levied and receyued of the Issues Revenues and proffectẹ of the landes and possessions belonging to the vicars of the foresaide Cathedrall churche of Saincte Andrewe in Wellẹ. . . . . iiij*li*. xiij*s*. iiij*d*.

Plate and Ornamtẹ. A chalice of silũ waying — xviij oz. do et do qrt.

Ornamentes praysed at — xxiiij*s*. viij*d*.

Memord. John Dyble clerke of the age of lxx yeres incũbent ther.

Ther ar belonging to this Almoschouse, landes and teñtẹ to the yerely value of xiij*li*. v*s*. iiij*d*. ob., oũ and besydes the foresaide priestẹ Salarie.

Somerset Chantries.

This Almoschowse was ordeyned and erected for the relief of one priest, and xxiiij poore men and women to praye for the sooles of the founders.

The Chapell of Saincte Andrie.

The rent of the same Chapell scituate in Southou in Welles aforesaide . . . . xij*d*. —Is yerely worthe in

The Chapell of saincte paule of Polsham.

The rente of the saide Chapell w{t} one acre of lande belonginge to the same . . . . xx*d*. —Is yerely worthe in

The Chapell of Southwaye late of Thomas Beckyt w{t}in the sayd parysh.

The rent of the saide Chapell w{t} ij acres of arable lande to the same Chapell belonging . . . . xij*d*. —Is yerely worthe in

The psonage ther is impropriate to the Deane and Chapiture Memord. of Welle.

The vicarage ther is wo{r}the yerely xxxiij*li.* xiij*s.* iiij*d.*, wherof Roger Edgewo{r}th clerke Docto{r} of Dyuinitie is nowe incūbent who findeth one priest or curate vnder hym to mynyster ther.

Partakers of the Lordes Holy Soop MM psones.

198. Dynder Prebendary.

Lyghte and obitte foundyd w'in the parysche churche ther.

Ar yerely worthe in
One teñt callyd Langhowse w⁺ ij acres of arable lande, and one roode of medowe in the occupying of Johan Thoms widowe ijs. viijd.

---

199. The Cathedrall Churche of Saincte Andrewe in Welles.

The College or Newe Hall in la Mount Roye w'in the Citie of Welles foundyd and erected for the mayntenñce of xviij chauntrie prieste celebratyng wythin the sayde Cathedrall churche.

Is yerely worthe in
Landes teñte and hereditam'e in the tenure of sondery psones as maye appere pticulerly more at large by the Rentall of the same . . . . xxiijli. iijs.

Wherof in

Rente resolute paide yerely to sondery psones . lxxiijs. iiijd.

And so

Remayneth clere . . . . xixli. ixs. viijd.

Plate and ornam'e.
Plate one chalice gilt—xvij oz.

Ornament'e, xiijs., viijd. and implem'te, praysed at iiijli. iiijs. vjd. — iiijli. xviijs. ijd.

Memard.
The College was erected for a comen howse or lyving of of xviij chauntrie prieste foundyd w'in the saide Cathedrall churche hereafter next following, who before the erection of the

same had no certeyne place of habitacōn, but lyved abrode in the Cure, wher they coulde get rowme for their money.

Ther was distributed yerely equally amongest the saide xviij chauntrie prieste xj*li*. viij*s*. viij*d*., pcell of the foresaid clere yerely value in mañ and fo^rme following, viz., for the comēn table, vj*li*. xvj*d*.; in augmentacōn of their salaries, ciiij*s*.; and for reding and resyting the names of their benefacto^rs iij*s*. iiij*d*., wch being equally devyded amounteth to xij*s*. viij*d*. for eůy of theym.

The incūbent in Ergehams Chauntrie herafter following, for the tyme beinge, receyved yerely out of the same clere yerely value, for singing dayly morrowe masse w^tin the saide Cathedrall churche—xx*s*.

The rest of the proffecte wer imployed for the wages of thofficers of the howse, as the Receyvo^rs, Cooke, Launder and others, and for their fewell woode and other necessaries, and repacōns of the saide College, and the the xth yerely due for the same.

Too Chauntries foundyd by Robte Burnell and Walter Hasilshewe sometyme bysshops of Bathe and Welles wtin the sayde cathedrall churche.

Redy money to be paide by the Deane and Chapiture of the Cathedrall churche of Welle aforesaide, of the Issues, Revenues and proffecte of the psonage of Burneham appropried to the saide Deane and Chapiture, viz., to either priest incūbent in the same Chauntrie, v mrke by the yere . . . . vj*li*. xiij*s*. iiij*d*. 　*Ar yerely worthe in*

None but a chalice guilt—xv oz. 　*Plate and ornamte.*

Robte Dyrant of the age of liiij yeres and Thomˉs Bugley of the age of lviij yeres incūbente ther. 　*Memord.*

Somerset Chantries.

Too Chauntries foundyd wt'in the same Cathedrall Churche by Henry Husey sometyme Deane of the same.

Ar yerely worthe in Redy money to be paide by the same Deane and Chapiture of the Issues, Revenues and proffecte of the Manor of Northcory and Knappe, viz., to either priest incūbent in the saide Chauntries v mrke by the yere. . . . . vj*li.* xiij*s.* iiij*d.*

Plate and Ornamte. Plate none but a chalice guilt — xv oz.

Ornamentes praysed at vj*s.* vij*d.*

Memord. John Erington of the age of xliiij yeres and John Broke of the age of lx yeres incūbente ther.

Too Chauntries foundyd by William Wellyngton wt'in the same churche.

Ar yerely worthe in Redy money to be paide by the foresaide Deane and Chapiture, of the Issues, Revenues and proffecte of their saide Manor of Northcory, viz., to either priest incūbent in the saide Chauntries, v mrks by the yere . . . . vj*li.* xiij*s.* iiij*d.*

Plate and Ornamte. A chalice of silu waying — xv oz.

Ornamente praysed at — iiij*s.* ij*d.*

Memord. Henry Bancke of the age of liiij yeres, and Richard Meryfelde of the age of lx yeres, incūbente ther.

Too Chauntries foundyd by Robte Corymaples and John Drokenesforde.

Ar yerely worthe in Redy money to be paide by the same Deane and Chapiture, of the Issues, Revenues and proffecte of their Manor of North-

Somerset Chauntries.

cory aforesaide, viz., to either incūbent in the saide Chauntries, v mrkẽ by the yere . . . . vj*li.* xiijs. iiij*d.*

None but a chalice guilt — xiiij oz. **Plate and Ornamtẽ.**

Thom̄s Rigby of the age of lxx yeres, and Thom̄s Clerke of the age of lvij yeres incūbentẽ ther. **Memord.**

One Chauntrie foundyd wtin the sayde churche by John Godley.

Redy money to be paide by the saide Deane and Chapiture **Is yerely worthe in** of the Issues Revenues and proffectẽ of the foresaide Manor of Northcory . . . . lxvjs. viij*d.*

None but a chalice — xiiij oz. **Plate and Ornamtẽ.**

Robte Sprie clerke of the age of l yeres incūbent ther. **Memord.**

One Chauntrie foundyd ther by Walter Hull.

Redy money to be paide by the saide Deane and Chapiture **Is yerely worthe in** of the Issues Revenues and proffectẽ of their landes and possessions . . . . iiij*li.*

None but a chalice — xvj oz. **Plate and ornamtẽ.**

William ffenwyke clerke of the age of lx yeres incūbent ther. **Memord.**

Ther is no landes assigned for the paym^t of this salarie, but out of the hole possessions, appertaynyng to the saide Deane and Chapiture.

One Chauntrie ther foundyd by Raffe Ergeham.

Redy money to be paide by the foresaide Deane and **Is yerely worthe in** Chapiture of the Issues, frutẽ and proffectẽ of the psonage of Poculchurche appropried to the same deane and chapiture . iiij*li.*

Somerset Chantries.

Plate and ornamt̃ẹ. None but a challice — vj oz.

Memord. Walter Sheperde clerke of the age of xxxvij yeres incũbent ther.

The same Incũbent songe or saide morrowe masse dayly wᵗⁿ the saide Cathedrall churche and receyued yerely therfore, out of the Revenues of the said College of la Mount Roy, xxs., as before is declared amongest the memorᵈ of the same College.

Foure Chauntries ther foundyde by Nicholas Bubwithe.

Ar yerely worthe in Redy money to be paide by the same Deane and Chapiture, as well of the Issues, frutes and proffectẹ of the psonages of Newton and Buckeland, appropried to the same Deane and Chapiture, as also of the Issues and Revenues of their Manoʳ of Bickenaller, viz. to cũy priest incũbent in the same Chauntries cvjs. viijd. by the yere . . . . xxjli. vjs. viijd.

Plate and ornamtẹ. None but a challice, xij oz. q̃ter ob. q̃ter.

Memord. John Pawle clerke of the age of xliiij yeres: William Burge clerke of the age of lj yeres: John Sheperde, clerke of the age of l yeres; and John Newes of the age of lv yeres incũbentẹ ther.

One other chauntrie foundyd wtin the same churche.

Is yerely worthe in Redy money to be paide by the saide Deane and Chapiture out of a pencõon of xli. due and payable yerely vnto the same Deane and Chapiture, by the Archedeacon of Wellẹ for the tyme beinge . . . . lxvjs. viijd.

Plate and ornamtẹ. None.

Memord. Robte Wether al Wellẹ of the age of lxviij yeres incũbent ther.

Somerset Chantries.

One Chauntrie foundyd ther belongyng to the Colacon of the Chauntor of the sayde Cathedrall churche.

Redy money to be paide by the same Chauntor of the Issues Revenues and ƥffectȩ of his office.............. iiij*li*. | Is yerely worthe in

None. | Plate and Ornamtȩ.

John Trowbridge clerke of the age of lx yeres incūbent ther. | Memord.

The Chauntrie ther callyd Martyns Chauntrie.

Redy money lately comyng out of the Issues and Revenues of the late dissolued Hospitall or priory of saincte Johañs in Wellȩ and nowe to be levied and receyved of the Issues and Revenues of the courte of Thaugmentacōn, by vertue of a Decre made in the same courte.................. iiij*li*. | Is yerely worthe in

A chalice of silu̇ waying, xv oz. | Plate and ornamtȩ.
Ornamentes none.

John Dible clerke of the age of lxx yeres incūbent ther. | Memord.

All the foresaid xviij chauntrie priestȩ ar resident in the saide College of La Mount Roye, and ǧve in the saide Cathedrall churche, according to their foundacōn, receyving eu̇y of theym suche Relief of the Revenues of the same College as before is declared amongest the memor[d] of the same.

The Chauntrie foundyd ther by John Stortewate callyd Stortewattes chauntrie.

- - Redy money to be paide by the foresaide Deane and Chapiture out of a pencōn of x*li*. due and payable yerely vnto the same | Is yerely worthe in

Somerset Chauntries.

Deane and Chapiture, out of the Issues, frutes, and proffecte of the psonage of Wrexall. . . . . vj*li*. xiij*s*. iiij*d*.

Plate and Ornamte. None.

Memord. Gyles Buttal clerke of thage of lxx yeres incūbent ther.

The saide yerely pencōn of x*li*. due to the foresaide Deane and Chapiture of Welle out of the psonage of Wrexall aforesaide, hathe ben w^{t}holden from the saide Deane and Chapiture, by the psones of the saide churche of Wrexall and Sir Edwarde Gorge, Knighte, patrone and fermo^r of the same by the space of vj or vij yeres.

Breade wyne and wex expendyd by the Incumbente of sondery the foresayde Chauntries.

Ar yerely worthe in Redy money to be paide by the foresaide Deane and Chapiture for breade wyne and wex expendyd by the incūbente of sondery of the foresaide Chauntries, videlt, The Chauntrie callyd Burnelle and Hasilshewes, iiij*s*.; Husies, iij*s*. viij*d*; Wellingtons, iiij*s*.; Godlees, xij*s*.; Ergehams, iij*s*. viij*d*.; Bubwithes, viij*s*.; and Stortewatte, xvij*s*. w^t the mayntenīnce of one lampe ther . . . . lij*s*. iiij*d*.

Obitte and Anniūsaries foundyd w^{t}in the said Cathedrall churche.

Ar yerely worthe in Redy money to be paide out of the Issues and Revenues frutes and proffecte of the landes and possessions belonginge to the foresaide Deane and Chapiture, by thandes of the Receyvo^r or comyno^r of the saide Cathedrall churche, for sondery obite and annivaries foundyd w^{t}in the same. . . . . xlviij*li*. xvj*d*.

Memord. The foresaide Deane and Chapiture of the saide Cathedrall

Somerset Chantries.

churche do distribute yerely to the poore people out of the Rentℯ and Revenues of their landes and possessions — xxj*li*. xvj*s*. vj*d*.

The same Deane and Chapiture of their ffree will kepe and maynteyne a free gramer Scole ther, and do paye to the M^r of the same Scole yerely for his stipend or wagℯ, xiij*li*. vj*s*. viij*d*., and to the vssher of the same Scole yerely — vj*li*. xiij*s*. iiij*d*.

END OF CERTIFICATE NO. 42.

DECLARATION

OF THE

Rental and Possessions

OF THE

CHANTRIES, COLLEGES, AND FREE CHAPELS

IN THE

County of Somerset.

(*Land Revenue Records, Vol. No.* 97.)

Deanery of Crukerne.

Ilminster.

The Chantry of St. Katerine within the parish church there, founded by John Wadham, esquier.

The house there of the same — xij*s.*

Kateryne Cuffe, widow, holds by indenture for her life the farm or messuage of Einston and land, meadow and hereditaments in the parish of Hengstrege, and renders per ann. — iiij*li.*

John Satchell holds a cottage with six acres of arable land in Stoke sub Hamden, and renders per ann. — vij*s.*

John Borde holds a cottage with two acres of arable land in Aldington juxta Burporte in the county of Dorset, and renders per ann. — xj*s*.

William Hunshill holds land, arable and meadow, in the parish of Simon Desborough in the county of Devon, and renders per ann. — xl*s*.

Christiana Lyde, widow, holds eight acres of arable land in the parish of Saltcombe in the county of Devon juxta Sedburie, and renders per ann. — xiiij*s*.

Richard Knolling holds a tenement with appurtenances in the parish of Hurberton in the county of Devon juxta Totneys, and renders per ann. — xl*s*.

Total — x*li*. iiij*s*.

Deduct in. — Rent resolute to Edward Duke of Somerset for the aforesaid house, per ann. — viij*s*.

Money paid to George Broke Kt., lord Cobham, for a private road (*pro uno chimino*) to the land in Symondsborowe, — xij*d*.

Total — ix*s*.

And remains over, per annum — ix*li*. xv*s*.

Land and possessions placed in fee for ever for the use and maintenance of three priests celebrating in the parish church there.

Thurston Golde holds certain free land and a tenement in Atherston, and renders per ann. — x*s*.

Thomas Downam and John Michell hold two tenements and xl acres of meadow land and pasture in Chelington, and render per ann. — xl*s*.

Somerset Chantries.

Richard Paule holds two acres of arable land in Chelworth, and renders per ann. — ij*s*.

William Pale holds two acres of land at Chelworth, and renders per ann. — vij*s*.

William Warryn holds a meadow called Cowlande mede containing by estimation two acres, also a burgage with appurtenances and a dove house in Willington, and renders per ann. — xiiij*s*. viij*d*.

The aforesaid William Warryn holds a burgage with appurtenances in Willington late in the tenure of Robert Wylle, and an acre of land there late in the tenure of William Shapcotte and also a house there called the clothe house late in the tenure of William Pyers, and renders per ann. — xvij*s*. viij*d*.

John Hartro holds a cottage with an acre and a half of land late Holtons, and renders per ann. — viij*s*.

John Gillinge holds a certain close of meadow and pasture in Hunspill containing by estimation viij acres — xiiij*s*. v*d*.

Nicholas Riche holds vj acres of land there, and renders per ann. — vj*s*. viij*d*.

Richard Gilling holds iij acres of more and meadow in Hunspill, and renders per ann. — vj*s*.

Thomas Elyott holds certain land there, and renders per ann. — v*d*.

John Mershall holds ij closes of land containing by estimation five acres in See, and renders per ann. — xxij*s*.

John Whyte holds a close at See containing iij acres, and renders per ann. — xij*s*.

Nicholas Pale holds a close at Dunpoll containing vj acres, and renders per ann. — xij*s*.

John Whitehorne holds a close at Dunpoll containing ij acres, and renders per ann. — vjs. viijd.

Agnes Thressher holds ten acres of pasture, and renders per ann. — xijs. iiijd.

William Gossome holds iij closes at Dunpoll containing iij acres and a half, and renders per ann. — viijs. iiijd.

Thomas Waldon holds ij acres and a half and a virgate of meadow in Langmede, and renders per ann. — vjs. viijd.

Richard Walden holds certain parcels of pasture and meadow at See and Dunpoll containing by estimation xiiij acres, and renders per ann. — xxjs.

John Messeld holds iiij acres of land at See and Dunpoll, and renders per ann — ijs. viijd.

John Barfote holds vj acres of land in Crikett, and renders per ann. — ijs.

Thomas Speke Knt. holds ten acres of land on Dowlish Downe, and renders per ann. — iijs. iiijd.

John Billinghaye holds a close containing viij acres in Crikett, and renders per ann. — viijs.

John Chike holds a certain parcel of pasture there containing v acres, and renders per ann. — ixs.

Lucy Walden holds a certain parcel of land at Chalkewill containing xxx acres, and renders per ann. — xxxvs. iiijd.

Nicholas Bragge holds ten acres of land there in Dowlishe Wake, and renders per ann. — xs.

    Total, xiiijli. xviijs. ijd.

Deduct in. — Rent resolute to the Bishop of Bath for the land in Willington — vijs. vd.

Somerset Chantries.

Rent resolute to the Earl of Brigewater for the land in Chelmyngton — vjs. viijd.

Rent resolute to the same Earl for suit of Court there — vjd.

Rent resolute to the Earl of Ormond for land in Hunspill, — ijs.

Rent resolute to the same Earl for suit of Court there — vijd.

Rent resolute to the said Earl for suit of Court there called the Water courte — iiijd.

Rent resolute to Thomas Speke Knt. for suit of Court for the lands in Crikett — vjd.

Total — xviijs.

And remains over, per annum — xiiijli. ijd.

Lands and possessions leased to farm for divers years and given for the use and augmentation of the fee or stipend of the aforesaid three chaplains or priests celebrating in the aforesaid parish church.

A house or edifice with three curtilages in Ilmyster, leased, granted and confirmed to Alexander de la Lynde esquire, John Rippe chaplain, Thomas Thorne and William Webbe, by John Cherde late Abbot of the Monastery of Muchelney in the county of Somerset and the convent of the same place, by indenture given under their convent seal in their Chapter House the 12th day of April, 1458, to have and to hold the aforesaid house and other premises to the use and maintenance of the chaplains aforesaid to the end of a term of 990 years next following after the date of the said indenture, rendering therefor annually to the aforesaid Abbot and convent and their successors during the term aforesaid xijd.

egal money of England at the iiij annual principal terms. And rendering per annum, beyond the aforesaid rent of xij$d$. to the said Abbot and convent and their successors annually during the term aforesaid paid and reserved, as set down in the book of Survey aforesaid — ij$s$. iiij$d$.

All those messuages, lands, tenements, meadow, pasture, and feed, with their appurtenances in the tithing of Winterhaye in the parish of Ilmyster called Modies tenement, by John Sherbourne, Abbot formerly of the Monastery of Muchelney aforesaid, and the convent of the same place, leased to farm to Henry Dawbeny, Kt., lord de Dawbeney, Thomas Speke, Hugh Paulet, Nicholas Wadham, junr., esquire, John Poole, Thomas Michell and John Battyn, clerk, John Bonvyle, John Balche, George Balche, John Chyke of Horton, senr., John Chike his son, Thomas Hawker, John Barfote, John Spicer and Thomas Radbere clerk, by deed of the same Abbot and convent given in their chapter house under the seal of the convent aforesaid the third day of November A.D. 1528, to have and to hold all and singular the premises with their appurtenances to the aforesaid Henry Dawbeney and the others aforenamed and their assigns for the term of a hundred and eighty years next following immediately after the death, surrender or forfeiture of Agnes wife of John Wilmote junr., who holds the same premises for the term of her life, Rendering therefor annually to the said Abbot and convent and their successors vij$s$. vij$d$. at the usual annual terms, with divers other covenants as in the said deed specified, and rendering per annum beyond the aforesaid rent of vij$s$. vij$d$. reserved — iiijli. vj$s$. vd.

John Chike holds, all those messuages, lands, tenements, meadow, pasture, and feed with appurtenances in Horton in the parish of Ilmyster, once in the tenure of John Rippe, clerk, which the aforesaid John Sherborne Abbot formerly of the Monastery of Muchelney and the unanimous consent of the convent of the same place by deed given under the common seal of their house the third day of November, A.D 1528, granted and confirmed to the aforesaid Henry Dawbeney, Kt., lord de Dawbeney and the others for the term of two hundred years to be fully completed next after the date of the said deed. Rendering annually therefor to the aforesaid Abbot and convent and their successors during the term aforesaid, iiij*s*. vj*d*. for all offices and services, with divers other agreements in the said deed specified. And renders per ann. beyond the aforesaid rent of iiij*s*. vj*d*. reserved to the aforesaid Abbot and convent annually,— iiij*li*. vj*s*. viij*d*.

Total — viij*li*. xv*s*. v*d*.

Land and possessions leased to farm for a term of years for the maintenance of a lamp with oil burning in the chancel of the parish church there.

A tenement in Lovelane in Ilmyster containing ten acres of meadow and pasture with appurtenances, also a tenement in Lovelane aforesaid containing five acres of land, meadow and pasture with appurtenances, and five acres of land of the lord's demesne in divers fields there, adjacent to the said two tenements; leased to farm, to John Marke and Richard Harrys *alias* Towker custodians or procurators for the perpetual maintenance of a lamp with oil burning to the honour and glory of Almighty God and the holy body of Christ in the chancel of the parish church aforesaid and to them annually and to their successors in the same offices, by John Sherborne Abbot formerly of the monastery of the blessed apostles Peter and Paul of Muchelney and the convent of the same, by indenture dated in the chapter house under their common seal, the 15th June, in the 15th year of Henry viij, to have and to hold to the aforesaid John Marke and Richard Harrys their successors and assigns for the term of eighty years next following and to be fully completed immediately after the death, surrender or forfeiture of John Sooper who then held the same for the term of his life, Rendering therefor annually to the said Abbot and Convent and their successors fourteen shillings and ten pence legal money of England at the four usual annual terms, with divers covenants in the same writing specified. And they render per annum beyond the above rent of xiiij*s.* to the said Abbot and convent reserved, — xxv*s.* ij*d.*

Charde.

The Fraternity of the blessed Mary there.

Thomas Symys holds a burgage with a garden and orchard adjacent containing an acre, and renders per ann. — xij*s.*

John Brewar holds a burgage with a garden containing half an acre, and renders per ann. — vj*s.* viij*d.*

Ralph Legge holds a burgage with a garden containing a rod of land, and renders per ann. — v*s.*

John Smyth holds a burgage with a certain piece of land containing half an acre, and renders per ann. — viij*s.*

Joan Welsheman holds a burgage with a garden containing a rod of land and renders per ann. — vj*s.* viij*d.*

Somerset Chantries.

Robert Blewett holds a burgage with a garden and an acre of land in Forman Downe and renders per ann. — iiij*s*.

Robert Webbe holds a burgage with a garden containing a rod of land and renders per ann. — viij*s*.

John Legge holds a burgage with half an acre of meadow and renders per ann. — viij*s*.

Richard Toker holds a burgage with a garden and renders per ann. — vj*s*.

William Moryn holds a burgage with a garden and renders per ann. — x*s*.

John Chapell holds a burgage there and renders per ann. — xvj*d*.

John Bagwell holds a burgage with a garden and renders per ann. — viij*s*.

Richard Tucker holds a burgage called the George with six acres of land there and renders per ann. — xl*s*.

Thomas Alston holds a burgage with an acre of meadow and renders per ann. — x*s*.

Richard Marshall holds a burgage with an acre of meadow and renders per ann. — xvj*s*.

Alice Bartelatt, widow, holds a burgage with a garden adjacent and renders per ann. — x*s*.

John Selwoode holds an acre of land and renders per ann. — xij*d*.

William Selwoode holds a burgage with a garden and renders per ann. — ij*s*. viij*d*.

Thomas Tyler holds a burgage with a garden and renders per ann. — viij*s*.

Somerset Chantries.

William Selwoode holds a burgage with a rod of land, and renders per ann. — vj*s*. viij*d*.

Henry Monday holds a burgage with a garden, and renders per ann. — x*s*.

John Selwoode holds a burgage with half an acre of land, and renders per ann. — v*s*.

William Selwoode holds a burgage with an acre of land and renders per ann. — viij*s*.

Robert Chanon holds a burgage and renders per ann. — x*s*.

Robert Steympe holds a burgage and renders per ann. — iij*s*. iiij*d*.

John Atkyns holds a burgage and renders per ann. — viij*s*.

Amia Cogan, widow, holds a burgage and renders per ann. — xx*s*.

John Whitehorne holds a burgage and three rods of land and renders per ann. — x*s*.

Joan Colyns, widow, holds a burgage and renders per ann. — vj*s*. viij*d*.

James Gregory holds a burgage and renders per ann. — vj*s*. viij*d*.

Joan Glover, widow, holds a tenement in Langham with ten acres of land by estimation and renders per ann. — viij*s*.

John Bayly holds two acres of land and renders per ann. — iiij*s*.

John Donster holds a meadow at Pysmarshe containing iij acres and renders per ann. — xij*s*.

Total — xiiij*li*. ix*s*. viij*d*.

Somerset Chantries.

The Chantry of St. Katerine in the parish church there.

The Bishop of Bath and Wells renders an annual free rent from a tenement in the tenure of John Pale, per ann. — viijs.

Nicholas Baynoff holds a burgage with a garden and renders per ann. — xiijs. iiijd.

John Bayly holds a burgage with an acre of land and renders per ann. — xxjs. iiijd.

Robert Petre holds an acre of land and renders per ann. — vs. iiijd.

John Whyteman holds a burgage with a garden and renders per ann. — xs.

Richard Tucker holds an acre of land and renders per ann. — ijs.

William Selwoode holds half an acre of land and renders per ann. — ijs.

John Touche holds four acres of land lying at Farnham Downe and renders per ann. — viijs.

John Kaye holds a burgage and renders per ann. — vjs. viijd.

Henry Payne holds a burgage and renders per ann. — xijs.

Walter Atkyns holds a burgage and an acre of land, and renders per ann. — xijs.

Richard James of Todworth holds certain land lying in Todworth and renders per ann. — xxvjs. viijd.

. . . . holds a cottage with a garden called Our Lady house in which the late incumbent lived, and renders per ann. — iijs. iiijd.

Total — vjli. xs. viijd.

Crukerne.

The Chantry of the blessed Mary in the Churchyard of Crukerne.

John Michell, clerk, late incumbent, holds the house with the garden and orchard of the said Chantry in Crukerne, and renders per ann. — iijs. iiijd.

Thomas Baker and others hold for their lives a cottage in the Forestrete of Crukerne; two cottages in the Southe strete there; a close of pasture called Hinderhayes; half an acre of meadow, and six acres of land in the common field of Crukerne, and render per ann. — xxxijs. viijd.

Walter Jeffray holds by copy for his life a cottage and eleven acres of land in the common field of Crukerne, and renders per ann. — xs.

Joan Laurence, widow, holds by copy for her life, a cottage with curtilage in the Southe street there, and renders per ann. — vjs. viijd.

Bernard Baker holds by copy a cottage with curtilage in the same street, and renders per ann. — vijs.

William Leche holds by copy a cottage with curtilage and two acres of land in Bowhaies, and renders per ann. — iijs. iiijd.

William Gill holds by copy a cottage with curtilage, and five acres of land in the common field of Crukerne, and renders per ann. — vs. viijd.

William Aishe holds half a mill called Padockes mill, and renders per ann. — iiijs.

Richard Hull holds by copy half a mill there called Cont mill, and renders per ann. — iijs. vjd.

John Pery holds by copy a cottage with appurtenances and eleven acres of land lying in the common field of Crukerne, and renders per ann. — vjs. viijd.

Joan Pittarde holds by copy a cottage and an acre of land lying in the common field of Crukerne, and renders per ann. — iijs. iiijd.

William Hullet holds by copy a cottage and an acre and a half of arable land lying in the common field of Crukerne, and renders per ann. — ijs.

Ralph Rowlande holds by copy a cottage with curtilage and eight acres of land in the common field of Crukerne, and renders per ann. — vjs. viijd.

Total — iiij*li.* xiiijs. xd.

The Chantry of the blessed Mary in the parish church of Crukerne.

Alexander Berde holds by indenture a dwelling house with a close adjacent and xij acres of land in the common field of Crukerne, and renders per ann. — iiijs.

Elenor Jeffery, widow, holds by indenture for the term of her life a close of pasture called Vynleghe, containing by estimation fifty acres, and renders per ann. — ls.

Richard Meryfeld holds by copy for his life a close of pasture called Segecomb, and renders per ann. — xxs.

John Baker holds by copy for his life another close of pasture called Segecomb, and renders per ann. — xviijs.

Richard Cogyn holds by copy for his life a cottage there, and renders per ann. — xvjd.

John Benet holds by copy three acres of pasture called Hynde Hayes, and renders per ann. — vs.

Total — iiij*li.* xviijs. iiijd.

Deduct in.—Rent resolute to the Lord the King as of his manor of Crukerne, viz., for half a pound of pepper. — xiiij*d*.

And remains over — iiij*li.* xvij*s.* ij*d.*

The late Chantry of the Holy Trinity now the Free School there.

Robert Rawys holds by indenture a close of pasture called Temple landes lying at Pillesdon in the county of Dorset, and renders per ann. — 1*s.*

John Golde, esquire, holds a close of pasture called Maydens-well, and renders per ann. — iiij*s.*

Henry Cryke holds by copy six acres of land in the common field of Crukerne, and renders per ann. — iij*s.*

Thomas Baker holds an acre of land in the common field, and renders per ann. — v*d.*

Robert Hawkyns holds a cottage with a garden annexed, a close of pasture, iij virgates of meadow in Great Blacknyll and an acre of land, and renders per ann. — x*s.* j*d.*

John Brayne holds a cottage with curtilage and xiiij acres of land in the common field of Crukerne, and renders per ann. — xiij*s.* iiij*d.*

Robert Sherlocke holds a cottage with a garden, and renders per ann. — vj*s.* viij*d.*

John Byrde holds a cottage with a virgate of meadow in Great Blacknyll and renders per ann. —x*s.*

Joan Lawrence holds by copy a cottage and iij acres of land in the common field of Crukerne, and renders per ann. — viij*s.*

James Grenewaye holds a cottage and xx acres of land in the common field of Crukerne, and renders per ann. — xiij*s.* iij*d.*

Somerset Chantries.

Alexander Berde holds by copy a cottage and ij acres of arable land, and renders per ann. — vj*s*. viij*d*.

William Browne holds a close of land called the Westoners, and renders per ann. — ix*s*.

John Mason holds at will half an acre of land in the common field, and renders per ann. — iij*d*.

Laurence Colles holds a close of pasture and an acre of meadow lying in Sturmyster Marshall in the county of Dorset, and renders per ann. — viij*s*.

William Wattes holds a tenement with appurtenances lying at Mayden Newton in the county of Dorset, and renders per ann. — x*s*.

James Bayly holds a close of pasture containing by estimation ij acres and renders per ann. — iiij*s*.

John Dawbeny holds an annual rent coming from Combe seynt reigne, and renders per ann. — xxiij*s*. iiij*d*.

Total — ix*li*.

Deduct in.—Rent resolute to the Lord the King for free rent for the land called Comes landes with suit and service — xj*s*. j*d*.

Rent resolute to the Lord the King for free rent and for the land called Temple landes. — vj*s*.

Rent resolute to Hugh Pawlet, Kt., for free rent — xx*d*.

Total — xviij*s*. ix*d*.

And remains over — viij*li*. xv*d*.

Customary lands demised by copy of Court Roll to Hugh Paulet, Kt., and Henry Creke to the use of the Trinity and the maintenance of the aforesaid Free School by Henry late Marquis of Exeter of High Treason attainted, once of the demesne of the manor of Crukerne now in the hands of the Lord the King.

Hugh Paulet, Kt., and Henry Creke hold by copy of Court roll for their lives to the use aforesaid two parts of the land lying in Crukerne aforesaid called Craft and render per ann. beyond xl*s.* annually payable to the Lord the King as of his manor of Crukerne for the rent or farm of the aforesaid ij parts of the land called Craft — xxxiij*s.* iiij*d.*

Land and possessions granted for the observance of an annual Anniversary in the parish church there.

John Bevyn holds a close of land in Meriet called Hannynge Haye, and renders per ann. — iij*s.* iiij*d.*

Annual rent granted for the maintenance of a lamp and a light burning in the parish church there.

Hugh Paulet, Kt., renders annually from his land and tenements in Crukerne aforesaid, per ann. — x*s.*

The Chapel of Misterton within the parish of Crukerne.

Land given to the use and maintenance of a light burning in the Chapel aforesaid.

. . . . holds an acre of land there, and renders per ann. — viij*d.*

South Petherton.

The Free Chapel of Saint John there.

John Kingman holds the dwelling house with garden and orchard adjacent and renders per ann. — viijs.

Walter Helyer holds a tenement there, and renders per ann. — xiiijs. iiijd.

Richard Capper holds another tenement there, and renders per ann. — xijs.

John Wylly holds divers lands, meadow, pasture and feed there, and renders per ann. — xxvjs. iiijd.

John Forte holds certain land there with appurtenances, and renders per ann. — ijs. viijd.

William Collyn holds an acre of land there, and renders per ann. — xvjd.

Richard Burnet and Richard Wylly hold divers meadows, pasture and feed, and render per ann. — xlviijs.

Total — vli. xijs. viijd.

Deduct in.—Money annually paid to the rector of the parish church there — ijs.

Money annually paid to the Vicar of the same church — xiiijs.

Total — xvjs.

And remains clear — iiijli. xvjs. viijd.

The Chauntry in the parish church there.

Redy money to be annually received at the foure annual terms by equal portions out of the Issues, Revenues, and profits of the manor of South Petherton aforesaid by the hands of the bailiff of the saide manor for the time being, so founded and granted by Henry late Earl of Brigewater, by deed dated Henry viij, per ann. — vj*li.* xiij*s.* iiij*d.*

Land and possessions given to the use and maintenance of a lamp and a light burning in the parish church there.

The Churchwardens hold four acres of arable land lying in the fields of South Petherton and Sevington Saint Michael, and render per ann. — ij*s.* viij*d.*

The Chapel of Lopon.

Robert Sanforde holds certain land with appurtenances and renders per ann. — xiij*s.* iiij*d.*

Total — xiij*s.* iiij*d.*

Deduct in.—Rent resolute to the church of South Petherton for repairs of the same, per ann. — vj*s.* viij*d.*

Rent resolute to the Chief lord of the same, for free rent of the said land, per ann. — xij*d.*

Total — vij*s.* viij*d.*

And remains over — v*s.* viij*d.*

Curry Rivell.

The Chantry of Wykeperham.

Thomas Hill and others hold for their lives a cottage with appurtenances and render per ann. — viijs. iiij*d*.

The same Thomas Hill holds by copy two acres of meadow in Smethyt furlong and xij virgates of meadow towards Bullingham, and half an acre of meadow next les Whytebare, and renders per ann. — vijs. iiij*d*.

John Hemmyng and others hold by copy a tenement there containing viij acres of arable land and vij acres of meadow and one les Whitebarre, and pasture for two oxen in Smethyt, and render per ann. — xxs.

John Morforde holds by copy a tenement called Lakehouse containing xiij acres and a half of arable and vj acres of meadow, and pasture for four oxen in Bullingham, and pasture for four oxen in Smethyt, and renders per ann.— xviijs. iiij*d*.

Thomas Morforde holds by copy three acres of meadow lying in Wykemede with appurtenances, and renders per ann. — vjs.

Thomas Hill holds by copy two acres of meadow and four acres of arable land with appurtenances, and renders per ann. — vjs. viij*d*.

Total — lxvjs. viij*d*.

Land and possessions as well in Curry Rybell as in divers other towns in the same County, belonging to the Free School or Chantry founded by Margaret late Countess of Richmond and Derby within the late College of Wymborne in the county of Dorset.

John Godybarne *alias* Sheres holds all the manors, lands, tenements, rents, reversions, and services, with all and singular their appurtenances, situate and lying in the county of Somerset to the said Free School of Wymborne belonging so to him leased for xxj years, by indenture dated xviij Feb., 35 Henry viij, under the seal of Richard Hosier, clerk, late Master there, rendering in equal parts at the usual four quarter days, per ann. — xj*li.* xiiij*s.*

Land and possessions given for the maintenance of a Light burning in the church there.

The Rector of the parish chruch aforesaid holds a parcel of arable land containing v acres and renders per ann. — v*s.*

Myrpett.

Land and possessions given for the maintenance of a lamp there.

An acre of land with appurtenances there — iiij*s.* (*All cancelled.*)

Somerset Chantries.

Kyngesbury.

Land and possessions given for the observance of an annual obit there.

The Wardens of the parish church there hold a certain parcel of land there given by John Nabbe, and render per ann. — x*s*.

Curry Mallett.

The Free Chapel of St. James there.

John Copston holds at will the chapel aforesaid and fifty and iij acres of land and meadow there and renders per ann. — xlvj*s*. v*d*.

Abbottes Pele.

Land and possessions given to the use and maintenance of a Light burning in the parish church there.

Robert Baker holds half an acre of meadow there lying in Ilmore, and renders per ann. — xij*d*.

Fyffett.

Land and possessions there given by John Speke, Kt., to the Dean and Chapter of the Cathedral church of St. Peter Exeter, in the county of Devon to the use and maintenance of a Chantry founded in the same Cathedral.

Margaret wife of John Dolman and Thomas Taylor son of the same Margaret hold by indenture for their lives, a messuage, land, tenement, meadow, pasture, and feed there, with appurtenances, called Langforde Farm, and render per ann. — ix*li*. ixs. ij*d*.

John Taylor and Thomas Taylor hold by indenture, for their lives, thirty acres of meadow in Ilmore, and render per ann. — xlvjs. viij*d*.

Total — xj*li*. xvs. x*d*.

Deduct in.—Rent resolute to the Duke of Suffolk as of the Hundred of Bulston for chief rent for the farm of Langford — ijs. vj*d*.

And remains over — xj*li*. xiijs. iiij*d*.

Shepton Beauchamp.

Land and possessions given for the maintenance of a Light burning in the parish Church there.

The inhabitants hold a house called the Church house, and render per ann. — iijs. iiij*d*.

Christopher Rowsewell holds two acres of land in the common fields there, and renders per ann. — ijs. viij*d*.

The same Christopher holds half an acre of meadow there called Bulmeade, and renders per ann. — xij*d*.

Total — vijs.

Beare Crocombe.

Land and possessions given for the maintenance of a lamp burning in the church ther.

Richard Tyse holds three closes of land there called Pack- were lying next Yernehill containing v acres, and renders per ann. — xiijs. iiijd.

Wynsham.

Annual rents given to the use and maintenance of a light burning in the parish church there.

An annual rent coming from a close there called Vythra, viz., for ij lbs. of wax, per ann. — xijd.

Donyett.

The Chantry founded within the Park there.

Ready money annually received from the profits and revenues of the manor of Donyet, per ann. — xxxjs. ijd.

Money annually received from the profits and revenues of the Court of Augmentation of the Crown, by the hands of the Receiver General in the County of Somerset, by virtue of a certain Decree of the same Court in that behalf made — lxvj*s.* viij*d.*

Total — iiij*li.* xvij*s.* x*d.*

Total of the Deanery of Crukerne per ann. — cxxvj*li.* iij*s.* viij*d*

Deduct in.—Reprises and rents resolute in divers modes as before particularly shown — lxxiij*s.* j*d.*

And remains over, per annum — cxxij*li.* x*s.* vij*d.*

Deanery of Taunton.

Town of Taunton.

The Chantry of the blessed Mary in the parish of St. Mary Magdalen there.

.... holds the dwelling house in which the Cantarist formerly lived, and renders per ann. — x*s*.

John Buckethort holds a burgage there, and renders per ann. — xxxiij*s*. iiij*d*.

Robert Wyther holds a burgage there in the Churche lane, and renders per ann. — x*s*.

The same Robert holds a tenement there in Mawdelyn lane, and renders per ann. — x*s*.

Magdalen Fyssher holds a burgage in the High Street there, and renders per ann. — x*s*.

John Skotte holds a shamble in the market place there, and renders per ann. — xiij*s*. iiij*d*.

Thomas Muddesleighe holds a shamble in the market aforesaid, and renders per ann. — xij*s*.

William Percy holds a shamell in the same market, and renders per ann. — xij*s*.

Robert Newbery holds a garden in the High Street, and renders per ann. — x*s*.

Somerset Chantries.

Robert Boyer holds a garden in the same street, and renders per ann. — ij*s*.

Adam Bucher holds a cottage in the way there called Polle street, and renders per ann. — v*s*.

John Saunders holds a cottage there, and renders per ann. — v*s*.

. . . . Walthiane holds a cottage in Churche Lane, and renders per ann. — iiij*s*. iiij*d*.

Edmund Cockes holds according to the custom of Taunden a meadow in Monketon containing by estimation v acres, and renders per ann. — xvij*s*.

Christopher David holds according to the same custom an acre and a half of meadow in Hyde, and renders per ann. — iiij*s*.

. . . . Sooper, gent, holds an acre of meadow in Paules field, and renders per ann. — xvj*d*.

. . . . Loveles holds a window in the market there, and renders per ann. — xiij*s*. iiij*d*.

Roger Lyddon holds three windows in the market aforesaid with a chamber to the same, and renders per ann. — xxx*s*.

John Glose renders annually a free rent, viz., for a lb. of wax, per ann. — vj*d*.

Total — x*li*. iij*s*. ij*d*.

Deduct in.—Rent resolute to the Bishop of Winton for free rent of the ij shamells in the middle of the market, ij*s*.; for a burgage on the Cornehill, vj*d*.; for a garden in the High Street, ix*d*.; for the aforesaid chamber and three windows, xij*d*.; per ann. — iiij*s*. iij*d*

Rent resolute to the Lord Fitzwaren for rent of the same chamber and iiij windows there — xx*s*.

Total — xxiiij*s*. iij*d*.

And remains over, per annum — viij*li*. xviij*s*. xj*d*.

The Chantry of St. Nicholas *alias* Busshoppes Chauntry in the parish aforesaid.

. . . . holds the dwelling house there in which the incumbent lately lived, and renders per ann. — iij*s*. iiij*d*.

Thomas Davige holds a burgage in Taunton called les Three Cuppes, and renders per ann. — xx*s*.

Richard Roydon holds a burgage in Este strete there, and renders per ann. — xx*s*.

Elizabeth Pomery holds a burgage in Este strete aforesaid, and renders per ann. — xij*s*.

William Furryor holds a burgage there, and renders per ann. — xx*s*.

Henry Grene holds a burgage there, and renders per ann. — xviij*d*.

John Spiringe and Peter Leighe hold a shamell there, and render per ann. — xxiiij*s*.

The same hold another shamell in the middle of the market there, and render per ann. — viij*s*.

John Arundell holds a cottage there, and renders per ann. —v*s*.

William Charde holds an orchard there, and renders per ann. — v*s*.

Robert Gyle holds a shop in Mercery Lane, and renders per ann. — ijs. viijd.

William Swinger holds a shop in Mercery Lane aforesaid, and renders per ann. — ijs.

William Goughe holds a burgage there, and renders per ann. — xvjs.

John Pardoner holds a tenement there, and renders per ann. — ixs. iiijd.

William Lambert holds according to the custom of Taunden certain lands and tenements called Serney, Pyley, and Oke, in the parish of Trull in the county aforesaid, and renders per ann. — xxiijs.

James Spiring holds according to the custom aforesaid certain land and pasture in Trull aforesaid, and renders per ann. — xls.

John Smyth holds according to the custom aforesaid certain land there, and renders per ann. —xxvjs. viijd.

Robert Smyth holds according to the custom aforesaid a certain parcel of land there, and renders per ann. — xxxvs. viijd.

John Buncombe holds according to the custom aforesaid a meadow there containing vj acres — xs.

John Lane holds a parcel of land there, and renders per ann. — xs.

John Bowring holds certain lands and meadows there, and renders per ann. — xxxvjs.

Robert Smyth holds divers parcels of land there, and renders per ann. — xxs.

John Togood renders an annual free rent from his manor of Pyley and Oke, per ann. — x*s.*

Total — xviij*li.* ij*d.*

Deduct in.—Rent resolute to the Bishop of Winton for the above said burgages and shamells, per ann. — xj*s.* x*d.*

Rent resolute to the same Bishop for the lands aforesaid in Serney, Pyley, and Oke, per ann. — xx*s.*

Total — xxxj*s.* x*d.*

And remains over, per annum. — xvj*li.* viij*s.* iiij*d.*

The Chantry of the name of Jesu in the parish aforesaid.

Roger Yde holds a burgage there lying in Este strete, and renders per ann. — xx*s.*

Anthony Garrat holds a burgage there, and renders per ann. — xx*s.*

Philip Arther holds a burgage there, and renders per ann. — xviij*s.*

John Dolman holds a burgage there, and renders per ann. — xx*s.*

. . . . holds a burgage in Mercery lane, and renders per ann. — vj*s.* viij*d.*

. . . . Mante, of the county of Devon, holds a little house next the east gate there (in the tenure of Thomas Nosse), and renders per ann. — vj*s.* viij*d.*

Robert Marler holds a burgage there, and renders per ann. — xx*s.*

William Randall holds a window in the market place there, and renders per ann. — iiij*s.*

Roger Decher holds a window there, and renders per ann. — vj*s*.

Laurence Boyton holds a window there, and renders per ann. — vj*s*. viij*d*.

John Hurman holds a window there, and renders per ann. — vj*s*.

John Hooke holds a window there, and renders per ann. — iiij*s*. iiij*d*.

John Yonge holds a burgage in Newerton, and renders per ann. — vj*s*. viij*d*.

Maurice Daber holds a tenement there, and renders per ann. — v*s*.

William Skoryar holds a meadow lying next Newerton aforesaid, and renders per ann. — v*s*.

John Newport holds a burgage in Brigewater, and renders per ann. — xiij*s*. iiij*d*.

Total — viij*li*. viij*s*. iiij*d*.

Deduct in.—Rent resolute to the Bishop of Winton for free rent of the premises, per ann., viz.—for the tenement of John Harrys, ij*s*.; the tenement of Roger Ide, xviij*d*.; for the tenement of Philip Arther, ij*s*.; the tenement of John Dolman, xij*d*.; for the tenement in Mercery lane, viij*d*.; the tenement of Mande, j*d*.; and for the tenement in Powles strete, xij*d*. — viij*s*. iij*d*.

Rent resolute to Lord Fitzwaren for free rent for the land next Newerton, per ann. — xiij*d*.

Total — ix*s*. iiij*d*.

And remains over, per annum. — vij*li*. xix*s*.

Somerset Chantries.

The Chantry of the Trinity there in the parish aforesaid.

Christopher Wilkyns holds two acres and a half of pasture, and renders per ann. — x*s*.

John Sooper holds an acre of pasture in Haymede, and renders per ann. — iij*s*.

Thomas Mors holds a burgage, and renders per ann. — x*s*.

Hugh Whitcherte holds a burgage there, and renders per ann. xxvj*s*. viij*d*.

John Messolyn holds a burgage there, and renders per ann. — xvj*s*.

John Walforde holds certain land in Wilton, and renders per ann. — xiij*s*. iiij*d*.

Thomas Doble holds certain land in Crowcombe, and renders per ann. — xx*s*.

Henry Newbery holds a burgage, and renders per ann. — iij*s*. iiij*d*.

Thomas Holmes holds a burgage there, and renders per ann. — iij*s*. iiij*d*.

Anthony Lambert holds a burgage, and renders per ann. — iij*s*. iiij*d*.

Robert Boucher holds a cottage, and renders per ann. — v*s*.

John Cobler holds a cottage, and renders per ann. — v*s*.

John Pears holds a ruined and vacant cottage, and renders per ann. — v*s*.

John Jennynge holds a cottage and two acres of land in the parish of Ede juxta Exiter, and renders per ann. — xj*s*.

Total — vj*li*. xvj*s*.

Deduct in.—Rent resolute to the Bishop of Winton for free rent of all the burgages aforesaid, per ann., for the burgage of Hugh Whitehorne — iij*s.*; for the burgage of John Messeleyn — ij*s.* ij*d.*; for the burgage in decay — xviij*d.*; the cottage of Robert Bouche — vij½*d.*; the burgage of Henry Newbery — xij*d.*; the cottage of John Cobler — vij½*d.*; the burgage of Thomas Holmes — xij*d.*; and the burgage of Anthony Lambert — xij*d.*

Total — x*s.* xj*d.*

And remains over, per annum.— vj*li.* v*s.* j*d.*

The Chantry of Saint Andrew there in the parish aforesaid.

The dwelling house in the churchyard in which the Cantarist lived, per ann. — ij*s.* viij*d.*

Ralph Wilkins, clerk, holds a burgage in the churchyard aforesaid, and renders per ann. — x*s.*

John Workman holds a burgage, and renders per ann. — vj*s.* viij*d.*

John Wethercote holds a burgage, and renders per ann. — v*s.*

Ivota Glaston, widow, holds a burgage, and renders per ann. — iiij*s.*

John Stonderd holds a burgage, and renders per ann. — ij*s.*

Katherine Day holds two burgages, and renders per ann. — xx*s.*

Thomas Bartlet holds a burgage, and renders per ann. — xiij*s.* iiij*d.*

Richard Harding holds a parcel of vacant land, and renders per ann. — xx*d.*

Alice Piers holds a burgage, and renders per ann. — vj*s.*

Somerset Chantries.

John Lawrence holds a burgage, and renders per ann. — xj*s*.

Joan Bellamy holds a burgage, and renders per ann. — iiij*s*.

William Vyny holds an acre of land in Wilton, and renders per ann. — iiij*s*.

William Charde holds an acre of land, and renders per ann. — iij*s*. iiij*d*.

Edward Score holds a certain piece of vacant land, and renders per ann. — iiij*s*.

William Okar holds a cottage and thirty-four acres of land in Durston, and renders per ann. — xxiiij*s*.

William Hoper holds eleven acres of land in Durston, and renders per ann. — vij*s*.

Total — vj*li*. viij*s*. viij*d*.

Deduct in.—Rent resolute to the Bishop of Winton for all the burgages aforesaid, per ann., viz.:—for the burgage in the churchyard — ij*s*. vj*d*.; for the burgage in the tenure of John Lawrence — xij*d*.; for the parcel of vacant land — vij½*d*.; for the burgage in the tenure of Alice Piers — ij*s*.; for the burgage in the tenure of Katherine Daye — ij*s*. ij*d*.; for the burgage in the tenure of Thomas Bartelet — iij*s*.; for the burgage in the tenure of Joan Belamy — xij*d*.; and for the parcel of vacant land in the tenure of Edward Skore — ij*s*.

Total — xiiij*s*. iij½*d*.

And remains over, per annum.— cxiiij*s*. iiij½*d*.

The Chantry there called Swinges Chantry in the parish aforesaid.

The dwelling-house of the Chantry in the churchyard there, per ann. — ij*s*.

James Eston holds a tenement in the High Street, and renders per ann. — xviijs. vjd.

John Adam holds a tenement in the same street, and renders per ann. — xvijs.

Joan Pheppyn holds a tenement in Mercery Lane, and renders per ann. — vijs.

John Hause holds two chambers with appurtenances in Fore strete, and renders per ann. — ixs. iiijd.

John Gill holds a shamell in the market place, and renders per ann. — xiijs. iiijd.

Simon Farewell holds a shop in the said market place, and renders per ann. — vjs. viijd.

John Hurle, John Brewer, Richard Prior, John Keche, John Crosse, and Nicholas Hare hold six shops in the Fore strete, and render per ann. — xijs.

William Stadyn and John Stadyn hold two windows in the Fore strete, and render per ann. — xiiijd.

Total — iiijli. vijs.

Deduct in.—Rent resolute to the Bishop of Winton for free rent of all the tenements aforesaid, per ann., viz. : for the tenement of James Eston — xviijd.; for the tenement of John Adam — iijs.; for the tenement in Mercery Lane — ixd.; for the two chambers with appurtenances — xd.; for a shamell — iiijd.; for a shop — ½d.; and for the six shops aforesaid — ijd.

Total — vjs. vij½d.

And remains over, per annum.— iiijli. iiij½d.

The Chantry of St. Etheldrede there in the parish aforesaid.

William Hodges holds a tenement with appurtenances in Oack, and renders per ann. — iiij*li*. x*s*. x*d*.

John Tanner holds a tenement with appurtenances there, and renders per ann. — xl*s*.

John Kytforde holds a tenement with appurtenances there, and renders per ann. — vij*s*.

William Huyshe holds a tenement with appurtenances there, and renders per ann. — xiij*s*. iiij*d*.

Alexander Walforde holds a tenement with appurtenances, and renders per ann. — ix*s*.

Total — viij*li*. ij*d*.

Deduct in.—Money paid for suit to the Hundred of Cannyngton, per ann. — vj*d*.

And remains over, per annum. — vij*li*. xix*s*. viiij*d*.

The Fraternity of the High Cross there in the parish aforesaid.

Robert Walles holds a burgage in North strete, and renders per ann. — xviij*s*. iiij*d*.

William Horsey holds a burgage in the same strete, and renders per ann. — xx*s*.

The same William holds a burgage in the same strete, and renders per ann. — xxvj*s*. viij*d*.

Richard Wharton holds a burgage, and renders per ann. — viij*s*.

Somerset Chantries.

Cornelius Hayes holds a burgage there, and renders per ann. — xvjs.

Robert Shaldon holds a burgage there, and renders per ann. — xxs.

Gregory Pers holds a burgage there, and renders per ann. — xiijs. iiijd.

Joan Marteyne holds a burgage there, and renders per ann. —xvjs. viijd.

James Hurtnell holds a shamell there, and renders per ann. — xiijs. viijd.

John Tanner holds a burgage in the High street there, and renders per ann. — xvjs.

William Charde holds an acre of land in Charforde, and renders per ann. — xviijd.

Total — viijli. xs. ijd.

Deduct in.— Rent resolute to the Bishop of Winton for free rent of the burgages aforesaid, per ann. — vjs.

And remains over, per annum. — viijli. iiijs. ijd.

The Fraternity of the Sepulchre there in the parish aforesaid.

Nicholas Browne holds a burgage in North strete, and renders per ann. — xxvjs. viijd.

Richard Borforde holds a burgage in Highe strete, and renders per ann. — xiijs. iiijd.

William Denys holds a burgage in Silver strete, and renders per ann. — xs.

William Hoper holds a burgage in Pollestreet, and renders per ann. — xs.

Somerset Chantries.

Robert Marlent holds a burgage there, and renders per ann. — x*s.*

Robert Bargen holds a burgage there, and renders per ann. — viij*s.*

Alice Pers, commonly called mother Alice, holds a burgage there, and renders per ann. — viij*s.*

John Eyer (late Roger Bedman) holds a burgage in the churchyard there, and renders per ann — xij*s.*

John Eyer holds a burgage there, and renders per ann. — x*s.*

Robert Browne clerk, holds a burgage there, and renders per ann — x*s.*

William Trowbrige clerk, holds a burgage there, and renders per ann. — x*s.*

John Kape holds a meat shamell in Fore strete, and renders per ann. — xviij*s.*

Elias Saunderley holds a shamell, and renders per ann. — x*s.*

William Dorston senr. holds a certain parcel of land in Sherwoode, and renders per ann. — xvj*s.*

William Dorsten junr. holds a tenement with appurtenances in Sherwoode, and renders per ann. — vj*s.* viij*d.*

Robert Hegens holds a little parcel of land, and renders per ann. — iiij*d.*

Total — viij*li.* xix*s.*

Deduct in.—Rent resolute to the Bishop of Winton for free rent for the premises, per annum. — ix*s.* iij*d.*

And remains over, per annum. — viij*li.* ix*s.* ix*d.*

The Service of the Blessed Mary in the parish church of St. James.

John Horsey holds a burgage there according to the custom of Taunton, and renders per ann. — xjs. vjd.

Richard Swyton holds a burgage there according to the custom of Taunton, and renders per ann. — viijs.

Avicia Brouscombe holds a burgage according to the custom of Taunton, and renders per ann. — viijs.

John Chilcote holds a burgage, and renders per ann. — vs.

John Skose holds a burgage, and renders per ann. — vs.

Richard Longe holds two burgages, and renders per ann. — xiijs.

Richard Colforde holds a burgage, and renders per ann. — viijs.

William Rede holds a burgage, and renders per ann. — viijs.

Thomas Crowde holds a burgage, and renders per ann. — viijs.

Edward Plumer holds a burgage, and renders per ann. — viijs.

Henry Vuall holds a burgage, and renders per ann. — vjs. viijd.

John Wynesland holds a burgage, and renders per ann. — vjs. viijd.

Philip Solye holds a burgage there, and renders per ann. — xijs.

The same Philip holds a burgage, and renders per ann — iijs. iiijd.

Walthian Johns holds a burgage, and renders per ann. — ij*s*. viij*d*.

John Whyte holds a burgage there, and renders per ann. — x*s*.

Henry Nyneacre holds a burgage, and renders per ann. — x*s*.

John Cornewall holds a piece of ground to the said service belonging, on which he has built a wall, and renders per ann.— ij*d*.

William Carter holds two acres of land in Bromhayes, and renders per ann. — vj*s*.

Richard Gale holds six acres of arable customary land in Dodmere, the gift of John Mylle, and renders per ann. — xxj*s*. viij*d*.

John Gale holds a meadow called Pyntleymede containing seven acres, and renders per ann. — xiij*s*. iiij*d*.

Philip Solewe holds a meadow called Ilbare mead (customary) containing ij acres, and renders per ann. — x*s*.

William Charde holds land in Grassmead, and renders per ann. — xxj*s*.

. . . . holds a little house there called the clerks house, and renders per ann. — ij*s*. viij*d*.

Total — x*li*. viij*s*. viij*d*.

Deduct in.—Rent resolute to the Earl of Bath for free rent of the premises, per ann. — iij*s*.

Rent resolute to the Bishop of Winton for free rent, per ann. — xviij*d*.

Rent resolute to the aforesaid Bishop for the land called Bondlande, per ann. — x*s*. vj*d*.

Total — xv*s*.

And remains over, per annum. — ix*li*. xiij*s*. viij*d*.

A *marginal note to the holding of William Charde, reads* :—
xiiij*s*. parcel of the some of xxj*s*., is parcel of the said Chantry, and viij*s*. remaining belong to Henry Bercomb as parcel of the customary lands.

North Curry.

The Chantry there.

. . . . holds the dwelling house with a garden adjacent, and renders per ann. — ij*s*.

Divers persons there hold divers lands, tenements, cottages, meadows, feed and pasture, to the said chantry belonging, and render per ann. — lxvij*s*. j*d*.

The Dean and Chapter of the Cathedral Church of Wells render annually to the incumbent celebrating in the same Chantry (of their free will or grace) in augmentation of the salary of the incumbent, per ann. — xl*s*.

Total — cix*s*. j*d*.

Deduct in.—Rent resolute to the Dean and Chapter of Wells aforesaid issuing from vj acres and a half of meadow, per ann.— ij*s*. vj*d*.

Rent resolute to the same Dean and Chapter issuing from half a burgage in Newporte, per ann. — vij½*d*.

Rent resolute to the same Dean and Chapter issuing from a certain meadow called Knappemede, per ann. — vj*d*.

Total — iij*s*. vij½*d*.

And remains over, per annum.— cv*s*. v½*d*.

The Service of a priest there called a Brotherhedd priest.

Elena Wiche holds a tenement with appurtenances, and xvij acres of land, and an acre of meadow in Wrentage, and renders per ann. — x*s*.

William Zely, sen., holds two acres of land in Langdowne, and renders per ann. — iij*s*.

Thomas Ivery holds an acre of land there, and renders per ann. — ij*s*.

William Bale holds a rod of meadow in Brodemede, and renders per ann. — xij*d*.

Alice Batyn holds a burgage with appurtenances in Newporte, and renders per ann. — v*s*.

John Androse holds a burgage with appurtenances, and an acre of meadow in Colcetes, and an acre of wood in Lustokewoode, and renders per ann. — v*s*.

Total — xxvj*s*.

Wellington.

The Service of a perpetual chaplain there.

William Cape holds a burgage there, and renders per ann. — v*s*. iiij*d*.

William Gyfforde holds half a burgage there, and renders per ann. — v*s*.

John Budde holds half a burgage there, and renders per ann. — iiij*s*.

Somerset Chantries.

Robert Husye holds half a burgage there, and renders per ann. — vs.

Thomas Royoll holds half a burgage there, and renders per ann. — xij$s$.

William Frye holds an acre of land there, and renders per ann. vj$d$.

John Mondye holds half a burgage, and renders per ann. — vs. iiij$d$.

William Byrrye holds half a burgage there, and renders per ann. — iij$s$.

William Gyfforde holds half a burgage there, and renders per ann. —vj$s$. viij$d$.

John Baker holds a tenement there, and renders per ann. — iiij$s$. viij$d$.

John Gaylarde holds a shop there, and renders per ann. — xij$d$.

Andrew Hewet holds a tenement there, and renders per ann. — vs.

Robert Mogridge holds half a burgage there, and two half acres of land, and renders per ann. — viij$s$.

Thomas Lynke holds half a burgage, and renders per ann. — vs.

An annual rent coming from the revenues of a tenement there, in the tenure of Margaret Budde, per ann. — ij$s$.

An annual rent from the revenues of a messuage and curtilage there in Chipping strete in the tenure of Laurence Frie, per ann. — iij$s$. iiij$d$.

Total — lxxv$s$. xd.

Deduct in.—Rent resolute to the Manor of Wellington for all the burgages, land and tenements, &c., per ann. — viij*s*. iiij½*d*.

And remains over, per annum.—lxvij*s*. v½*d*.

West Buckland.
Chapel annexed to the parish church of Wellington.

The Service of a priest there called a Brotherhedd priest.

Divers persons there hold four tenements with gardens adjacent in Wellington, also vij acres and a half of land lying in the fields there, and render per ann. — lviij*s*. iiij*d*.

Total — lviij*s*. iiij*d*.

Deduct in.—Rent resolute to the Bishop of Bath and Wells as of his manor of Wellington, per ann. — ix*s*. viij*d*.

And remains over, per annum.— xlviij*s*. viij*d*.

Bysshoppes Lydyarde.

The Chapel of the blessed Mary there called Sandylan.

.... holds the said chapel with half an acre of land to the same appertaining, and renders per ann. — xvj*d*.

Kingeston and Cotherston.

Land and possessions customary, given and assigned for the maintenance of a chaplain there called a Brotherhed priest.

Robert Farthing holds two acres of meadow called Slapemede, and renders per ann. — xv*s.*

Thomas Branchflower holds ten acres of land called Whitefeld, and renders per ann. — vij*s.* iiij*d.*

The same Thomas holds a cottage there, and renders per ann. — vj*s.*

Thomas Hill holds a cottage there, and renders per ann. — v*s.* viij*d.*

Thomas Cornyshe holds two acres and a half of land here, and renders per ann. — v*s.*

Total — xxxix*s.*

Deduct in.—Rent resolute to the Bishop of Winton for the rent and farm of all the premises, per ann. — xij*s.* j*d.*

And remains over, per annum.— xxvj*s.* xj*d.*

Pytminster.

Land and possessions customary, given and assigned for the maintenance of a stipendiary chaplain.

The dwelling house there in which the late incumbent lived, per ann. — iij*s.* iiij*d.*

Somerset Chantries.

Divers persons there hold according to the custom of Taunden five cottages with four acres and a half of land to the same belonging, and render per ann. — liij*s*. iiij*d*.

Total — lvj*s*. viij*d*.

Deduct in.—Rent resolute to the Bishop of Winton for rent of the cottages, per ann. — xxj*s*.

And remains over, per annum.— xxxv*s*. viij*d*.

Staplegrove.

Land given for the observance of an annual Obit in the parish church there.

John Knyght holds three rods of meadow there called Lowsemedowe, and renders per ann. — iiij*s*.

Deduct in.—Rent resolute to the Bishop of Winton for free rent for the same, per ann. — vij½*d*.

And remains over, per annum.— iij*s*. iiij½*d*.

Thornefawcon.

Land given for the maintenance of a Light burning in the parish church there.

Gilbert Bradshawe clerk holds four acres of land there, and renders per ann. — iiij*s*.

Total — iiij*s*.

Somerset Chantries.

Bradford.

The Chantry within the parish there.

Thomas Crowe holds by indenture an inn or burgage and half a burgage in Wellington called the Swanne, and renders per ann. — xxx*s*.

Divers persons hold by copy all the messuages, land, and tenements, meadows, feed and pasture and other hereditaments in Sampford Parva to the said Chantry belonging, and render per ann. — xxxiij*s*. iiij*d*.

Divers persons hold by copy all the messuages, land, tenements, feed, and pasture and other hereditaments in Langford and Rymton to the said Chantry belonging, and render per ann. — liiij*s*. viij*d*.

Total — cxviij*s*.

Deduct in.—Money paid to the Lady the Queen for suit and service for the land in Romington, per ann. — xij*d*.

Money paid to the Bailiff of Herforde for suit and service for the land in Langford, per ann. — xij*d*.

Money paid to Thomas Speke, Kt., for suit and service for the land in Samford, per ann. — xij*d*.

Money paid to the Bishop of Bath for suit and service for the land in Wellington, per ann. — xij*d*.

Total — iiij*s*.

And remains over, per annum. — cxiiij*s*.

Somerset Chantries

Westmonketon.

The Service of the blessed Mary there.

John God, junior, holds half an acre of meadow lying in Bromehay, and renders per ann. — xviij*d.*

The Service of a chaplain celebrating in the chapel belonging to the Hospital for the Poor there.

Money annually received from the profits and revenues of the Court of Augmentation of the Crown, by the hands of the Receiver General of the same in the County of Somerset, by virtue of a certain Decree of the same Court, per ann. — lxvj*s.* viij*d.*

Combe Flory.

The Chantry there.

Hugh Sampforde and Elinor his wife held for term of their lives a tenement or burgage with appurtenances in Combeflory, and render per ann. — xlij*s.* v*d.*

William Fraunces, Kt., holds common of pasture in Combdowne for fifty sheep, and a dovecot there, and renders per ann. — xxiij*s.* iiij*d.*

Geoffrey Arundell holds a parcel of meadow there, and pays per ann. — xv*d.*

The said Hugh Sampforde holds a close at Pawlinges feldes containing five acres of arable land, and renders per ann. — iij*s.* iiij*d.*

Total — lxx*s.* iiij*d.*

Somerset Chantries.

The Chapel there.

Edmund Turnour clerk, rector of the parish church there, holds three acres and a half of land in one close there, and renders per ann. — vjs. viijd.

Langford Budfelde.

Land and possessions given to the use and maintenance of a Light perpetually burning in the parish church there.

. . . . holds a tenement with seven acres of land there to the same belonging, and a piece of land containing half an acre called Mary hayes in Langford, and renders per ann. — iiijs. vjd.

John Sydenham of Dulverton, gent., pays an annual rent coming from a tenement in the parish of Milverton in the tenure of Walter Coram, per ann. — ixd., viz.: in ready money — iijd., and for the price of a lb. of wax, annually — vjd.

Total — vs. iijd.

Deduct in.—Rent resolute to John Luttrell, esquire, as of his manor of Carehampton, for free rent for the said tenement, per ann. — xviijd.

And remains over, per annum.— iijs. ixd.

Aishebrittle.

The Fraternity of the blessed Mary there.

Richard Capron holds by indenture for term of his life a tenement with appurtenances there, and renders per ann. — x*s.*

John Sherlonde and John Capron hold two tenements there containing a virgate of land, and render per ann. — x*s.*

Alexander Wood pays an annual rent from the revenues of his land and tenements there, per ann. — iiij*s.* x½*d.*

Total — xxiiij*s.* x½*d.*

Milverton.

The Chantry of the blessed Mary there.

. . . . holds a house and garden with a brewhouse there, and renders per ann. — vj*s.* viij*d.*

John Combe holds by copy a tenement with garden there, and renders per ann. — ij*s.* iiij*d.*

Sabina Covent, widow, holds a tenement and garden with a toft of land there, and renders per ann. — ix*s.* iiij*d.*

John Quanto holds a tenement there, and renders per ann. — v*s.* iiij*d.*

Margaret Reynolds holds a tenement with garden and an acre of land there, and renders per ann. — v*s.* iiij*d.*

Roger Kent holds by copy a tenement with garden there, and renders per ann. — vj*s.* iiij*d.*

Robert Olyver holds by copy a tenement with divers parcels of land adjacent, and renders per ann. — xviij*s*. vj*d*.

Maurice John holds by copy a tenement with garden there, and renders per ann. — iij*s*. iiij*d*.

John Hodges holds by indenture a tenement with iij acres of land there, and renders per ann. — xv*s*. iiij*d*.

William Chaplyn holds by copy an acre of land called Oldehall, and renders per ann. — ij*s*.

Richard Gunfeld holds a tenement with a garden there, and renders per ann. — v*s*.

Christiana Lyne, widow, holds a tenement with a garden there, and renders per ann. — vj*s*. viij*d*.

Ludovic Fyllye holds a tenement there, and certain land called Cage, also a certain parcel of land there called Herne, and renders per ann. — xv*s*. vj*d*.

William Foureaker holds a tenement with a garden there, and renders per ann. — iiij*s*.

Roger Zule holds a tenement with a garden and orchard there, and renders per ann. — vj*s*.

Richard Drewe holds a tenement with a garden there, and renders per ann. — iiij*s*.

William Sengleton holds a tenement with a garden, and renders per ann. — iiij*s*.

Thomas West holds a tenement with a garden and orchard, and renders per ann. — viij*s*.

Robert Toker holds a tenement with a garden and two acres of land, and renders per ann. — vj*s*. viij*d*.

Somerset Chantries.

William Lancaster holds a tenement with a garden and orchard and an acre and a half of land there, and renders per ann. — xiijs. iiijd.

John Perys holds a tenement with a garden, and renders per ann. — vjs.

William Sherelaude, late held a tenement there, vacant and in the hands of the lord, per ann. — viijd.

Alice, wife of John Sprete, holds a barn with a close of land to the same annexed, and renders per ann. — vijs.

Edward Richardes holds certain land in Halselake and Halseyerde within the manor of Milverton, and renders per ann. — iiijs.

Thomas Thorne holds certain land in Langford Bodefelde, and renders per ann. — xvjd.

Libanus Atwaye holds a certain parcel of land there, and renders per ann. — vjd.

The heir of .... Hurcombe renders a certain annual rent from his land and tenements there, per ann. — vd.

Total — viijli. vijs. vijd.

Deduct in.—Rent resolute to the Provost of the borough of Milverton, per ann. — xxs. xj½d.

Rent resolute to John Sydenham of Dulverton, per ann. — xijd.

Rent resolute to the farmer of Buckland St. Mary, per ann. — vijd.

Rent resolute to the heir of John Coke, per ann. — vj½d.

Total — xxiijs. jd.

And remains over, per annum.— vijli. iiijs. vjd.

Somerset Chantries.

Annual rent given for the maintenance of a Light in the parish church there perpetually burning.

The heir of William Tanner, late of Milverton, pays annually from a tenement there situate in the street called Southstrete, in the tenure of Thomas Tanner, per ann. — v*s*. iiij*d*.

Total for the Deanery of Taunton, per ann. — cxxxij*li*. xxj½*d*.

Deduct in.—Reprises and rent resolute in divers modes as particularly shown. — x*li*. xj*s*. xj½*d*.

And remains over, per annum. — cxxj*li*. ix*s*. x*d*.

Deanery of Dunster.

Hawkerigge and Wethypoll.

Annual rent given as well to the use and maintenance of a Light perpetually burning in the parish church there, as for the observance of an annual Obit to be sung or said in the aforesaid church.

.... Southcote renders annually from the issues and revenues of his land there for the use aforesaid. — ij*s*.

Selworthie.

Land and possessions given as well to the use and maintenance of divers Lamps and Lights burning in the parish church there, as for the observance of an annual Obit there.

Annual rent from the revenues of certain land there, parcel of the possessions of the late dissolved house of St. John of Buckland, in the county of Somerset, as the price of vij lbs. of wax at the rate of v*d*. per lb., per ann. — ij*s*. xj*d*.

Money annually paid from the same land, per ann. — iiij*d*.

.... Brattons gent. renders annually from his land and tenements lying in Estlinche for a lb. of wax, per ann. — v*d*.

Somerset Chantries.

John Arundell, (*trekes*), Kt., renders annually from the revenues of his land and tenements lying in Honycote for half a lb. of wax. — ij$\frac{1}{2}$d.

. . . . Hensley, gent., renders annually from the revenues of his land and tenement in Honycote for half a pound of wax. — ij$\frac{1}{2}$d.

. . . . Whyttyns, gent., renders annually from the revenues of his land and tenement called Atwill for wax, per ann. — vj*d*.

. . . . Sydenham, gent., renders annually from his lands at Brosington for wax, per ann. — iij*d*.

Richard Horne holds an acre of arable land in Allerford, and renders per ann. — xx*d*.

Rent of a house and a virgate of land with a little garden, per ann. — iiij*s*. ij*d*.

. . . . Stevinges, gent., renders annually from the revenues of the manor of Honycote in ready money, per ann. — ij*s*.

The Churchwardens of the parish church of Selworthie hold a house there commonly called the Churchhouse, and render per ann. — xvj*d*.

Total — xiiij*s*.

Deduct in.—Rent resolute to John Arundell, Kt., for free rent of the house called the Churchhouse, per ann. — j*d*.

Rent resolute to . . . . Steyninge for free rent of the house containing a virgate of land with a little garden, per ann. — j*d*.

Total — ij*d*.

And remains over, per annum. — xiij*s*. x*d*.

Dunster.

The Chantry of St. Laurence within the parish church there.

The dwelling house with a garden to the same adjacent, per ann. — iijs. iiijd.

Alexander Voysey holds land and a tenement there, and renders per ann. — iiijs.

Roger Hoper holds land there, and renders per ann. — xiiijs.

Robert Goffe holds land there, and renders per ann. — xs.

Thomas Joyner holds land there, and renders per ann. — xiijs. iiijd.

The same Thomas holds other land there, and renders per ann. — iiijs.

John Sexton holds certain land there, and renders per ann. — ijs.

Thomas Holcombe holds certain land there, and renders per ann. — xjs.

The same Thomas holds other land there, and renders per ann. — xvjd.

Edmund Stibbe holds certain land there, and renders per ann. — iiijs.

Troilus Hayne holds certain land there, and renders per ann. — ijs.

Rise Gouffe holds land there, and renders per ann. — ijs.

Henry Crane holds land there, and renders per ann. — vjs.

Walter . . . . , clerk, holds a house there, and renders per ann. — iijs.

The Wardens of the parish church there hold a house there called the Churchhouse, and render per ann. — iijs.

Morgan Howell holds land there, and renders per ann. — vs.

John Sutton holds land there, and renders per ann. — vijs. viijd.

Thomas Capner holds land there, and renders per ann. — vjs.

Thomas Make holds land there, and renders per ann. — iiijs.

Katerine Lowdon holds a house there, and renders per ann. — vjs. viijd.

John Borge holds land there, and renders per ann. — xijs.

William Hyndon holds land there, and renders per ann. — viijd.

John Lyolle holds land there, and renders per ann. — vjs.

William Lowlys holds land there, and renders per ann. — xs.

John Williams holds land there, and renders per ann. — xijs.

David Arter holds land there, and renders per ann. — iiijs.

William Carran holds land there, and renders per ann. — iiijs.

John Mawhoude holds land there, and renders per ann. — iiijs.

John Cottrill holds land there, and renders per ann. — vs. iiijd.

Christiana Sole holds land there, and renders per ann. — vjs.

Nicholas Browne holds land there, and renders per ann. — vjs.

The heir of . . . . Bartelott holds certain free lands, and renders per ann. — viijd.

Total — ix*li*. viijs. iiijd.

Deduct in.—Rent resolute to John Luttrell Kt. chief lord there for free rent for the premises, per ann. — xxs.

And remains over, per annum. — viij*li*. viijs. iiijd.

Land and possessions assigned to the use and maintenance of a chaplain there, celebrating in the Chantry of the Trinity or St. George.

Divers persons hold ten tenements and five acres and a half of land there, and render per ann. — iij*li*.

Total — iiij*li*.

Deduct in.—Rent resolute to John Luttrell Kt. for free rent for the premises, per ann. — vij*s*.

And remains over, per annum. — lxxiij*s*.

Land assigned to the use and maintenance of a Light perpetually burning in the parish church there.

. . . . holds half an acre of land lying in Watchet, and renders per ann. — xviij*d*.

Deduct in.—Rent resolute to . . . . Fulforde, Kt., for free rent for the same half acre of land per ann. — vj*d*.

And remains over, per annum. — xij*d*.

Nettlecombe.

The Chantry of St. John Baptist within the parish church there.

. . . . holds the capital dwelling house with a garden and orchard adjacent, and a little meadow there, and renders per ann. — iij*s*. iiij*d*.

.... hold all messuages, lands, tenements, meadow, feed and pasture and other hereditaments whatsoever in Sampforde Brytt belonging to the said Chantry, per ann. — xxxix$s$. iiij$d$.

.... holds certain messuages, land, tenements, cottages, meadow, feed and pasture and other hereditaments in Cutcombe to the said Chantry belonging, and renders with ix$s$. iiij$d$. customary rent there, per ann. — lxxiij$s$. iiij$d$.

Thomas Hawten holds by copy a cottage with a mill there, and renders per ann. — xviij$s$. viij$d$.

Bernard Duffelde holds by indenture two tenements with appurtenances in Est Ellysworthy and West Ellysworthy to the said Chantry belonging, and renders per ann. — xxj$s$.

Isabella Michell holds by indenture two cottages with appurtenances in Nettlecombe, and renders per ann. — vs. iiij$d$.

Total — viijli. xij$d$.

Perquisites of Court and other Casualities there one year with another. — vs.

Deduct in.—Money paid to the Lord the King at his Cour of Exmoor, per ann. — xd.

Rent resolute to the manor of Sampford Brytte, per ann. — iij$s$.

Rent resolute to the Earl of Brigewater for fine and suit of Court to his manor of Wythecombe, per ann. — vij$d$.

Rent resolute to the Castle of Dunster, and for fine and suit of Court to the Hundred of Charhampton, per ann. — iiij$\frac{1}{2}d$.

Rent resolute to .... Pym for fine and suit of Court at Cutcombe, annually, — vij$d$.

Somerset Chantries

Fee to John Englyshe, steward there, granted by Letters Patent whose date is 4th October, anno xxviij Henry viij, per ann. — vjs. viijd.

Total — xijs. ½d.

And remains over, per annum. — vij*li.* viijs. xj½d.

Land and possessions granted to the use and observance of an annual Obit held in the parish church there.

John Darlinge holds a house in Taunton, and renders per ann. — xviijs.

Porlocke.

Two Chantries within the parish church there.

Rents of assise and free rents in Ugborowe, in the county of Devon, per ann. — xiij*li.* xvs.

Rent of all tenements held at will according to the custom of the manor of Ugborowe, per ann. — vj*li.* ijd.

Rent of a messuage with divers other cottages in Porlocke demised by copy, per ann. — lxvjs.

Rent of a dwelling house called the Two Chantries with a garden, per ann. — vs.

Total — xxiij*li.* vjs. ijd.

Deduct in.—Rent resolute to the Rector of the parish church there, per annum.— iiij½d.

Money paid annually to the same Rector for an acre of land there. — ijs. vjd.

Rent resolute to John Arundell esquire of Treryse for land in Porlocke as the price of two capons annually, — vij*d*.

Money paid for a fee to the Steward holding the Court there annually by the foundation, — xiij*s*. iiij*d*.

Total — xvj*s*. ix½*d*.

And remains over, per annum. — xxij*li*. ix*s*. iiij½*d*.

Land and possessions granted to the use and maintenance of a Lamp perpetually burning in the parish church there.

John Goulde, junr., holds a house there, and renders per ann. — iiij*s*.

Total for the Deanery of Dunster, per ann. — xlix*li*. xvij*s*. vj*d*.

Deduct in.—Reprises and rents resolute in divers modes as before particularly shown, — lviij*s*.

And remains over, per annum. — xlvj*li*. xix*s*. vj*d*.; and v*s*. for perquisites of Court in the Chantry of Nettlecombe aforesaid.

[This totals £46 15*s*. only. Some folios are missing. The amount may be made up by adding,—Wiveliscombe 6*s*. 8*d*.; Stogumer 8*s*. 8*d*.; Brushford 5*s*.; Elworthy 3*s*. 4*d*.; Cutcombe 3*s*. 8*d*.; Cleve 4*s*.; St. Decumans 27*s*.; Withycombe 1*s*. 7*d*.; Sampford Brett 2*s*. 4*d*.; and Carhampton 3*d*.]

Deanery of Bridgewater.

Gotehurst.

Land and possessions given to the use and observance of an Anniversary held annually in the parish church there.

John Reede holds by indenture twelve acres of land, and a rod of land and meadow there, and renders per ann. — viij*s*.

Coulve with Strengston annexed.

Annual rent given to the use and maintenance of a Lamp perpetually burning in the parish church there.

John Rogers Kt. renders annually from the issues and revenues of his tenement there, in the tenure of Henry Hastell, per ann. — vj*d*.

Stokegurcy with Lylstocke annexed.

The Guilde of the blessed Mary the Virgin there.

Elizabeth Walforde holds two closes of pasture there called Wynkeldons, and renders per ann. — ix*s*.

Deduct in.—Rent resolute to . . . Strode for free rent of the same per ann. — vj*d*.

And remains over, per annum. — viij*s*. vj*d*.

Land and possessions given as well to the use and maintenance of a Light and a Lamp burning in the parish church there, as for the observance of an Annibersary to be held there for ever.

John Colforde holds a burgage and an acre of land there, and renders per ann. — iiijs. viijd.

John Marys and Richard Toker hold two burgages and the fourth part of a burgage there, also half a burgage there, and render per ann. — viijs. iijd.

Elizabeth Steyninge holds a cottage there, and renders per ann. — xvjd.

John Strange holds an acre of land at Stilewaye, and renders per ann. — xijd.

Total — xvs. iijd.

Deduct in.—Rent resolute to the manor of Stokegurcy viz., for the said burgage and an acre of land — ijs. iiijd.

For the two burgages and the fourth part of a burgage — ijs. iijd.

And for the half burgage — vjd.

Total — vs. jd.

And remains over, per annum. — xs. ijd.

Lynge.

The Free Chapel of St. Michael at Borowe within the parish there.

The Chapel aforesaid with a close called Chapel haye containing an acre with a road leading to the same, per ann. — ijs.

Sparton.

Annual rents and other possessions given to the use and maintenance of a Light burning in the parish church there.

William Hody renders annually from his land and tenements lying in Tuxwill for a lb. of wax — v*d*.

James Tylley renders annually from his lands and tenements lying in the parish aforesaid for 1 lb. of wax — v*d*.

John Legatt and his wife and Thomas their son, hold for term of their lives certain arable land there called Churchelandes with appurtenances, and render per ann. — iiij*s*.

Total — iiij*s*. x*d*.

Cannington.

The Free Chapel of Ichestoke within the parish there.

.... holds the dwelling house there with a close containing three acres of land, and renders per ann. — v*s*.

Robert Silke and Andrew Lovell hold six acres of land there, and render per ann. — viij*s*.

John Gaye holds by indenture certain land in Stokegurcy, and renders per ann. — xvj*s*.

Richard Bickcham holds a meadow there by indenture, and renders per ann. — xj*s*.

John Hatcher holds by indenture certain land there, and renders per ann. — vij*s*.

Somerset Chantries.

John Crampleyne holds by indenture a certain parcel of land there, and renders per ann. — vs. xd.

William Bucke holds an acre of land there, and renders per ann. — xijd.

John Burlande and William Bytforde hold certain land there, and render per ann. — xviijs.

John Poole holds a parcel of land there, and renders per ann. — vs.

Robert Everet holds a certain parcel of land there, and renders per ann. — xlviijs.

William Bydforde holds a parcel of land there, and renders per ann. — viijs.

William Poole holds two acres of land there, and renders per ann. — ijs. viijd.

Total — vjli. xvs. vjd.

Land and possessions given to the use and maintenance of a Lamp in the parish church there perpetually burning.

Walter Stone holds at will ten acres of land in Spaxton, and renders per ann. — viijs.

Deduct in. — Rent resolute to the Duke of Somerset as of his manor of Tuckeswell, per ann. — xv½d.

And remains over, per annum. — vjs. viij¼d.

Chedzoy.

Land and possessions given and assigned to the use and maintenance of a perpetual stipendiary priest celebrating in the parish church there.

Richard Stronge holds by indenture a tenement in Kirton (Crediton), in the county of Devon, and renders per ann. — x𝑠.

Anthony Stewarde holds a tenement in the parish of Chedzoy aforesaid, and renders per ann. — x𝑠.

John Cokipe holds a tenement in Axbridge, and renders per ann. — vij𝑠.

. . . . holds a tenement in Brigewater, and renders per ann. — iiij𝑠.

Total — xxxj𝑠.

Deduct in.— Rent resolute to the chief lord of Brigewater for free rent for the tenement there, per ann. — iij𝑑.

And remains over, per annum. — xxx𝑠. ix𝑑.

Land and possessions given to the use and maintenance of a Lamp and a Light in the parish church there perpetually burning.

John Constable holds a cottage in Chedzoy at will, and renders per ann. — vj𝑠. viij𝑑.

Richard Lacy holds an acre of land there at will, and renders per ann. — xviij𝑑.

Total — viij𝑠. ij𝑑.

The Town of Bridgewater.

The Chantry of St. George within the parish church there.

Ralph Benet holds by indenture seven acres of arable land lying in Blacklonde, and renders per ann. — xiiijs.

The same Ralph and Robert Castleman hold sixteen acres of arable land called Goodwell, and render per ann. — xvjs.

The said Ralph and Thomas Holcombe hold the fourth part of a burgage lying outside the west gate southward, and an acre of meadow in Chilton more, and render per ann. — ijs. viijd.

Robert Benet holds by indenture a house with a quarter burgage land lying in Fryerne strete, and renders per ann. — iijs. iiijd.

Alice Bysshop holds a house with divers burgage lands and two acres of arable land in Blacklonde — xs. (*Cancelled.*)

Robert Gregory holds half a burgage land lying outside the west gate northward there, and renders per ann. — viijd.

Maurice Morell holds a house with half a burgage, and renders per ann.— viijs.

William Tracy holds a little house with a quarter burgage there, and renders per ann. — iijs.

John Bonde holds a house there called a slaughter house, and renders per ann. — iijs.

John Page holds a workshop in the fish market there, and renders per ann. — vjs. viijd.

Richard Tydell holds a barn there called Cocke's barne and a burgage there, and renders per ann. — ijs.

Somerset Chantries.

John Hodges holds a workshop (*officinam*) there, and renders per ann. — vs. iiijd.

John Cothins holds a workshop there at will, and renders per ann. — vs. iiijd.

Richard Michell holds a workshop there, and renders per ann. — xijs.

John Pyers holds a little chamber above a shamble there, and renders per ann. — iijs.

John Coleford holds an acre of meadow called Blackmede in the parish of Wemdon, and renders per ann. — ijs.

Joan Sadler holds a little chamber above a shamble there, and renders per ann. — iijs.

John Everet holds a house with a little garden there lying next the churchyard, and renders per ann. — vjs. viijd.

James Vant clerk holds a tenement with a little garden there, and renders per ann. — viijs.

William Grendon holds the third part of a house there, and renders per ann. — iiijs.

Alice Bysshop holds the third part of a stable there, and renders per ann. — ijs. vjd.

William Carver holds a house with a little garden there, and renders per ann. — vjs. viijd.

Agnes Hull holds a garden there, and renders per ann. — xvjd.

John Nethewaye holds half a burgage and a quarter of a burgage there, and renders per ann. — xijd.

John Newporte holds half a burgage there, and renders per ann. — ijs.

John Woode holds an acre of pasture lying next Crophill, and renders per ann. — xij*d*.

Geoffrey Arundell holds half a burgage land lying in the south part of the bridge there near St. John's Gate — xij*d*.

John Nethercote holds a rod of meadow lying in Chelton More, and renders per ann. — vj*d*.

Total — vij*li*. iiij*s*. viij*d*.

Deduct in.—Rent resolute to the King as of the Monastery of Athelney, per ann. — iiij*s*.

Rent resolute to .... Michell, Esq., per ann. — iiij*d*.

Money paid to the Bailiff of the Borough of Bridgewater — xvij*s*. x*d*.

Total — xxij*s*. ij*d*.

And remains over, per annum. — vj*li*. ij*s*. vj*d*.

The Chantry of the blessed Mary within the parish church there.

John Oder holds a house there, and renders per ann. — xx*s*.

Richard Burne holds a house there, and renders per ann. — xxj*s*.

William Alen holds a house there, and renders per ann. — x*s*.

Nicholas Kyrys holds a house there, and renders per ann. — iij*s*. iiij*d*.

John Oder holds a tenement there, and renders per ann. — xij*s*.

Richard Terell holds certain land there by indenture, and renders per ann. — iiij*s*.

Somerset Chantries.

James Boyes holds half a burgage there, and renders per ann. — xij*d*.

William Gowlde holds a quarter burgage there, and renders per ann. — viij*s*.

Peter Carde holds a burgage and a half there, and renders per ann. — iij*s*.

Dionisius Cogon holds a burgage and a half there, and renders per ann. — ij*s*.

John Pittock holds by indenture five acres of land there, and renders per ann. — v*s*. viij*d*.

John More holds an acre of meadow there, and renders per ann. — ij*s*.

John Day holds a burgage there, and renders per ann. — ij*s*.

William Shorys holds a house there, and renders per ann. — xij*s*.

George Walys holds a house there, and renders per ann. — xv*s*.

. . . . holds a house there situated before the porch (*coram hostio*) of the church, and renders per ann. — vj*s*. viij*d*.

John Gappers holds a house there, and renders per ann. — vj*s*. viij*d*.

John Newman holds a house there, and renders per ann. — vj*s*. viij*d*.

John Clementes holds a house there, and renders per ann. — vj*s*.

William Curryer holds a house there, and renders per ann. — x*s*.

Thomas Glandfeld holds a house there, and renders per ann. — xij*s*.

John Stayners holds a house there, and renders per ann. — vijs.

John Horne holds a burgage land there, and renders per ann. — vjs. viijd.

. . . . holds the dwelling house in which the Cantarist lived, per ann. — vjs.

Total — ixli. viijs. viijd.

Deduct in.—Rent resolute to the Bailiff of the town of Brigewater for the lord of the fee there, per ann. — xxviijs.

And remains over, per annum. — viijli. viijd.

The Chantry of the Trinity within the parish church there.

Mariana Galwey holds by indenture a tenement with an acre and a virgate of meadow, and renders per ann. — xs.

The same holds a tenement there, and renders per ann. — iiijs.

William Shorye holds half a burgage there, and renders per ann. — ijs.

Tege Irysheman holds a tenement there, and renders per ann. — vjs. viijd.

William Walshe holds half a burgage there, and renders per ann. — xijd.

Thomas Welshe holds a tenement there, and renders per ann. — vijs. iiijd.

John Daye holds a burgage and a half there, and renders per ann. — xxd.

Somerset Chantries.

John Morley holds four acres of land and two burgages there, and renders per ann. — vij*s*.

William Grendon holds part of a tenement there, and renders per ann. — ij*s*.

Agnes Hosteler holds a tenement there, and renders per ann. — iiij*s*.

Henry Cony holds a tenement there, and renders per ann. — viij*s*.

Denis Makeway holds a tenement and a burgage there, and renders per ann. — vj*s*. viij*d*.

John Wake holds a tenement there, and renders per ann. — vj*s*. viij*d*.

John Goughe holds a tenement there, and renders per ann. — vj*s*. viij*d*.

John Longe holds by indenture a tenement with a stable, and renders per ann. — xiij*s*. iiij*d*.

Thomas Hall holds a tenement and half a burgage with four acres of pasture, and renders per ann. — xv*s*. vj*d*.

John Pagge holds an acre and a half of meadow, and renders per ann. — iij*s*.

Margaret Geffery holds a tenement and a burgage, and renders per ann. — iiij*s*.

William Jenkyns holds a tenement there, and renders per ann. — vj*s*. viij*d*.

John Champayne holds a tenement there, and renders per ann. — x*s*.

John Smyth holds a tenement there, and renders per ann. — iiij*s*.

Somerset Chantries.

Lucy Hore holds a tenement, and renders per ann. — iiij*s.*

John Spicer holds a tenement, and renders per ann. — iij*s.*

John Gye holds a tenement there, and renders per ann. — iij*s.*

Richard Martyn holds a tenement, and renders per ann. — vj*s.* viij*d.*

Thomas Graynger holds a tenement, and renders per ann. — vj*s.* viij*d.*

John Laurence (Thomas Holcombe) holds a tenement and half a burgage, and renders per ann. — xiiij*s.* iiij*d.*

Alexander Skelton holds half a burgage and half an acre of land, and renders per ann. — iiij*s.*

Christiana Kerell holds a tenement, and renders per ann. — iiij*s.*

Robert Somerton holds a tenement, and renders per ann. — v*s.*

William Goolde holds a tenement and half a burgage, and renders per ann. — v*s.*

John Craddock holds by indenture a tenement, a stable, and iij burgages there, and renders per ann. — x*s.*

John Danyell holds by indenture five acres of land, and renders per ann. — vj*s.* vj*d.*

Thomas Bydgood holds three acres of meadow, and renders per ann. — iij*s.*

Matilda Rowde holds two acres of meadow, and renders per ann. — ij*s.*

Richard Gatcombe holds an acre of meadow, and renders per ann. — xvj*d.*

Somerset Chantries.

Alice Busshop holds part of a tenement there, and renders per ann. — xviij*d*.

Nicholas Came holds an acre of land, and renders per ann. — xij*d*.

John Saunders junr., holds part of a tenement there, and renders per ann. — vj*d*.

John Norman, clerk, holds a stable, and renders per ann. — xij*d*.

Thomas Noke holds by indenture ten acres of land there, and renders per ann. — ij*s*. vj*d*.

Richard Terryll holds half a burgage, and renders per ann. — xij*d*.

Thomas Hopkyns holds a kitchen there, and renders per ann. — x*d*.

.... holds the dwelling house in which the Cantarist formerly lived, and renders per ann. — xx*d*.

Total — x*li*. xviij*s*. viij*d*.

Deduct in.—Rent resolute to the Bailiff of the town of Brigewater for the lord of the fee of the Borough, per ann. — xxiiij*s*.

And remains over, per annum. — ix*li*. xiiij*s*. viij*d*.

An annual rent given as well to the use and observance of an Annibersary held in the parish church there, as to the use and maintenance of a Light there perpetually burning.

The Mayor, Bailiff, and Burgesses of Brigewater aforesaid render annually from the profits and revenues of certain their lands lying in Stower Estover in the county of Dorset in the tenure of Thomas Bolston, per ann. — xiiij*s*.

Northe Petherton.

The Free Chapel of Sherston within the parish there.

John Togood holds a tenement in Sherston, and renders per ann. — iiij*s*.

John Ryvers holds a tenement there, and renders per ann. — xij*s*.

Robert Nowell holds two tenements there, and renders per ann. — xx*s*. ij*d*.

William Howse holds a tenement there, and renders per ann — vj*s*. iiij*d*.

Joan Prate, widow, holds a tenement there, and renders per ann. — v*s*. ij*d*.

John Cosyn holds a grain mill and eight acres of land, and renders per ann. — vj*s*. viij*d*.

The same John Cosyn holds a tenement there, and renders per ann. — xj*s*.

Thomas Hichefeld holds a tenement there, and renders per ann. — ij*s*. vij*d*.

Joan Vynycombe holds a tenement there, and renders per ann. — ij*s*. viij*d*.

Total — lxx*s*. vij*d*.

The Chantry of Newton Placy within the parish there.

. . . . , holds the dwelling house of the Chantry with a garden adjacent, and renders per ann. — v*s*.

Somerset Chantries.

Simon Courte holds by indenture for his life eight acres of land in Newton Placy, and renders per ann. — xiijs. iiijd.

Robert Raufe and John Pye hold by indenture eight acres of meadow there, and render per ann. — viijs.

John Pye and others hold by indenture three acres of land there, and render per ann. — iijs.

Richard Pye and others hold by indenture three acres of land there, and render per ann. — ijs. viijd.

Stephen Batte holds a cottage and eight acres of land in Michell Churche, and renders per ann. — viijs.

Nicholas Morrice holds a cottage and four acres of land there, and renders per ann. — iiijs.

John Babbe holds a cottage and two acres of land there, and renders per ann. — ijs.

. . . . holds the tithes of agistments in the Warren of North Petherton one year with another and renders per ann. — xls.

. . . . holds the tithes of agistment of certain pasture called Woodmede, and renders per ann. — vs.

. . . . holds the tithes of agistment of certain pasture called Perkesfeld, and renders per ann. — xijd.

. . . . holds the tithes great and small from eight inhabitants of the said Town to whom the chaplain there late incumbent ministered all holy offices and sacraments, one year with another. — liijs. iiijd.

(Decimas tam maiores quam minores octo inhabitantium dicte ville quibus capellanus ibidem nuper incumbens ministrat omnia sacramenta et sacramentalia, et reddit communibus annis, — liij*s.* iiij*d.*)

Total — vij*li.* v*s.* iiij*d.*

Deduct in.—Rent resolute to Alexander Popham Esq., for certain land called Culverfelde, per ann. — vj*s.* viij*d.*

And remains over, per annum. — vj*li.* xviij*s.* viij*d.*

A marginal note to Simon Courte's holding reads—Leased to the said Simon by indenture 5th April, xxxvj Henry viij, rendering per ann. — viij*s.*

The Chantry of the blessed Mary within the parish church there.

FREE RENTS.

William Paulet, Kt., lord Seint John holds certain lands there called Pawlettes landes in the occupation of Richard Biggegood, and renders per ann. — viij*s.*

The heir of John Whitinge holds certain (land) there, and renders per ann. — x*s.* vj*d.*

Edmund Wynter holds certain land there, and renders per ann. — xv*d.*

. . . . holds the land once John Michell's, and renders per ann. — viij*s.*

Alexander Popham holds certain land in Horlocke, and renders per ann. — xiij*s.* iiij*d.* (*A marginal note reads,*—now the Lady Portman's.)

John Hare holds certain land in Ernesham, and renders per ann. — iiij*d.*

John Horle holds certain land, and renders per ann. — iiij*d.*

Somerset Chantries.

. . . . holds certain land in Newton late Marmaduke Mauncell's, and renders per ann. — ij*s*.

Stephen Wheler holds certain land there and renders per ann. — v*s*.

William Birge holds certain land, and renders per ann. — iiij*s*.

John Scare holds certain land called Nicolles landes, and renders per ann. — ij*s*.

Held for term of life.

John Caine holds a certain parcel of meadow there, and renders per ann. — xiij*s*. iiij*d*.

John Bulpan holds a certain parcel of meadow there in Horlock, and renders per ann. — xiij*s*. iiij*d*.

William Norton holds a burgage, with a fruit garden and a garden, and three acres of land, and renders per ann. — xj*s*. vj½*d*.

John Kelley holds a burgage with a garden and orchard adjacent in North Petherton, and renders per ann. — viij*s*. viij*d*.

Robert Rousewell holds a burgage with a fruit garden and orchard, and one acre of land, and renders per ann. vj*s*. viij*d*.

Robert Budde holds a burgage there with a garden adjacent, and renders per ann. — vj*s*. viij*d*.

John Baldwyn holds a burgage there with a fruit garden and orchard and one acre of land adjacent, and renders per ann. — vj*s*. viij*d*.

Richard Dible holds a burgage there with a garden, and renders per ann. — iiij*s*. iiij*d*.

John Benett holds a burgage there with a garden adjacent, and renders per ann. — v*s*. vj*d*.

John Wheler holds a burgage there with a garden, and renders per ann. — iiijs. viijd.

Christopher Harvey holds a burgage with a garden, and renders per ann. — iiijs.

Henry Canne holds a piece of land lying within the land of said Henry himself, and renders per ann. — ijs. viijd.

John Swinger holds the dwelling house of the Chantry, and renders per ann. — xijd.

    Total — vijli. iijs. ix½d.

Deduct in.—Rent resolute to the lord the King as of his manor of Durleighe parcel of the Duchy of Lancaster, per ann. — vj½d.

Rent resolute to Roger Blewet, Kt., per ann. — xxd.

Fee to Alexander Popham, steward there, per ann. — xs.

Fee to Robert Godyn, bailiff there, per ann. — vjs. viijd.

    Total — xviijs. x½d.

And remains over, per annum. — vjli. iiijs. xjd.

Annual rent given to the use and maintenance of a Lamp in the parish church there perpetually burning.

An annual rent coming from certain land at Rydon within the parish aforesaid once Marmaduke Mauncelles — iijs. iiijd.

Total for the Deanery of Brigewater per ann. — lvijli. xjs. iij½d.

Deduct in.—Reprises and rents resolute in divers modes, as before particularly shown — cvjs. xd.

And remains over, per annum.— lijli. iiijs. v½d.

Deanery of Paulet.

Hunspill.

The Service of the blessed Mary in the parish church there.

Matilda now wife of Richard Phelps holds by Indenture a certain parcel of land containing xxiiij acres of meadow and pasture lying in the parishes of Hunspill and Paulet, and renders per ann. — xxiiijs.

John Martyn holds by indenture seven acres and one virgate of land in the same parish of Hunspill, and renders per ann. — vijs. iijd.

John Golde holds at will a house in the said parish and half an acre of land to the same appertaining, called our lady's howse, and renders per ann. — ijs.

Total — xxxiijs. iijd.

Deduct in.—Rent resolute to the chief lord there for free rent for the vij acres and one virgate of land, per ann. — ijs. xd.

And remains over, per annum. — xxxs. vd.

The Service of St. Nicholas in the parish church there.

John Dune of Morrewe holds for term of his life two acres of land there, and renders per ann. — ijs.

Wullavington.

The Chantry of St. John Baptist in the churchyard there.

The third part of the house, with a third part of a common garden adjacent in Wullavington, in which three Cantarists lived, per ann. — xx*d*.

The third part of four acres and a half of meadow there to the said three Cantarists in common belonging, per ann. — ij*s*.

The third part of twenty-four acres of land there with appurtenances, per ann. — vj*s*.

The third part of a close of pasture there called Priston Close, containing twelve acres, per ann. — xj*s*.

Alice Norman holds the third part of a tenement in Brigewater, and renders per ann. — vj*d*.

John Bentley holds the third part of a burgage there, and renders per ann. — iiij*d*.

Money received annually from the Court of Augmentation in the county of Somerset as by Decree of the same Court — iiij*li*. xvij*s*. iiij*d*.

Annual rent from the Manor of Newnam in the parish of Stokegurcy in the hands and possession of William Hody, gent., per ann. — xxvj*s*. viij*d*.

Total — vij*li*. v*s*. vj*d*.

Deduct in.—Rent resolute to the King — ij*d*.

Rent resolute to John Tychet, Kt., lord de Audeley — ij*d*.

Total — iiij*d*.

And remains over, per annum. — vij*li*. v*s*. ij*d*.

Somerset Chantries.

The Chantry of the Trinity there.

The third part of the house, with the third part of a garden adjacent, per ann. — xx*d*.

The third part of four acres and a half of meadow there, per ann. — ij*s*.

The third part of twenty-four acres of land with appurtenances there, per ann. — vj*s*.

The third part of a close of pasture called Priston Close, per ann. —xj*s*.

Alice Norman holds the third part of a tenement in Brigewater, and renders per ann. — vj*d*.

John Bentley holds the third part of a burgage there, and renders per ann. — iiij*d*.

Money received annually from the Court of Augmentations in the said County of Somerset by virtue of a Decree of the same Court — lxxiij*s*. iiij*d*.

Annual rent from the manor of Newnam in the parish of Stokegurcy — xxvj*s*. viij*d*.

Total — vj*li*. xviij*d*.

Deduct in.—Rent resolute to the lord the King — ij*d*.

Rent resolute to Lord Audeley — ij*d*.

Total — iiij*d*.

And remains over, per annum. — vj*li*. xiiij*d*.

The Chantry of St. Katerine there.

The third part of the house with the third part of a common garden adjacent — xx*d*.

The third part of four acres and a half of meadow there, per ann. — ij*s*.

The third part of twenty-four acres of land with appurtenances there, per ann. — vj*s*.

The third part of a close of pasture called Priston Close, per ann. — xj*s*.

Alice Norman holds the third part of a tenement in Brigewater, and renders per ann. — vj*d*.

John Bentley holds the third part of a burgage in Brigewater, and renders per ann. — iiij*d*.

Money received annually from the Court of Augmentation by virtue of a Decree of the same Court — lxxiij*s*. iiij*d*.

Annual rents received from the Manor of Newnam in the parish of Stokegurcy — xxvj*s*. viij*d*.

Total — vj*li*. xviij*d*.

Deduct in.—Rent resolute to the lord the King — ij*d*.

Rent resolute to Lord Audeley — ij*d*.

Total — iiij*d*.

And remains over, per annum. — vj*li*. xiiij*d*.

Polett.

Annual rent given to the use and maintenance of a Light perpetually burning in the parish church there.

The heir of Margerie Golde renders annually from the issues and revenues of certain land in Hunspill late in the tenure of Richard Whyte as for the price of ij lbs. of wax, per ann. — xiiij*d*.

Cosyngton.

Land given to the use and maintenance of a Light burning in the parish church there.

Roger Joyce holds an acre of land there, and renders per ann. — vj*d*.

Bawdrybe.

The Free Chapel of Forde within the parish there.

Richard Brent and others hold for term of their lives a tenement or burgage in Stowell in the parish of Murlinche, and render per ann. — xxvj*s*. viij*d*.

Total for the Deanery of Paulet aforesaid per ann. — xxij*li*. xij*s*. j*d*.

Deduct in.—Reprises and divers rents resolute as before particularly shown — iij*s*. x*d*.

And remains over, per annum. — xxij*li*. viij*s*. iij*d*.

Jurisdiction of Glaston.

Budleyghe.

Annual rent given to the use and maintenance of an Obit annually held in the parish church there.

The heir of John Camell renders annually from the issues and revenues of certain his lands in Budleighe, per ann. — iiij*s.*

Weston.

The Service of the Blessed Mary there.

William Godfrey holds iiij acres and a half of land lying in the fields of Myddelsoy, and renders per ann. — viiij*s.* vj*d.*

Murlynche.

The Chantry of Catcote in the parish there.

Richard Hodshon clerk, holds the dwelling house with a garden adjacent and xxiiij acres of land, meadow, and pasture, also the Chapel of the said Chantry, and renders per ann. — xiij*s.* iiij*d.*

William Coke holds all the tithes of Catcote aforesaid except the sheaf tithes there, reserved to the Rector of the parish church of Murlinche, and renders per ann. — lxvj*s.* viij*d.*

Total — iiij*li.*

Strete.

Annual rent given to the use and observance of an annual Obit to be held in the parish church there for ever.

The Churchwardens of the parish render annually from the issues and revenues of four acres of land in Glastonbury given to the use and reparation of the parish church of Strete aforesaid, per ann. — xvj$d$.

Glaston.

The Chantry there.

Redy money annually paid by the hands of the General Receiver of the Lord the King from the Revenues of the Attainted late Monastery of Glaston, by virtue of a certain Decree made thereupon by the General Surveyor of the lands of the Lord the King in his chamber called the Prince's Council Chamber, as shown by the same Decree of the Commissioners, per ann. — vjli. iij$s$. iiij$d$.

Total of the Jurisdiction of Glaston aforesaid, per annum — xli. xvij$s$. ij$d$.

Deanery of Axbrige.

Wedmour.

The Chantry of the blessed Mary there.

William London, clerk, late incumbent, holds a house there with a garden, and renders per ann. — iiij*s*.

Thomas Corell holds a tenement and an acre of land, and renders per ann. — iij*s*. iiij*d*.

John Cubbery holds certain land, and a tenement there, and renders per ann. — v*s*.

Christopher Roo holds a piece of land there, and renders per ann. — j*d*.

Thomas Isaake holds certain land there, and renders per ann. — iiij*s*.

Alice Longe holds a house there called St. Mary House, and renders per ann. — iij*s*. viij*d*.

Peter Williams holds a tenement, and renders per ann. — iiij*s*.

Williams Morice holds certain land there, and renders per ann. — v*s*. viij*d*.

Agnes Cubbery holds a tenement there, and renders per ann. — iij*s*. viij*d*.

The said William Morice holds a tenement there, and renders per ann. — xviij*d*.

Somerset Chantries.

Robert More holds a tenement, and renders per ann. — v*s*.

Robert Algar holds a tenement, and renders per ann. — ij*s*.

The same Robert Algar holds certain land there, and renders per ann. — vj*s*.

John Howper holds certain land there, and renders per ann. — ix*s*.

John Cooke holds certain land there, and renders per ann. — xij*s*.

John Champney holds a tenement, and renders per ann. — iiij*s*.

The same John holds a certain parcel of land, and renders per ann. — xxij*d*.

Edmund Champney holds a tenement, and renders per ann. — x*s*.

The same Edmund holds certain land at Stonyng brige, and renders per ann. — iiij*s*.

Robert Tynkwell holds a piece of land, and renders per ann. — iij*d*.

John Brownyng holds a tenement, and renders per ann. — iiij*s*.

Humfry Cosyn holds certain land, and renders per ann. — x*s*. viij*d*.

John Penarde holds certain land, and renders per ann. — xij*d*.

John Bulting holds certain land, and renders per ann. — xx*d*.

The same John holds a piece of land there, and renders per ann. — x*d*.

John Swayne of Alverton holds certain land, and renders per ann. — xx*d*.

Somerset Chantries.

Agnes Blake holds certain land there, and renders per ann. — ij*s*.

William Blake holds a piece of land there, and renders per ann. — x*d*.

John Shelcroft holds a piece of land there, and renders per ann. —iiij*d*.

Richard Kirkeby holds certain land there, and renders per ann. — viij*d*.

John Vowles holds certain land there, and renders per ann. — vij*d*.

John Randall holds certain land there, and renders per ann. — vij*d*.

Isabella Kirkeby holds certain land there, and renders per ann. — iij*s*. iiij*d*.

The same holds certain land there, and renders per ann. — vij*s*.

Agnes Culbery holds certain land there, and renders per ann. — xij*d*.

John Algar of Westham holds certain land there, and renders per ann. — vj*s*. viij*d*.

The same John holds certain other land there, and renders per ann. — ij*s*

John Bayly holds certain land there, and renders per ann. — x*d*.

Edmund Champy holds a piece of land there, and renders per ann. — vj*d*.

John Hodges holds certain land there, and renders per ann. —-xij*d*.

Somerset Chantries.

Robert Alger holds certain land there, and renders per ann. — iij*s.*

John Squyre of Alverton holds certain (land) there, and renders per ann. — xviij*d.*

John Ager de Stowton holds certain land there, and renders per ann. — ix*s.*

Isabella Galgaye holds certain land there, and renders per ann. — vj*s.*

John Lambert holds certain land there, and renders per ann. — xiij*d.*

John Gorwey holds certain land there, and renders per ann. — xij*d.*

Nicholas Dowse of Marke holds certain land there, and renders per ann. — xiiij*s.*

Katerine Feoffer holds a shop there, and renders per ann. — xx*d.*

Richard Alger holds certain land there, and renders per ann. — viij*d.*

William Michell holds certain land there, and renders per ann. — v*d.*

John Bayly of the Sonde holds certain land there, and renders per ann. — xij*d.*

Total — viij*li.* xvij*s.* vj*d.*

Deduct in.—Rent resolute to the Dean of Wells for a common fine in Bempston per ann. —xiiij*d.*

Money paid to the same Dean for free suit of his Court of Bempston aforesaid, per ann. — iiij*d.*

Rent resolute to the said Dean for rent of certain lands in Wedmore, per ann. — xviij*s.* ij*d.*

Rent resolute to the same Dean for land called Blokesham, per ann. — v*s.* vj*d.*

Rent resolute to the same Dean for a tenement called Kinges Place, per ann. — ij*s.*

Rent resolute to the said Dean for a tenement called Bulles house in Churche londe, per ann. — xviij*d.*

Rent resolute to the aforesaid Dean for the dwelling house of the aforesaid Chantry, per ann.—j*d.*

Rent resolute to the same Dean for suit of the Borough Court of Wedmore, per ann.—ij*d.*

Rent resolute to William Stone for the land of Peter Milborne in Wedmore aforesaid, per ann. — iij*d.*

Rent resolute to William Councell for a piece of land called Smockelande, per ann. — vj*d.*

Total — xxix*s.* viij*d.*

And remains over, per annum. — vij*li.* vij*s.* x*d.*

The Free Chapel of Blackeforde in the parish there.

. . . . holds the chapel, with the tithes of corn and hay of Blackeforde aforesaid, and renders per ann. — vj*li.*

The Service of St. Anne in the parish church there founded for a term of years.

. . . . holds certain lands, tenements, meadow, feed, pasture, fishing and other hereditaments with their appurtenances in Wedmore, by William Cosyn, sometime Dean of the Cathedral Church of St. Andrew of Wells, leased to farm to Thomas Cornyshe vicar of Wedmore, Baldwin Malet, Richard Renyon, gents., John Champoney, John Westoner and divers others guardians of the parish church aforesaid, by Indenture given under the seal of the aforesaid Dean the first day of September, A.D. 1509, and in the first year of the reign of King Henry viij for the term of ninety-nine years next following to be fully completed. And which the said Dean and the Chapter of the same place with common consent ratified, approved and confirmed in their Chapter House under their common seal the third day of November in the year aforesaid. Under this condition that the above named and their assigns shall find and continue during the term aforesaid a fit Chaplain celebrating mass at the altar of St. Anne in the said church of Wedmore three times a week, with divers other covenants in the same Indenture specified and expressed. And they render per annum, beyond lxvj$s$. x$\frac{1}{2}d$. to the aforesaid Dean and his successors for the rent and farm of the premises during the term aforesaid annually reserved, as in the same Indenture is more fully clear. — vjli. iiij$s$. iij$\frac{1}{2}d$.

The Service of a priest in the parish church there celebrating for a term of years.

Ready money given by Walter Stone clerk, in his last Will to the use and maintenance of a priest celebrating in the parish church there for the good estate of Walter himself, for the space of vij years beginning at the Feast of St. John Baptist in the first year of the reign of the now King Edward vj, rendering annually by the hands of the Executors of his Testament or last Will aforesaid during the term aforesaid — vjli.

Annual rent given to the use and maintenance of an annual mass in the parish church there called Jesus masse.

Thomas Broke renders annually from the issues and revenues of a piece of land in the parish aforesaid called Chaterly in the tenure of Thomas himself — ij*s*.

Chedder.

The Chantry of the Holy Trinity in the parish church there.

STOKE IN THE PARISH OF CHURCHEULL.

John Lache holds by copy a tenement there, and renders per ann. — xxj*s*.

The same holds another tenement there, and renders per ann. — iij*s*. iiij*d*.

John Johans holds a tenement there, and renders per ann. — xx*s*.

John Maide holds a tenement there, and renders per ann. — viij*s*.

John Edys holds a tenement there, and renders per ann. — ij*s*. iiij*d*.

John Bustell holds a tenement there, and renders per ann. — v*s*. iiij*d*.

Katherine Horte holds a tenement there, and renders per ann. — iiij*s*. viij*d*.

Thomas Brownyng holds a tenement there, and renders per ann. — v*s*. iiij*d*.

Somerset Chantries.

Thomas Lovell holds a tenement there, and renders per ann. — vs. iiijd.

Thomas Walle holds a tenement there, and renders per ann. — vjs. viijd.

THE CITY OF WELLS.

Christopher Whyte holds by indenture for a term of years a tenement and a cottage there, and renders per ann. — xiijs. viijd.

Walter Marchaunt holds by indenture a tenement there, and renders per ann. — vs.

Agnes Bowe widow, holds by indenture a tenement there, and renders per ann. — iijs. iiijd.

. . . . holds at will two cottages there, and renders per ann. — vs. iiijd.

. . . . lately held a cottage there, now vacant, and rendered per ann. — ijs. viijd.

Total — cxijs.

Deduct in.—Rent resolute to John Seintlowoe Kt. for suit of Court in his manor of Churchehull for the land aforesaid in Stoke, per ann. — iiijd.

Money paid to the Dean of Wells for suit of Court in Alrington, per ann. — iiijd.

Rent resolute to the Bishop of Bath and Wells for free rent for the land aforesaid in Wells, per ann. — ijs. jd.

Decayed rent for the aforesaid cottage now vacant, per ann. — ijs. viijd.

Total — vs. vd.

And remains over, per annum. — cvjs. vijd.

Somerset Chantries.

The Chantry of the blessed Mary in the parish church there.

Ready money annually paid from the issues and profits of the land and possessions of the Lord the King from his Court of Augmentation in the county of Somerset, by the hands of the Receiver General of the same in the same county, by virtue of a certain Decree in the same Court made, per ann. — vj*li*. xiij*s*. iiij*d*.

Land and possessions placed in feoffment to the use and observance of an annual Obit to be held in the parish church there for ever.

William Parsons holds by indenture for the term of his life a tenement there, and renders per ann. — xiij*s*. iiij*d*.

John Boole holds a barn with certain land to the same annexed, and renders per ann. — viij*s*.

Total — xxj*s*. iiij*d*.

Deduct in.—Rent resolute to the Vicars of the Cathedral Church of Wells, per ann. — v*s*.

And remains over, per annum. — xvj*s*. iiij*d*.

Banwell.

The Fraternity there.

Richard Ratclyffe holds a certain parcel of land in Wolforde Hill and Burstfurlong — xij*s*., also a meadow called Aptmede — xvij*s*., and an acre of meadow in Estons mede, and also an acre in Corne More — iij*s*., and renders per ann. — xxxij*s*.

John Marys of Axbridge holds a piece of land lying next the end of the town there, and renders per ann. — xx*d*.

Margaret Northon holds a garden there, and renders per ann. — xij*d*.

Thomas Wylley holds a close of pasture called Whytecroft, and renders per ann. — x*s*.

John Bowden holds iiij acres and a half of land in the parish of Keustoke, and renders per ann. — xiij*s*.

Walter Nedes holds a certain parcel of land in Kingston, and renders per ann. — x*s*.

The Wardens of the said late Fraternity hold two acres of land there, and render per ann. — iij*s*. iiij*d*.

Total — lxxj*s*.

Deduct in.—Rent resolute to Thomas Payne esquire for free rent of the premises as of his manor of Rolston, per ann. — iij*d*.

And remains over, per annum. — lxx*s*. ix*d*.

The Chapel of St. George within the parish there.

. . . . holds the chapel aforesaid, with a little piece of land containng a rod in which the same chapel is situate, and renders per ann. — vj*d*.

South Brent.

Annual rent given to the use and maintenance of an annual Obit to be held in the parish church there for ever.

John Gillings renders annually from the issues and revenues of his lands and tenements lying in the borough of Axbridge, per ann. — xiij*d*.

Somerset Chantries.

Marke.

The Service of the blessed Mary the Virgin in the parish church there founded for a term of years.

. . . . holds certain land, tenements, cottages, meadow, feed, pasture and fishing, and all other hereditaments with their appurtenances lying and being in the manors of More, Southyoke and Merke, in the county aforesaid, leased to the parishioners or inhabitants of the town of Marke, by John Gunthorpe sometime Dean of the Cathedral Church of St. Andrew of Wells, by indenture given under his seal the twentieth day of October in the year of the reign of King Edward the fourth after the Conquest of England the nineteenth, for a term of ninety-nine years next following to be fully completed : and by the same Dean and the Chapter of the same place unanimously ratified approved and confirmed in their Chapter House under the common seal the xxv day of October Anno Domini 1479; to the use and maintenance of a fit chaplain celebrating at the altar of the blessed Mary the Virgin in the parish church of Marke aforesaid with divers other covenants in the same indenture specified and expressed : and they render per annum, beyond lxs. vij$\frac{1}{2}d$. to the aforesaid Dean and his successors for the rent or farm of the premises annually during the said term reserved, as in the aforesaid indenture is more particularly clear — cxvs. x$\frac{1}{2}d$.

Overwere.

The Free Chapel of Aileston Sutton within the parish there.

Thomas Bocher holds the chapel aforesaid with the tithes of corn of certain acres of land in Aileston aforesaid, and the tithes of hay of certain acres there, and renders per ann. — xxiij*s.* iiij*d.*

Blagdon.

Land and possessions given to the use and maintenance of a Light perpetually burning in the parish church there.

Margaret Priste, widow, holds an acre of arable land there, and renders per ann. — ij*s.*

John Osen holds an acre of arable land there, and renders per ann. — ij*s.*

Walter Whyte holds an acre and a half of meadow, and renders per ann. — vj*s.*

Total — x*s.*

Criston.

Land given to the use and observance of an annual Obit there.

John Payne holds two acres of land lying on the common hill there (*super communem montem*), and renders per ann. — xvj*d.*

Loxton.

Land and possessions given as well to the use and observance of an annual Obit to be held in the parish church there, as to the use and maintenance of a Light in the same church perpetually burning.

Divers persons there hold vj acres of land, meadow and pasture there, and render per ann. — vj*s.*

Bageworthe.

Land given to the use and observance of an annual Obit to be held in the parish church there for ever.

. . . . holds two acres of pasture lying in Hartefeld, and renders per ann. — iij*s.* iiij*d.*

Westbury.

Land and possessions given to the use and maintenance of divers Obits to be held in the parish church there.

John Hickes holds a house there, and renders per ann. — ij*s.*

John Brent holds a house there, and renders per ann. — ij*s.*

John Bromewiche holds a house there, and renders per ann. — ij*s.*

Thomas Golde holds a house on Frye Hill, and renders per ann. — ij*s.* viij*d.*

Somerset Chantries.

Richard Pytman of Yardley holds four acres of land, and an acre and a half of meadow in the parish of Woky, and renders per ann. — v*s.*

Total — xiij*s.* viij*d.*

Deduct in. — Rent resolute to the Almshouse in the city of Wells, per ann. — j*d.*

Money paid for the fabric or reparation of the parish church of Westebury aforesaid, per ann. — xij*d.*

Total — xiij*d.*

And remains over, per annum. — xij*s.* vij*d.*

Burnehame.

The old Chapel there.

. . . . holds the said Chapel with an acre of land in which the same Chapel is situate, and renders per ann. — xx*d.*

Wynscombe.

The Chapel of Sampforde within the parish there.

. . . . holds the said chapel with a certain parcel of land, by estimation a rod, in which the same chapel is situate, and renders per ann. — xij*d.*

Axbridge.

Land and possessions given to the use and maintenance of an annual Obit in the parish church there to be held for ever.

Joan Howell, widow, holds a tenement there, and renders per ann. — v$s.$

John Morowe holds a tenement there, and renders per ann. — viij$s.$

John Egill holds by indenture a tenement and a morehaye there, and renders per ann. — x$s.$

Thomas Hopkyns holds a tenement and a morehaye there and renders per ann. — vj$s.$ viij$d.$

Nicholas Hunt holds a tenement there, and renders per ann. — ij$s.$

Thomas Gye holds a cottage and a shamble, and two acres and a half of reed, and renders per ann. — v$s.$

. . . . holds a piece of land there in which formerly was situate a tenement lately burned by fire and decayed, and renders per ann. — iiij$d.$

Total — xxxvij$s.$

Total in the Deanery of Axbridge, per ann. — liiij$li.$ xvij$s.$ iij$d.$

Deduct in.—Reprises and rents resolute in divers modes as before particularly shown. — xlj$s.$ v$d.$

And remains over, per annum. — lij$li.$ xv$s.$ x$d.$

Deanery of Beomyster.

Clyvedon.

The Free Chapel of Hydall within the parish there.

John Bulbecke holds for a term of lxiij years, by indenture dated xij day of March in the xxvj year of the late King Henry viij, a messuage called Hydall being in the vill of Clyvedon aforesaid, with all and singular the land, meadow, feed, and pasture to the same messuage appertaining, and renders per ann. — iiij*li.*

Lyttleton.

Land and possessions given to the use and maintenance of a Light burning in the parish church there.

John Hodges holds half an acre of pasture in Framboroughe and renders per ann. — xij*d.*

Wrexall.

Land and tenements given to the use and maintenance of an Obit to be held in the parish church there.

.... holds two tenements with gardens in Temple strete within the city of Bristoll, and renders per ann. — xiij*s.* iiij*d.*

Norton Hawtfeld.

The Free Chapel there.

Arthur Payton holds the said Chapel with four acres of arable land, an acre of pasture, and all and singular the demesne lands, also the tithes and oblations and profits to the said Free Chapel appertaining, so to him leased by Thomas Elice late incumbent there, by indenture, for the term of five years and so from five years to five years during the life of the said Thomas, and renders per ann. — xxvj*s.* viij*d.*

Eston in Gordano.
The parish of St. George there.

Land and possessions given to the use and maintenance of an Obit to be held in the parish church there.

The inhabitants of the vill there hold a house there called the Churche Howse, and render per ann. — iij*s.* iiij*d.*

Clutton.

Land and possessions given to the use and maintenance of a Light burning in the parish church there.

Thomas Lokey holds four acres of land there, and renders per ann. — ij*s.*

Chelworth.

Land and possessions given as well to the use and maintenance of a Light burning in the parish church there, as for the observance of an annual Obit to be held there.

Robert Elme holds an acre of land there, and pays per ann. — xij*d*.

Richard Parsones holds three virgates of land there, and renders per ann. — j*d*.

Total — xiij*d*.

Pryston.

Land and possessions given to the use and maintenance of a Light burning in the parish church there.

The parishioners there hold an acre of land, and render per ann. — ij*s*.

Henton Blewett.

Land and possessions given for four masses in the parish church there annually to be celebrated for ever.

. . . . holds a piece of land there called Kentescrofte, and renders per ann. — ij*s*.

Wynforde.

The Chapel of the blessed Mary there.

.... holds the said Chapel with a certain piece of land in which the same Chapel is situate, and renders per ann. —vj*d*.

Land and possessions given to the use and maintenance of a Light burning in the same Chapel of the blessed Mary there.

Thomas Amysbury holds an acre and a half of land there, and renders per ann. —viij*d*.

Walketon.

An Annual rent given to the use and maintenance of a Light burning in the parish church there.

Richard Burrett renders annually from the issues and revenues of a tenement with its appurtenances there in the tenure of himself, for a lb. of wax, per ann. — vj*d*.

Backewell.

Annual rent given to the use and maintenance of an Obit to be held annually in the parish church there.

..... Trystram renders annually from the issues and revenues of his lands and tenements there —vj*d*.

Chew Magna with the Chapel of Dundre annexed.

Annual rent given to the use and maintenance of an Obit to be held annually in the parish church there.

John Horsington renders annually from the issues and revenues of his lands and tenements there — xiij*s.* iiij*d.*

The Chapel of Dundre aforesaid.

Land and possessions given to the use and maintenance of a Lamp in the same Chapel burning.

. . . . , holds four acres of land there, and renders per ann. — xvj*d.*

Patton.

The Free Chapel of Clareham within the parish there.

Alice Graunt holds two acres of meadow there, and renders per ann. — iij*s.* iiij*d.*

William Wamperfelde holds an acre and a half of meadow there, and renders per ann. — iiij*s.*

Mr. Capell holds an acre of meadow there, and renders per ann. — xx*d.*

Divers persons there render one year with another for divers agistments, and for the tithes to the same Free Chapel appertaing or belonging, viz.: Thomas Wale — xviij*s.*; John Barnes — viij*s.*; Joan Hilman — v*s.*; Joan Bradmer — ij*s.*; Joan Erle — xviij*d.*; Mr. Capell for the tithe of hay of Hilsey — vj*s.* viij*d.*; Joan Hilman for tithe of hay and agistments — vij*d.*; John Brodmer — xij*d.*; John Craddock — xij*d.*; Joan Erle — ix*d.*; John Vynpeny — ij½*d.*; John Morfeld — ij*d.*; William Croke — v*d.*; John Fyssher — viij½*d.*; William Wamperfelde — viij*d.*; Edward Avery — j*d.*; William Sergaunt — ij*d.*; William Bene — ij*d.*; Thomas Antony — j½*d.*; Walter Somer — vj*d.*; Alexander Harrys — v*d.*; Alice Graunt — iiij*d.*; John Pascall — ix*d.*; and John Hilman — v*d.*—in all, per ann. — xlix*s.* vij½*d.*

Total — lviij*s.* vij½*d.*

Deduct in.—Rent or pension annually paid to the Vicar of Yatton aforesaid for the time being — x*s.*

And remains over, per annum. — xlviij*s.* vij½*d.*

Compton Dando.

Annual rent given to the use and maintenance of a Lamp in the parish church there perpetually burning.

Agnes Tucker, widow, renders annually from the issues and revenues of a house called Tucker's house, lying within the parish of Compton Dando aforesaid — vj*s.*

Portebury, parish of St. Mary.

The Chantry or Free Chapel of the blessed Mary there.

John Corbet holds a toft there, called a roveles thinge, with a close of land or pasture containing by estimation iij acres of land called le Orcharde, and two acres of meadow land lying in the meadow of Portebury, with all and singular the appurtenances to the same toft belonging, and renders per ann. — iiij*s*.

Richard West holds a messuage lying in Portebury aforesaid, and an acre of pasture at Dykelake, with all and singular their appurtenances, and renders per ann. — xij*s*.

John Crocke holds all that messuage situate and lying in Hame Grene in the parish of Portebury, with all its appurtenances, to the said Chantry or Free Chapel belonging, and renders per ann. — vj*s*.

William Harding holds v acres of pasture with their appurtenances lying in the parish of Portebury aforesaid, and renders per ann. — v*s*.

Total — xxvij*s*.

The Chapel of St. Katerine there.

. . . . holds the said Chapel with a certain parcel of land there called a stiche, viz., a rod of land in which the same Chapel is situate, and renders per ann. — xvj*d*.

Somerset Chantries.

Land and possessions given to the use and maintenance of a Trental in the parish church there, to be sung three times per annum for ever.

.... holds three tenements within the city of Bristol, situate in the street called Balam strete, and renders per ann. — xlvs.

Bedmpster.

The Free Chapel or Hospital of St. Katherine there.

Richard Hall holds the scite and demesne lands of the said Hospital, and renders per ann. — vij*li*.

Alice Sparrer holds two acres of meadow in Lookemoor, and renders per ann. — iijs. iiijd.

John Coke holds one acre of meadow in Wademore, one acre of meadow in Boenmede, and one acre of meadow in Rodmede, and renders per ann. — vjs. iiijd.

Divers persons hold as well according to custom as at will, divers lands and tenements in Bedmyster and Aisheton in the county of Somerset, and in Barkeley in the county of Gloucester, to the said Hospital belonging, and render per ann. — xiij*li*. xvijs. viijd.

.... holds a certain tenement in the city of Bristoll, and renders per ann. — viijs.

.... holds iij little cottages called Almoshouses in the parish of Redclyff in the suburbs of Bristoll, and renders per ann. — *nil*, because they are inhabited by paupers.

Total — xxj*li*. xvs. iiijd.

Somerset Chantries.

Deduct in.—Money paid to the Lord the King as for the price of a lb. of pepper, per ann., for chief rent — iiijs. iiijd. Money paid to the said Lord the King for suit of Court to be annually performed — xijd.

Total — vs. iiijd.

And remains over, per annum. — xxjli. xs.

The Free Chapel of Knolle within the parish there.

. . . . holds the said Chapel with an acre of arable land and an acre of pasture, also all fruits, tithes, oblations, and other profits whatsoever to the said Free Chapel appertaining or belonging, and renders per ann. — lxvjs. viijd.

The Chapel situate in the churchyard of the parish church there.

The parishioners of the same town hold the said Chapel, and render per ann. — xijd.

The Chapel of St. Peter of Bisporte within the parish there.

. . . . holds the said Chapel with a piece of land included, in which the same Chapel is situated, containing a rod of land, and renders per ann. — xxd.

Annual rent given to the use and maintenance of a Lamp in the parish church there burning.

John Kemys of Knolle renders annually from the issues and revenues of his land and tenements there — vjd.

Longe Aisheton.

The Chantry within the parish church there founded by Richard Choke, Kt.

. . . . holds the dwelling house with a garden and orchard adjacent, and renders per ann. — v*s*.

John Baber holds for term of his life a messuage or farm with appurtenances, called Barrowe farm juxta Bathe in the county aforesaid, and renders per ann. — iiij*li*.

John Wheler holds by indenture for a term of years a close of pasture called Gages lease, a meadow called the Great mede, and another meadow called Little mede in Keynsham, with a piece of land called Harrys lande, and renders per ann. — xxiiij*s*.

John Gaye and Thomas Whippey hold by indenture for a term of years a messuage or farm with its appurtenances, called Stockewoodes ferme in Keynsham aforesaid, and render per ann. — xlij*s*. viij*d*.

John Cheryton holds by indenture for term of life, a tenement with appurtenances in Wokey within the parish of Wells, and renders per ann. — xvj*s*.

Total — viij*li*. vij*s*. viij*d*.

Deduct in.—Rent resolute to John Rodney, esquire, as free rent for the said farm called Barrowe farme, viz., for one lb. of pepper — ij*s*. ; and xij*d*. for suit of Court, per ann. — iij*s*.

Rent resolute for the aforesaid land within the parish of Wells, per ann. — viij*s*.

Total — xj*s*.

And remains over, per annum. — vij*li*. xvj*s*. viij*d*.

Land and possessions placed in feoffment by Nicholas Chocke and Henry Chocke for the use and maintenance of a perpetual chaplain celebrating mass three times a week in the chapel of the blessed Mary there, called Merwattes Chapell.

Richard Gilling holds by indenture a tenement with appurtenances in Hunspill, and renders per ann. — xlijs.

.... Getter holds a tenement with appurtenances there, and renders per ann. — xxvijs. iiijd.

Alice London, widow, holds a tenement, with appurtenances, there, and renders per ann. — iijs. vjd.

John Martyn holds ij acres of pasture there, and renders per ann. — vs. xd.

John Leye holds a piece of land there, called a pocke juxta the mill, and renders per ann. — iiijd.

John Parker holds by indenture a tenement with appurtenances in Stone Eston, and renders per ann. — xxviijs.

The Wardens of the parish church of Hunspill aforesaid, render a free rent annually from the issues and revenues of the land and tenements appertaining to the said church — xviijd.

Total — cviijs. vjd.

Deduct in.—Rent resolute to the Earl of Bath for free rent of the premises, per ann. — vjs. iiijd.

Money paid to the same Earl for suit of Court, per ann. — vd.

Rent resolute to Lord Salinger for free rent, per ann. — iijs.

Money paid to the same Lord Salinger for suit of his Court, per ann. — vd.

Rent resolute to the lord Marquis of Dorset for free rent as the price of a lb. of cummin, per ann. — iiij*d*.

Total — x*s*. vj*d*.

And remains over, per annum. — iiij*li*. xviij*s*.

Annual rent given to the use and maintenance of a Lamp and a Light burning as well in the said Chapel called Merpattes — ij*s*., as in the parish church there. — iij*s*. viij*d*.

Thomas Lyons esquire renders annually from the issues and revenues of his lands and tenements called Ludsyat lying within the parish of Wynyfrede, per ann. — ij*s*.

William Evered senr. renders annually from the issues and revenues of his land and tenements called Nethewayes in the tenure of Thomas Evered, per ann. — iij*s*. viij*d*.

Total — v*s*. viij*d*.

Land and possessions given to the use and maintenance of an annual Obit to be held in the parish church there for ever.

The inhabitants of the vill of Long Aisheton aforesaid hold a tenement there called the Churchehouse with a garden adjacent containing half an acre of land, and an acre of land with a little grove of wood at the Knolle, also a virgate of land lying under Butterclyff, all which Thomas Stevyns formerly held, and they render per ann., with xij*d*. for the rent of a house on a piece of the same land, lately built for the dwelling of the priest there — vij*s*. viij*d*.

Deduct in.—Rent resolute to John Smythe for free rent of the premises, per ann. — v*s*.

And remains over, per annum. — ij*s*. viij*d*.

Somerset Chantries.

Total for the Deanery of Bedmyster aforesaid, per ann. — liiij*li.* x½*d.*

Deduct in.—Reprises and rents resolute in divers modes as before particularly shown — xxxvj*s.* x*d.*

And remains over, per annum. — lij*li.* iiij*s.* ½*d.*

Deanery of Frome.

Farley Hungerforde.

The Chantry of St. Leonard within the Castle there.

Anthony Besye holds by copy the capital messuage or farm situate and lying in Tellysforde with all and singular its appurtenances called Tellysforde Farm, and renders per ann. — lxiijs. iiijd.

The same holds a cottage with its appurtenances there called Showlecroft, and renders per ann. — xliijs. iiijd.

Thomas Tucker holds a fulling mill there called a Tokingmylle, and renders per ann. — lxvjs. viijd.

. . . . holds a tenement with its appurtenances there, and renders per ann., with iiijd. for rent of a garden there. — viijs. iiijd.

Total — ixli. xxd.

Land and possessions given to the use and maintenance of a Lamp in the parish church there perpetually burning.

The Wardens of the parish church aforesaid hold ij acres of arable land there, and render per ann. — xxd.

Philippes Norton.

Annual rents given to the use and maintenance of divers Lights burning in the parish church there.

Henry Clerke renders annually from the issues and revenues of his land and tenements there as for the price of ij lbs. of wax, per ann. — xij$d$.

John Vigar of Hemyngton renders annually from the issues and revenues of his lands and tenements as for the price of one lb. of wax, per ann. — vj$d$.

Total — xviij$d$.

Camerton.

Annual rent given to the use and maintenance of a Light burning in the parish church there.

Richard Bawne renders annually from the issues and revenues of his land and tenement there as for the price of a lb. of wax, per ann. — iij$d$.

Laverton.

Annual rent given to the use and maintenance of a Light burning in the parish church there.

The Master of the Hospital of Mary Magdalen in Bathe renders annually from the issues and revenues of a tenement there, per ann. — xij$d$.

Holcombe.

Land and possessions given to the use and observance of an annual Obit to be held within the parish church there.

William Portaunt holds certain land there, per ann. — xiijs. iiijd.

Wulverton.

Annual rent given to the use and maintenance of a Light burning in the parish church there.

. . . . Horton, gent., renders annually from the issues and revenues of a certain parcel of pasture land in Rode called Hawkyns Hamme. — vjd.

Merston.

Annual rent given to the use and maintenance of a Light burning in the parish church there.

The Lord Stourton renders annually from the issues and revenues of a meadow there called Bynhill in the occupation of Joan Smythwyke, widow, — ijs.

Kilmersdon.

Land and possessions, with an annual rent, given to the use and maintenance of a Light burning in the parish church there.

Thomas Riche holds an acre of land there, once John Russell's, and renders per ann. — xij*d*.

Richard Wydcombe holds an acre of land there, once William Lotsome's, and renders per ann. —xij*d*.

The Lord of the Manor of Kylmersdon aforesaid renders annually from the issues and revenues of the same as paid by the hands of his provost there for the time being, per ann. — vj*s*. viij*d*.

Total — viij*s*. viij*d*.

Radstocke.

Annual rent given to the use and maintenance of a Light burning in the parish church there.

Lord Thomas Howarde as heir of Lord Marney renders annually from the issues and revenues of his three tenements in the occupation of John Harrys, John Savage, and John Dowlour, per ann. — vj*d*.

Chuton.

Land and possessions given to the use and maintenance of a Light burning in the parish church there.

John Elys holds a house there called Barrowe house, and renders per ann. — xx*d*.

Rode.

Annual rent given to the use and maintenance of a Light burning in the parish church there.

John Sturgies, gent., renders annually from the issues and revenues of his land and a tenement there, viz., from a close of land there in the tenure of John Lugge, and from a tenement in the tenure of . . . . Myller, widow, per ann. — xviij*d*.

Nunney.

The Chantry there.

. . . . holds the dwelling house of the said Chantry with a garden adjacent situate, lying, and being within the Castle of Nunney aforesaid, and renders per ann. — xij*d*.

John Pye and John Chancellour hold two tenements or cottages with a virgate of land to the same annexed and adjacent at Trutoxhill in the parish of Nunney aforesaid, also iij acres of meadow there, all which John Bagge gave to the said Chantry anno viij Henry vj for a term of cxx years next following and to be completed (as it is said), and they render per ann. — xvjs.

William Paulet, Kt., Lord sainct John renders annually from the issues, profits, and revenues of the lordship or manor of Fyssherton Dalamer in the county of Wilts, by the hand of the receiver, bailiff, provost, farmer, or other officer or minister of the same Lord Seinct John of his manor aforesaid for the time being, per ann. — vj*li*. xiijs. iiijd.

Total — vij*li*. xs. iiijd.

Deduct in.—Rent resolute to Roger Mawdeley, gent., for free rent of the aforesaid two tenements or cottages and other premises granted for a term of years, per ann. — iiijs. vjd.

And remains over, per annum. — vij*li*. vs. xd.

Land and possessions given to the use and maintenance of a Light and a Lamp burning in the parish church there.

The Wardens of the church aforesaid hold an acre of land there called Lampe acre, and render per ann. — vjd.

John Thynne, Kt., renders annually from the issues and revenues of a tenement there called Longlete in the tenure of Geoffrey Clymer as for the price of one lb. of wax, per ann. — vjd.

Total — xijd.

Barkeley.

Land and possessions given as well to the use and maintenance of a Light burning in the parish church there, as for the maintenance of an annual Obit to be held there.

John Golweige holds a piece of land there called Saincte George lande, and renders per ann. — iiij*d*.

John Mody holds a close of pasture there called Churche close, and renders per ann. — iiij*s*.

Annual rent from the issues and revenues of a close of pasture there called Marmons, per ann. — vij*s*.

Total — xj*s*. iiij*d*.

Deduct in.—Rent resolute to John Newborowe, gent., for free rent of the said close called Churcheclose, per ann. — x*d*.

And remains over, per annum. — x*s*. vj*d*.

Midsomer Norton.

The service of a chaplain celebrating in the Chapel of the Guilde of the blessed Mary in the parish church there for the souls of all the faithful deceased.

John Dando, Joan his wife, and John their son, hold for term of their lives a certain parcel of land lying in Halowtre within the parish of Lytleton, and render per ann. — x*s*.

Froome Selwoode.

The Free Chapel of saincte Katerine there.

William Bayly holds the capital messuage or dwelling house there, and two tenements with all land, meadow, feed and pasture to the same appertaining, and renders per ann. — lxs.

Walter Newman holds three tenements with their appurtenances and a close there, and renders per ann. — xxijs. viijd.

William Selvey holds iiij tenements with their appurtenances and a close there, and renders per ann. — xxvijs. iiijd.

Andrew Cadbery holds a tenement and a garden there, and renders per ann. — vs.

Thomas Freestone holds a tenement with a garden in Froome situate in the street called Katerine Strete there, and renders per ann. — vjs.

Total — vjli. xijd.

The Chantry of St. Andrew alias St. John Baptist there.

.... holds the dwelling house there with a garden and orchard adjacent, and renders per ann. — viijs.

William Gentes holds by indenture two tenements with all land, meadow, feed and pasture and other commodities to the same appertaining, and renders per ann. — ls.

Divers persons hold by indenture divers lands, closes, meadows, feed and pasture there, and render per ann. — lxs.

Somerset Chantries.

Divers persons hold at the will of the lord, all the burgages, tenements and cottages there, with the gardens and other their appurtenances whatsoever in Froome aforesaid to the said Chantry appertaining, and render per ann. — xl*s*. x½*d*.

Total — vij*li*. xviij*s*. x½*d*.

Deduct in.—Rent resolute to William Lord Stourton, per ann. — iiij*s*. ix*d*.

Rent resolute to Robert Leversage, esquire, per ann. — xviij*d*.

Rent resolute to Edward Twynhoo, esquire, per ann. — v*d*.

Total — vj*s*. viij*d*.

And remains over, per annum. — vij*li*. xij*s*. ij½*d*.

The Chantry of St. Nicholas within the parish church there.

Divers persons hold by indenture divers burgages, lands, tenements, cottages, meadow, feed and pasture and other hereditaments with their appurtenances to the said Chantry appertaining in the said parish of Froome, and render per ann. — liij*s*. iiij*d*.

Thomas Fowey and others hold iiij burgages with iiij gardens to the same appertaining in Froome aforesaid, and render per ann. — liij*s*. iiij*d*.

Divers persons hold at the will of the lord divers other burgages with little gardens adjacent there, and render per ann. — xlix*s*. viij*d*.

Total — vij*li*. xvj*s*. iiij*d*.

Deduct in.—Rent resolute to Robert Leversage, esquire, issuing from the burgages aforesaid and other premises paid annually at the Feast of St. Michael archangel, — iiij*s*. viij*d*.

And remains over, per annum. — vij*li*. xj*s*. viij*d*.

The Chantry of the blessed Mary within the parish church there.

Divers persons hold certain free land and a tenement there, and render per ann. — ijs. iiijd.

Divers persons hold at will divers tenements and cottages with gardens adjacent in the parish of Froome Selwoode aforesaid, and render per ann. — lxvijs. viijd.

Divers persons hold by indenture, as well for term of their lives as for a term of years, certain land, tenements, meadow, feed and pasture and other hereditaments whatsoever in the said parish of Froome to the said Chantry appertaining, and render per ann. — lxxixs. viijd.

Total — vijli. ixs. viijd.

Deduct in.—Rent resolute to Robert Leversage, esquire, annually from the lands aforesaid, — vs.

And remains over, per annum. — vijli. iiijs. viijd.

Annual rent given to the use and observance of an annual Obit there.

The Wardens of the parish church of Trowbridge for the time being render annually from the issues and revenues of land and a tenement there given by Margaret Osbourne, per ann. — xs.

Land and possessions given to the use and maintenance of a Light burning in the parish church there.

Andrew Gadbury and Ralph Cooper hold two tenements there, given by the prior and convent of the late Priory of Bradleghe, and render per ann. — xvjs.

Somerset Chantries.

Total for the Deanery of Froome aforesaid — xlix*li.* xviij*s.* ix½*d.*

Deduct in.—Reprises and rents resolute in divers modes as before particularly shown — xxj*s.* viij*d.*

And remains over, per annum. — xlviij*li.* xvij*s.* j½*d.*

Deanery of Ilchester.

Mountague.

Annual rent given to the use and maintenance of a Light in the parish church there perpetually burning.

Thomas Philips esquire renders annually from the issues and revenues of half a burgage and a dovecot there, as the price of ij lbs. of wax, per ann. — xij*d*.

Northeperotte.

Annual rents given to the use and maintenance of a Light in the parish church there perpetually burning.

Edward Duke of Somerset, lord of the manor of Northperot aforesaid, renders annually from the issues of the same by the hand of his bailiff there. — viij*s*.

John Geyre renders annually from the issues and revenues of his land and tenements there, per ann. — iij*s*. iij*d*.

Total — xj*s*. iij*d*.

Aller.

The Chantry of the blessed Mary the virgin there.

Thomas Clerke holds xlij acres of pasture there and xviij acres of arable land with the dwelling house (*mans*) of the said Chantry with appurtenances by indenture for term of life, and renders per ann. — vj*li*.

. . . . holds a *domum parlarii*, (?) a parlour or meeting room, with a chamber in the aforesaid dwelling house (*mans*) and the third part of all the fruit growing in the orchard to the same Chantry belonging reserved to the incumbent by the said indenture, and renders per ann. — ij*s*.

Total — vj*li*. ij*s*.

Annual rent given to the use and maintenance of a Light in the parish church there perpetually burning.

The heir of . . . . Courtney renders annually from the issues and revenues of his manor of Bere within the parish aforesaid as for the price of x lbs. of wax, per ann. — v*s*.

Northover.

Land and possessions given to the use and maintenance of a Light in the parish church there perpetually burning.

The Wardens of the parish church there hold half an acre of meadow there, and render per ann. — xiiij*d*.

Ilchester.

The Free Chapel of the Holy Trinity of Whitehall in the Borough of Ilchester.

Thomas Duporte holds all the said Free Chapel called Whitehall with all and singular its members, rights, and appurtenances, and also all and singular the houses, buildings, messuages, tofts, cottages, curtilages, mills, lands, tenements, meadows, pasture and other profits, commons, woods, underwood, rents, reversions, services, waters, pools, rivulets, fishing, moors, marshes, Courts leet with perquisites and other profits to the same, heriots, estrays, reliefs, and all and singular other profits and advantages whatsoever to the said Free Chapel belonging or in any manner appertaining, or reputed, accepted, used, occupied, or acknowledged as part, parcel or member of the said Free Chapel or possessions of the same, situate, lying, and being, coming, contingent, emergent or growing, within the towns, parishes, hamlets, and fields of Ilchester, Northover, Lymyngton, and Taunton, or in any of them, or in other places in the county of Somerset, so to him leased, by George Carowe clerk, archdeacon . . . . and Master of the said Chapel, by indenture given under the seal of the said George xxviij day of June in the xxxviij year of the late King Henry viij. To have and to hold the said Free Chapel with all and singular the houses, messuages, lands, tenements, meadows, feed, pasture, woods, and all and singular the other premises before expressed and specified, with all and singular its appurtenances to the aforesaid Thomas Duporte and his assigns from the Feast of the Annunciation of the blessed Mary the virgin last past before the date of the said indenture, to the end and termination of xl years then next and immediately following and fully to be completed: Rendering therefor annually to the aforesaid George Carowe or his successors to be paid at the four annual terms in equal portions — xvj*li*. x*s*.

The Chapel there called Mychelles Bowe.

. . . . holds the said Chapel with a virgate of land and a dovecote there, taxed per ann. — iiij*d*.

Lympngton.

The Chantry of the blessed Mary within the parish church there.

. . . . holds the dwelling house of the said Chantry with a garden adjacent and iij acres of arable land and an acre of meadow there, and renders per ann. — viij*s*.

The lord Marquis of Dorset renders annually from the issues and revenues of his manor of Lymyngton aforesaid by the hands of his bailiff, provost, farmer or other officer or minister of his manor aforesaid, per ann. — lxxij*s*.

Total — iiij*li*.

Land and possessions given to the use and maintenance of a Light in the parish church there perpetually burning.

John Eston holds ij acres of arable land there, and renders per ann., for a lb. of wax, — vj*d*.

Somerset Chantries.

John Lye renders annually from the issues of his land in Lymyngton aforesaid called Lye's land, as for the price of the oil lately burning in a Lamp in the parish church there, per ann. — iiij*d.*

Total — x*d.*

Martocke.

The Chantry of Martocke within the parish church there.

Walter Godderde holds a messuage with its appurtenances in Bradforde, Brande, and Barnardley within the parish of Wynbourne in the county of Dorset, by indenture for a term of years, per ann. — lxxvj*s.* viij*d.*

Walter Godderde aforesaid holds a tenement with its appurtenances there, and renders per ann. — lxx*s.*

Thomas Prior holds certain arable land there, and renders per ann. — viij*s.*

Richard Cockes holds a pasture there, and renders per ann. — vij*s.* ij*d.*

John Godderde holds ij closes and ij acres of arable land there, and renders per ann. — xj*s.* viij*d.*

John Hannham holds a tenement or burgage there, and renders per ann. — ix*s.* viij*d.*

John Davy holds a tenement or burgage there, and renders per ann. — xviij*s.* viiij*d.*

Richard Russell holds a tenement or burgage there, and renders per ann. — xxxj*s.* iiij*d.*

Philip Barons holds a tenement or burgage there, and renders per ann. — xlj*s.*

John Abbotte holds a tenement or burgage there, and renders per ann. — x*s.*

.... hold the dwelling house of the said Chantry, and render per ann. — iiij*d.*

Total — xiiij*li.* v*s.* iiij*d.*

Deduct in.—Rent resolute to George Antill, per ann. — vj*li.* xiij*s.* iiij*d.*

Rent resolute to Edward Twynho' for free rent, per ann. — v*s.*

Fee to Edward Rogers, Kt., general Surveyor there by Letters Patent granted for term of his life, per ann. — xiij*s.* iiij*d.*

Fee to the bailiff there, per ann. — x*s.*

Total — viij*li.* xx*d.*

And remains over, per annum. — vj*li.* iij*s.* viij*d.*

Land and possessions given for a term of years to the use and maintenance of a chaplain celebrating in the parish church of Martocke as below.

.... hold xxiij acres of arable land, iij acres and a half of meadow, and pasture for vj oxen in Cotehey within the parish of Martocke aforesaid, leased, granted, and confirmed to John Belde, John Genys, William Master, and Roger Kele, by Thomas Harris treasurer of the Cathedral church of Saint Andrew of Wells and propriator of the parish church of Martocke aforesaid to the same treasurership united and annexed, by indenture dated in the Feast of St. Martin, bishop, v Henry vij; to have and to hold the aforesaid xxiij acres of arable land, three acres and a half of meadow, and pasture for six oxen in Cotchey aforesaid, with all appurtenances, to the said John Belde, John Genys, William Master, and Roger Kele their executors or assigns from the Feast of Easter next following after the date of the said indenture, to the end of a term of ninety and nine years next following and to be fully completed; for the support (*ad exhibitionem*) and maintenance of a chaplain celebrating at the altar of St. Thomas within the parish church of All Saints of Martocke aforesaid during the term aforesaid, rendering therefrom annually to the aforesaid Thomas Harrys and his successors, — vj*s.* viij*d.* legal money of England to be paid at the four annual principal terms in equal portions, with divers other covenants in the same indenture specified: which indenture and the contents of the same, John Gunthorpe then Dean of the Cathedral church of Wells aforesaid and the Chapter of the same, accepted, ratified, and according to the form and effect the same confirmed by their writing given in their Chapter House under their common seal on the morrow of S. Marttin, bishop, in the year above written. And they render per annum beyond the aforesaid vj*s.* viij*d.* — lij*s.* iiij*d.*

The Service of a stipendiary priest there.

The Duke of Suffolk renders annually from the issues and revenues of his manor of Martocke aforesaid paid by the hands of the receiver or bailiff of the same Duke of his manor aforesaid, per ann. — xl*s.*

Annual rent given to the use and maintenance of a Lamp burning in the parish church there.

Thomas Pike renders annually from the issues and revenues of a tenement with its appurtenances in Pike's Ashe, per ann.— viij*d.*

Annual rent given to the use and maintenance of a Light burning in the Chapel of Stapleton within the parish there.

The lord Marquis of Dorset renders annually from the issues of a meadow and pasture, with pasture for a beast feeding on the said pasture, belonging to a tenement in the Hamlet of Stapleton within the parish aforesaid in the tenure of John Borowe, and renders per ann. — xij*d*.

The Chapel of Longlode within the parish there.

. . . . holds the said Chapel with a piece of land called Chapell haye in which the same Chapel is situate, and a little cottage and an acre of arable land there called Mawdlyn forde to the said Chapel appertaining, and renders per ann. — xvj*d*.

Charlton Adam.

The Chantry or Free Chapel once called the Chapel of the Holy Ghost within the parish there.

John Larder esquire holds the said Chantry or Free Chapel with all and singular the land, meadow, pasture, common, issues, profits, advantages and all other conveniences, with appurtenances, to the same Chantry or Free Chapel belonging, by indenture given under the seal of Thomas Russell clerk, late incumbent, the last day of March xxxvj Henry viij for a term of xxj years then next following and fully to be completed, and renders per ann. — xxvj*s*. viij*d*.

Land and possessions given to the use and maintenance of an Obit in the parish church there annually to be held for ever.

.... holds a house there commonly called the Churche house, and renders per ann. — xij*d*.

Charleton Makerell.

The Chantry of Charleton Makerell.

John Drew holds eight acres of meadow lying in the common meadow there, and thirty acres of arable land lying in the common fields there, and renders per ann. — xxvj*s*. viij*d*.

Long Sutton.

The Chapel of Upton there.

.... holds the said Chapel, and renders per ann. — iiij*d*.

The Chapel of Knolle there.

.... holds the same Chapel, and renders per ann. — iiij*d*.

Stoke subtus Hamden.

The Free Chapel of St. Nicholas within the parish there.

John Kyes holds a messuage and iiij virgates of land there by indenture, and renders per ann. — vj*li.* xiij*s.* iiij*d.*

John Gardiner holds certain pasture and arable land lying in the fields and parish of Ilchester, and renders per ann. — xxvij*s.* ix*d.*

. . . . holds the tithes as well of the demesne land as of other lands lying and being in the parish of Shepton Beauchamp with certain customs and money called chursettes, and renders per ann. — lxvj*s.* viij*d.*

. . . . holds half an acre of meadow lying in the meadow of Ilchester, and renders per ann. — xx*d.*

Total — xj*li.* ix*s.* v*d.*

Deduct in.—Rent resolute annually to the Bailiff of the town of Ilchester — vj*s.* j*d.*

Rent resolute to the lord Marquis of Dorset for the aforesaid half acre of meadow, per ann. — vj*d.*

Total — vj*s.* vij*d.*

And remains over, per annum. — xj*li.* ij*s.* x*d.*

Ebilton.

The Free Chapel of Ebilton within the Lordship of Spekington.

William Hodgys junr., holds fifty-five acres of arable land meadow, and pasture with appurtenances there by indenture, and renders per ann. — xxxiijs. iiijd.

The same holds half of all the tithes, besides the tithe of sheaf corn and of hay coming from or growing on a certain farm in Spekington aforesaid in the occupation of John Souper esquire, and renders per ann. — vs.

The same holds the tithe from ten acres of land in the western field of the same vill to the same farm appertaining as often as they shall be sown, and renders per ann. — iijs. iiijd.

Total — xljs. viijd.

The Borough of Langporte *alias* Lamporte.

The Chantry of John Heron within the parish church there.

BYCKENELL.

Edward Brekempe holds a tenement there, iiij virgates of land in Edbare, an acre of meadow in Manemede, and two closes of pasture called Southbroke and Lye, and renders per ann. — xixs. xd.

William Kyche holds a tenement there called Pythouse, iij acres of arable land in Barrey and Horsepole, vj acres of meadow in Barrey and Newlande, and ij closes of pasture called Brodebere mede, and renders per ann. — xxxjs.

Somerset Chantries.

The same William Keche holds a cottage in Boleforde, and renders per ann. — xvj½d.

CURRY MALLET.

Peter Wever and others hold a toft there containing fifty-five acres of land and meadow there by indenture for term of life, and render per ann. — xxiiijs. viijd.

Robert Gurney holds free xxvj acres of land and pasture with appurtenances there, and renders per ann. — ijs.

FYFFED.

Isabella Taylour holds a tenement there with an orchard adjacent containing by estimation an acre, and xxiij acres of land and meadow lying in separate places of the fields there, and renders per ann. — xs. vjd.

SWELL.

Alexander Taylour holds a tenement there containing xxx acres of land and meadow lying in divers places of the fields there as by the rental thereof made on parchment is fully evident, and two closes of pasture, containing by estimation vij acres, of which one is called Trygelles Hamp and the other is called Shere Orcharde, and renders per ann. — xxvs. viijd.

NORTH PETHERTON.

Walter Whyte holds the moiety of a close of land and pasture called Showell there, and renders per ann. — xxvs. ½d.

Somerset Chantries.

NEWTON PLACY.

John Benet holds a tenement there with appurtenances, vij acres of land, and ix acres and iij rods of meadow, and renders per ann. — xvj*s*. iiij*d*.

. . . . holds certain land in Morelande there, and renders per ann. —vj*s*.

LAMPORTE.

. . . . holds a little garden or piece of vacant land there on which the dwelling house of the Cantarist of the said chantry was built, and renders per ann. — vj*d*.

Total — viij*li*. ij*s*. xj*d*.

Deduct in.—Rent resolute to William Portman, Kt., iij*s*. John Dorington iij*s*. and Thomas Buller, iij*s*. for free rent of the said land and tenements in Byckenell, per ann. — ix*s*.

Rent resolute to William Wadham for the said cottage in Bulforde, per ann. — ½*d*.

Rent resolute to the Lord the King as of his manor of Curry Mallet for the land and tenement there, as for the price of a lb. of wax, per ann. — iij*d*.

Rent resolute to Robert Walshe for the aforesaid land in Fyffed, per ann. — vj*d*.

Rent resolute to Thomas Newton as of his manor of Swell for the land and tenement there, per ann. — ix*s*.

Rent resolute to William Pawlet, Kt. lord Seinct John for the land and tenement aforesaid in North Petherton, with xij*d*. annually paid for the said land in Moreland, per ann. — xij½*d*.

Somerset Chantries.

Rent resolute to John Worthe for the aforesaid land in Newton Placy, per ann. — xij*d*.

Total — xx*s*. x*d*.

And remains over, per annum. — vij*li*. ij*s*. j*d*.

The Service of two priests or chaplains there called Fraternitie priestes.

The Provost and Commonalty of the Borough there render annually from the issues, profits, and revenues of their land, tenements and burgages there to be paid by the hand of the Receiver or Proctor of the same Provost and Commonalty per annum viz., for the salary or stipend of each priest or chaplain aforesaid annually cvj*s*. viij*d*., in all per ann. — x*li*. xiij*s*. iiij*d*.

Total of the Deanery of Ilchester aforesaid, per ann. — lxxxj*li*. xv*s*. vij*d*.

Deduct in.—Reprises and rents resolute in divers modes as before particularly shown — ix*li*. ix*s*. j*d*.

And remains over, per annum. — lxxij*li*. vj*s*. vj*d*.

Deanery of Cary.

Castell Cary.

Annual rent given for a term of years to the use and maintenance of an annual Obit to be held in the parish church there.

The executors or assigns of Henry Russe render annually from the issues, profits, and revenues of certain land called Hayes lying within the lordship of Bratton, which land the Lord Zouche by indenture under his hand and seal to the aforesaid Henry Russe granted and leased to farm, to hold to himself, his executors and assigns from the Feast of the Annunciation of the blessed Mary the Virgin, in the xxvj year of the reign of the late King Henry viij to the end and term of xlj years next following and to be fully completed under a certain rent in the same indenture specified &c. During which term the same Henry Russe granted and bequeathed to be paid from the issues thereof annually. — x*s*.

Pulton with the Chapel of Wotton annexed.

Land and possessions given to the use and maintenance of a Light in the same chapel burning.

John Alforde and Richard Kinge hold vj acres of land there, and render per ann. — x*s*.

Perlington.

Land and possessions given to the use and maintenance of a Light in the parish church there perpetually burning.

.... holds two acres of land in Galhampton within the parish of Cadbury, and renders per ann. — xvj$d$.

Hornebloughton.

Annual rent given to the use and maintenance of a Light in the parish church there perpetually burning.

Richard Marshall esquire renders annually from the issues and revenues of a certain pasture there called the Fostclose. — xij$d$.

Babcary.

The Free Chapel of Fodington within the parish there.

.... holds a close of pasture containing an acre and a half, and xxiij acres of arable land, and two acres and a half of meadow there, and renders per ann. — xv$s$. viij$d$.

.... holds the tithe of corn there, and renders per ann. — xx$s$.

.... holds the tithe of hay from xv acres of meadow there, and renders per ann. — iij$s$.

.... holds the small tithes there, and renders per ann. — xx$d$.

Total — xl$s$. iiij$d$.

Estpenmarde.

The Chapel called Stone Chapel within the parish there.

. . . . holds the Chapel aforesaid situate in a certain parcel of land belonging to George Mylbourne, gent., with a tenement and orchard adjacent containing half an acre of land which the chaplain celebrating there wholly inhabited, and renders per ann. — iijs.

Compton Paunsforde.

The Chantry within the parish church there.

William Due holds by indenture for term of life a tenement with appurtenances called Lighe in Bysshoppes Knoylle *alias* Este Knoylle in the county of Wilts, and renders per ann.— cxs. viijd.

Thomas Batte holds a tenement with appurtenances in Shaston in the county of Dorset, and renders per ann. — xs.

Divers persons there hold four gardens and a little piece of land in Shaston aforesaid to the same Chantry appertaining, and render per ann. — vijs.

Total — vjli. vijs. viijd.

Deduct in.—Rent resolute to the Bishop of Winton from the tenement of Lighe aforesaid, per ann. — vs.

Rent resolute to the same Bishop for fine (and) suit, for the said tenement of Lighe, per ann. — ixd.

Total — vs. ixd.

And remains over, per annum. — vjli. xxiijd.

Wyncaulton with Stabardell.

Two Chantries in the Chapel of the name of Jesus at Stabardell aforesaid.

Ready money received and levied from the issues, profits and revenues of Pytcombe and Colle belonging to the heir of Lord Zouche, to be paid by the hand of the Receiver or Bailiff of the said Lord Zouche of his manors aforesaid annually. — xiij*li.* vj*s.* viij*a.*

Annual rent given to the use and maintenance of an annual Obit in the parish church there.

The heir of William Sergaunt renders annually from the issues and revenues of a tenement with appurtenances there late in the tenure of John Balhedd. — iij*s.* iiij*d.*

Northe Cadbury.

Land and possessions given to the use and maintenance of a chaplain celebrating within the parish church there.

. . . . holds a cottage with its appurtenances, and a messuage with a virgate of land, a close of pasture and also a meadow lying in North Cadbury and Kylmersdon, and renders per ann. — lx*s.*

Somerset Chantries.

Land and possessions given to the use and maintenance of a Light burning in the parish church there.

Nicholas Walker clerk, rector of the church aforesaid, holds vj acres of land within the parish there, and renders per ann. — iiij*s*.

Shepton Mallet.

The Service of a priest celebrating in the parish church there, founded for a term of years.

. . . . holds a certain parcel of land and pasture called Smaldon, lying within the Lordship of Evercryche leased to Richard Renyon by Adriann late Bishop of Bath and Wells by indenture given in the year of our lord one thousand five hundred and five for the term of lxj years next following and to be fully completed. Rendering therefor annually to the aforesaid Bishop and his successors nine pounds sterling at the usual annual terms, with divers covenants in the same indenture specified; which Richard Renyon when he died gave and bequeathed by his last will the remainder of his term of years in the premises to the use and maintenance of a chaplain in the parish church of Shepton Mallet aforesaid to celebrate for the good estate of the said Richard himself. And renders per ann. beyond the aforesaid rent of ix*li*. to the Bishop aforesaid of Bath and Wells reserved during the term aforesaid. — vj*li*. vj*s*. viij*d*.

The Guilde or Fraternity of the Holy Trinity and St. John Baptist in the parish church there, founded for the maintenance of two chaplains celebrating there.

Divers persons hold certain lands and tenements in Aishewike, and render per ann. — xij*s*. iiij*d*.

John Rowse holds the farm or capital messuage there, together with all the land, meadow, feed, pasture, and common, to the same appertaining, and renders per ann. — lxiij*s*. iiij*d*.

Divers persons hold certain lands and tenements in Kylmersdon, and render per ann. — lxxviij*s*. vj*d*.

Divers persons hold certain lands and tenements in Shepton Mallet, and render per ann. — lviij*s*.

. . . . holds two messuages there in which the Cantarists now live, and renders per ann. — iij*s*. iiij*d*.

Divers persons hold certain lands and tenements in Stoke St. Michael, and render per ann. — xxvj*s*. viij*d*.

Divers persons hold certain lands and tenements in Holcombe, and render per ann. — x*s*.

Divers persons hold certain lands and tenements in Yevill, Elleston, and Barwyke, and render per ann. — xxvij*s*. iiij*d*.

Divers persons hold certain lands and tenements in Stoforde, and render per ann. — xxxv*s*. iiij*d*.

Total — xv*li*. xiiij*s*. vj*d*.

Deduct in. — Rent resolute to the Earl of Arundell for the land and tenements in Elston and Yevell, per ann. — vj*s*.

Rent resolute to the Earl of Huntington as of his manor of Kylmersdon, for certain lands and tenements of the said Guilde in Aishewike, per ann. — xij*d*.

Rent resolute to John Rogers, Kt., for the lands and tenements in Stoforde, per ann. — vj*s.* x*d.*

Rent resolute to Bartholomew Fortescue, esquire, as of his manor of Croscombe, for a tenement called Sharnchill in Shepton Mallet aforesaid, per ann. — iij*s.* iiij*d.*

Total — xvij*s.* ij*d.*

And remains over, per annum. — xiiij*li.* xvij*s.* iiij*d.*

Land and possessions given as well to the use and maintenance of a Light burning in the parish church there, as to the observance of an annual Obit and Anniversary to be held in the aforesaid church.

John Myller holds a close of pasture there containing by estimation two acres called Saint Edmund's close, and renders per ann. — v*s.*

Joan Broke and John her son hold a messuage or tenement there called Mortons tenement with certain land, meadow, and pasture to the same adjacent, and render per ann. — xxvj*s.* viij*d.*

Annual rent annually received and levied from the Master and Wardens of the craft or company (*artis sive consortis*) of Merchant Tailors of the City of London, per ann. — xl*s.*

Total — lxxj*s.* viij*d.*

Deduct in. — Rent resolute to the Lord De la Ware for free rent of the same messuages appertaining, per ann. — ij*d.*

And remains over, per annum. — lxxj*s.* vj*d.*

Corscombe.

The Guilde or Fraternity there.

EST HORRINGTON.

John Tyke holds by indenture for term of life the capital house or messuage there with all the demesne lands to the same appertaining, and renders per ann. — with ij*s.* the rent of a cottage in the occupation of the same John — lxij*s.*

William Lovell holds a tenement and xlij acres of land there, and renders per ann. — xx*s.* viij*d.*

John Lovell holds xl acres of land with appurtenances there, and renders per ann. — xxij*s.* vj*d.*

Thomas Chastell holds a tenement and fifty acres of land with appurtenances, and renders per ann. — xxxj*s.* viij*d.*

John Somerton holds a cottage and two acres of land there, and renders per ann. — x*s.* j*d.*

John Loxston holds a tenement with xlvj acres of land there, and renders per ann. — xx*s.*

John Marten holds a tenement and xl acres of land there, and renders per ann. — xxij*s.* ij*d.*

The Free Chapel of Esthorrington to the said Guilde united and annexed.

. . . . holds the said Chapel together with the dwelling house of the same and a close and certain arable land adjacent, with its appurtenances, also the tithes as well great as small of Est Horrington aforesaid to the said Free Chapel appertaining or belonging, and renders per ann. — lx*s.*

Somerset Chantries.

Durcote.

Divers persons hold free certain lands and tenements there, and render per ann. — iij*s*. j*d*.

John Hill holds divers lands, tenements, meadow, feed, and pasture, and other hereditaments in Durcote aforesaid, and renders per ann. — xl*s*.

John Rose holds a tenement with its appurtenances there, and renders per ann. — x*s*.

. . . . holds a cottage there, and renders per ann. — ij*s*.

The City of Wells with land in Tolveston and Noriche.

John Uskavayte holds a burgage with its appurtenances in the city aforesaid, to the said Fraternity or Guilde appertaining, and renders per ann. — vij*s*.

William Crowche holds all the lands, tenements, and other hereditaments, with their appurtenances in Tolveston and Noryche to the said Guilde or Fraternity appertaining or belonging, and renders per ann. — xiiij*s*.

Lake in the County of Wilts.

Divers persons hold free divers lands and tenements there, and render per ann. — xxvij*s*. iiij*d*.

Divers persons there hold certain lands and tenements according to the custom there, and render per ann. — lxix*s*. viij*d*.

Alice Duke holds divers arable lands of the lord's demesne there, and renders per ann. — lxxiij*s*.

Michael Duke and others hold by indenture for the term of their lives the capital messuage there with all houses, edifices, lands, tenements, feed, pasture, and common, and all hereditaments, advantages, and profits whatsoever to the said capital messuage appertaining, (except and altogether is reserved to the Wardens of the Guilde or Fraternity aforesaid, and their successors the heriots of all the tenants there,) and render per annum with vj*s*. viij*d*. for a good and fat swan annually in the Feast of St. Lucy the Virgin, per ann.—lxvj*s*. viij*d*.

The heriots from all the tenants in Lake aforesaid to the said Guilde appertaining, one year with another—xij*s*.

Total of the said Guild, xxviij*li*. xiij*s*. x*d*.

Deduct in.—Rent resolute to the Bailiff of the borough of Wells for the said burgage in Wells aforesaid, per ann.—ij*s*.

Rent resolute to Bartholomew Fortescue, lord of Corsecombe for the said lands and tenements in Tolveston aforesaid, for the price of 1 lb. of cummin and 1 lb. of pepper, per ann.—ij*s*. iiij*d*.

Total—iiij*s*. iiij*d*.

And remains over, per annum—xxviij*li*. ix*s*. vj*d*. with xij*s*. for the heriots from all the tenants in Lake one year with another.

Land and possessions given as well to the use and observance of an annual Obit to be held in the parish church there, as to the use and maintenance of a Lamp and a Light in the same church perpetually burning.

John Bysse and others hold all the messuages, lands, tenements, meadow, feed, pasture and other hereditaments whatsoever within the manor of Corscombe aforesaid and Shepton

Somerset Chantries

Mallet in the county aforesaid, given and placed in feoffment to the use and maintenance aforesaid by Walter Mayow and Joan his wife, and render per ann. — xxs.

Thomas Downes renders from the issues and revenues of his lands and tenements there, per ann. — iiijs.

Geoffrey Upton renders from the issues and revenues of his lands and tenements there, once . . . . Rynon's, per ann. — vjs. viijd.

Total — xxxs. viijd.

Deduct in. — Rent resolute to Bartholomew Fortescue esquire, for free rent of the aforesaid messuages and other premises, per ann. — xs. iiijd.

And remains over, per annum. — xxs. iiijd.

Total of the Deanery of Cary aforesaid, per ann. — lxxxvijli. xiiijs. ijd.

Deduct in. — Reprises and rents resolute in divers modes as before particularly shown — xljs. viijd.

And remains over, per annum. — lxxxvli. xjs. xjd.

[There seems an error here in the total; also Doulting and Cranmore and Stoke Lane, are omtited.]

Deanery of Marston.

Pevill.

The Chantry of the Holy Trinity within the parish church there.

.... holds the dwelling house there with a garden, and renders per ann. — vjs. viijd.

Lionel Carter holds by indenture a burgage there with a garden and an orchard adjacent containing by estimation ij acres, and xliiij acres and a half of arable land there, and renders per ann. — xxxiijs. iiijd.

Thomas Pynne holds by indenture a tenement in Kingestone juxta Yevill with a garden and an orchard adjacent containing by estimation half an acre, and two closes of pasture containing xvj acres and xxvij acres of arable land, and renders per ann. — xxviijs.

John Pynne holds by indenture a cottage in Kingeston aforesaid with a garden and an orchard adjacent containing iij rods of land, and vij acres of arable land there, and renders per ann. — xijs.

Richard Hacker holds by indenture half a rofeles tenement there with an orchard containing an acre, and xvij acres and a half of arable land, and renders per ann. — xvjs.

The same holds two burgages lying in Quedamstrete with a garden to the same appertaining, and renders per ann. — xijd.

Somerset Chantries.

John Locke holds by indenture a burgage with a garden and iiij acres of arable land, and renders per ann. — vs. iiij$d$.

Thomas Erlyche holds a burgage with a garden and iij acres and a half of arable land, and renders per ann.—vj$s$.

Stephen Trent holds a burgage with a garden there, and renders per ann. — ix$s$. iiij$d$.

John Pytman holds a burgage with a garden, an acre of meadow, and xj acres of arable land, and renders per ann. — xij$s$.

John Whitby holds a garden in Southstrete, and renders per ann. — iiij$d$.

William Hayne holds by indenture a burgage with a garden, and a close of pasture containing ij acres and iiij acres of arable land, and renders per ann. — xij$s$.

John Dowrede holds viij acres of land and pasture lying in Swyncombe within the manor of Kingeston, and renders per ann.— xvj$d$.

William Woodhele holds a garden in Pytlane, and renders per ann. — viij$d$.

William Bere holds a burgage with a close of pasture containing iiij acres, and renders per ann. — viij$s$.

Isabella Welfare widow, holds a burgage or Inn, with certain curtilages, called the Bell, and renders per ann. — xxxiij$s$. iiij$d$.

Alexander Yonge holds two burgages there with appurtenances, and renders per ann. — viij$s$. viij$d$.

William Delegryse holds a cottage with a garden and vj acres of arable land, and renders per ann.— viij$s$.

Thomas Lye holds a cottage with a garden and iij acres of arable land, and renders per ann. — viij$s$.

Thomas Gromes holds a burgage with a garden there, and renders per ann. — xx*d*.

Jone Marshe (late William Foche) holds a burgage with a garden, and renders per ann. — iij*s*. iiij*d*.

John Hotkins (late John Wolfe) holds a burgage and a garden, and renders per ann. — iiij*s*.

Robert Grobyn (late John Parker) holds a cottage with xij acres of land and pasture, and renders per ann. — xij*s*.

Total — xj*li*. xj*s*.

Deduct in.—Rent resolute to the Lady the Queen for free rent of the premises, per ann. — iij*s*.

Rent resolute to William Caraunt, Kt., for free rent, per ann. — xvj*d*.

Rent resolute to the Rector of Yevill for free rent, per ann. — viij*d*.

Total — v*s*.

And remains over, per annum. — xj*li*. vj*s*.

The Chantry of the blessed Mary the virgin within the parish church there.

. . . . holds the dwelling house of the said Chantry, and renders per ann. — iij*s*.

Hugh Cogen holds a tenement, and a cottage with a garden there, and renders per ann. — x*s*. viij*d*.

The same holds a garden in Southstrete with a virgate of meadow and iij virgates of arable land, and renders per ann. — ij*s*. viij*d*.

Somerset Chantries.

William Hayne holds a burgage with a garden, and renders per ann. — vj*s*. viij*d*.

William Slape holds a tenement with a garden and iij acres and a half of arable land, and renders per ann. — xx*s*.

The same holds a barn and a garden in Quedam strete, and renders per ann. — v*s*.

Philip Cromell holds a burgage with a garden lying in Grope Lane, and renders per ann. — vj*s*.

John Parker holds a burgage in South strete with a garden and iij acres and a half of arable land, and renders per ann. — iij*s*.

John Hacker, junior, holds a toft burgage there lying in South strete, and renders per ann. — xx*d*.

Walter Parker holds a burgage with a garden, and renders per ann. — ix*s*. vj*d*.

Mathew Abrell holds a burgage with a garden, and renders per ann. — x*s*.

John Hacker, senior, holds a burgage with a garden, and renders per ann. — xiij*s*. iiij*d*.

Walter Hasarde holds a cottage with a garden and ij acres of arable land, and renders per ann. — vj*s*. viij*d*.

John Jenys holds a burgage and a stable, with a garden, and renders per ann. — viij*s*. viij*d*.

John Fysshcr holds a burgage with a curtilage there, and renders per ann. — viij*s*.

John Whytbye holds a burgage with a garden and orchard adjacent containing by estimation iij virgates of land, and renders per ann. — xvj*d*.

Somerset Chantries.

John Marchaunt holds at the will of the lord a garden, and renders per ann. — viij*d.*

Nicholas Donne holds a stable in Gropelane, and renders per ann. — iij*s.* iiij*d.*

James Donne holds a cottage with a garden and half an acre of arable land, and renders per ann. — iiij*s.*

James Spede holds two burgages and a cottage with two gardens there, and renders per ann. — xxv*s.*

Joan Walter, widow, holds a cottage with a garden there, and renders per ann. — viij*s.*

Alice Evererd, widow, holds by indenture an Inn or tenement called the Angell, with a close of pasture containing ij acres and two pieces of meadow with iij virgates of arable land, also a cottage with a garden and iiij acres and a half of arable land to the same appertaining, and renders per ann. — lxvj*s.* viij*d.*

William Whytenoll holds a cottage with a garden, and renders per ann. — v*s.*

John Wyatt holds a cottage with an orchard adjacent containing half an acre of land, and renders per ann. — iiij*s.*

John Styckelynche holds a burgage and a garden, and renders per ann. — v*s.*

Giles Hacker holds a burgage situate in the High Street there, by divers persons by deed given to the use of the Chantry aforesaid for the term of eighty years beginning at the Feast of St. Michael archangel in the eighth year of the reign of King Edward iiij, and renders per ann. — xiij*s.* iiij*d.*

Total — xij*li.* xj*s.* ij*d.*

Somerset Chantries.

Deduct in.—Rent resolute to the Earl of Arundell for free rent annually — vij*s*.

Money paid annually by the Burgesses of the town of Yevill aforesaid for free rent — iij*s*. iiij*d*.

Total — x*s*. iiij*d*.

And remains over, per annum. — xij*li*. x*d*.

The Chantry of the name of Jesus within the parish church there.

Thomas Kyle holds by indenture the dwelling house of the said Chantry, and renders per ann. — viij*s*.

John Edmonde holds a burgage in the High Street there with appurtenances, and renders per ann. — xvj*s*.

Andrew Vauston holds a burgage with appurtenances there, and renders per ann. — xviij*s*.

William Stone holds a burgage in Pytlane, and renders per ann. — xiij*s*. iiij*d*.

The same William Stone holds a tenement and a cottage in Kingeston with an orchard containing an acre, and one acre of meadow and xxiij acres and a half of arable land, and renders per ann. — xxij*s*.

William Hayne holds ij closes and ij gardens there, and renders per ann. — iiij*s*.

The Wardens of the church hold a burgage there called the Corner House, and render per ann. — xiij*s*. iiij*d*.

Bartholomew Sewer holds a burgage with appurtenances, and renders per ann. — xxvj*s*. viij*d*.

Thomas Keyle holds a stable with a garden, and renders per ann. — ij*s*.

Somerset Chantries.

Henry Father holds a stable with a garden, and renders per ann. — ij*s*.

The same holds a burgage with a garden, and renders per ann. — iiij*s*. vj*d*.

John Howell holds at the will of the lord a burgage there, and renders per ann. — x*s*.

Edith Thressher holds a cottage with a garden there, and renders per ann. — iiij*s*.

John Turnour holds a burgage with a garden there, and renders per ann. — vij*s*.

Robert Hale holds a burgage with a garden in Stoforde, and renders per ann. — vj*s*. viij*d*.

James Meade holds half a tenement rofeles there, with an acre of meadow and ij little closes containing an acre, and xiij acres of arable land, and renders per ann. — x*s*.

Total — viij*li*. vij*s*. vj*d*.

Deduct in.—Rent resolute to the Burgesses of Yevill aforesaid, for free rent, per ann. — vj*d*.

Rent resolute to William Caraunt, Kt., for free rent, per ann. — ij*s*.

Total — ij*s*. vj*d*.

And remains over, per annum. — viij*li*. v*s*.

The Chantry of the Holy Cross there.

. . . . holds the dwelling house there, and renders per ann. — v*s*.

William Croft holds a tenement or burgage in Estlambroke, and renders per ann. — xl*s*.

Somerset Chantries.

The same holds two cottages there, and renders per ann.— viij*s*.

Robert Banton holds a tenement there, and renders per ann — viij*s*.

Robert Stuckey holds a tenement there, and renders per ann. — viij*s*.

William Pyttarde holds a tenement there, and renders per ann. — iiij*s*.

Robert Craft holds a tenement there, and renders per ann. — v*s*.

John Harvye holds a tenement in Galhampton, and renders per ann. — xxv*s*.

Richard Brownyng holds a tenement there, and renders per ann. — xiij*s*.

Thomas Vele holds a tenement there, and renders per ann. — xiij*s*. iiij*d*.

John Symes *alias* Robertes holds a tenement there, and renders per ann. — x*s*.

Henry Gaylarde holds a tenement in Chilterne Domer, and renders per ann. — ix*s*.

William Stone holds a tenement in Yevill aforesaid, and renders per ann. — xix*s*.

William Mason holds a cottage there at the will of the lord, and renders per ann. — v*s*.

William Woodhill holds a garden there, and renders per ann. — vj*d*.

Nicholas Donne holds a garden there, and renders per ann. — x*d*.

Richard Hacker holds ij acres of arable land there, and renders per ann. — ij*s*.

Total — viij*li*. xv*s*. viij*d*.

Deduct in.—Rent resolute to . . . . Bonvyle for free rent, per ann. — iij*s*.

Rent resolute to the Canons of Wells for free rent, per ann. — iiij*d*.

Rent resolute to the Burgesses of Yevill aforesaid for free rent, per ann. — iij*s*.

Rent resolute to the Lady the Queen for the land in Yevill, per ann. — vj*d*.

Money paid annually to the Provost there for superintending the performance of the Will of the founder as appears by the foundation, — vj*s*. viij*d*.

Total — xiij*s*. vj*d*.

And remains over, per annum. — viij*li*. ij*s*. ij*d*.

The Chapel or Rectory of Pytney *alias* Marshe or Kyngton within the parish there.

. . . . holds all the tithes as well great as small there to the said Chapel or Rectory of Pytney appertaining, and renders, one year with another, — vj*li*.

Milbourne Porte.

The Fraternity of St. John Evangeliste there.

William Sampson holds a close of land there, and renders per ann. — ij*s*.

Somerset Chantries.

Annual rent given to the use and maintenance of a Light burning in the parish church there.

The Burgesses of the town there render annually from the issues and profits of the lands and tenements appertaining to the commonalty of the same town there as for the price of ij lbs. of wax, per ann. — xij*d*.

William Hannam and Richard Longe render annually from the issues, profits, and revenues of their lands and tenements there as for the price of one lb. of wax, per ann. — vj*d*.

Total — xviij*d*.

Est Coker.

The Chantry within the parish church there.

. . . . holds the dwelling house or capital messuage with an orchard containing by estimation five virgates of land, and renders per ann. — iiij*s*. iiij*d*.

Thomas Cockes holds a barn with a little piece of land there called the Barton and half an acre of meadow, and renders per ann. — viij*s*.

William Whipping holds a tenement called a rofeles tenement with one little close containing one acre, and one close containing two acres of pasture, and also iij virgates of meadow and xvj acres of arable land, and renders per ann. — x*s*.

The same William holds a close containing ij acres of pasture, and renders per ann. — vj*s*.

Somerset Chantries.

John Collyns holds a tenement, xxvj acres of land with a close containing ij acres of pasture, and vj acres and a half of meadow, and renders per ann. — xv*s*.

William Howlewaye holds a tenement in West Coker, containing xiij acres and a half of arable land with a close containing five acres of pasture and an acre of meadow, and renders per ann. — x*s*.

John Jyles holds a cottage containing iij acres and a half of arable, and five acres of meadow, and renders per ann. — vj*s*.

Reginald Harryson holds a cottage containing an acre of arable land and iij virgates of meadow, and renders per ann. — v*s*.

William Danyell holds a cottage with a little garden, and renders per ann. — v*s*.

Thomas Jilles holds an acre and iij virgates of arable land, and ij acres of meadow, and renders per ann. — vj*s*. viij*d*.

Giles Penny, gent., holds four acres of meadow, and renders per ann. — viij*s*.

Thomas Wylles holds a close of pasture containing iij acres, and renders per ann. — xvj*s*.

Nicholas Jylles holds a close of pasture containing vij acres, and renders per ann. — xij*s*.

Edward Williams holds a close of pasture containing iij acres, and renders per ann. — ij*s*.

Certain annual receipts from the land of the Lord Cobham in Marshewoodevale called Yearde, per ann. — xv*s*.

Annual rent received from the land of Mr. Moreton in Est Coker, per ann. — iij*s*. iiij*d*.

Annual rent received from the land of John Strange in Est Coker aforesaid, per ann. — v*s*.

Annual rent received from the land of Nicholas Traske, per ann. — xiiij*d*.

Total — vj*li*. xvij*s*. vj*d*.

North Cherpton.

Land and possessions given to the use and maintenance of a Light burning in the parish church there, called the fount Taper.

Richard Saunders holds a virgate of land there, and renders per ann. — vj*d*.

Corton.

Annual rent given to the use and maintenance of an Obit to be held annually in the parish church there.

The heir of Tristram Storke pays annually from the issues, profits, and revenues of his lands and tenements in Corton aforesaid in the occupation of William Sooge of Holwaye, per ann. — vj*s*. viij*d*.

Horsington.

The Free Chapel of South Cheryton within the parish there.

Elizabeth Fitz James of Temple Combe, widow, holds the chapel aforesaid with half an acre of land in which the same chapel is situate, with all houses, edifices, lands, tenements, meadows, feed and pasture, and all other profits and advantages whatsoever to the said Free Chapel appertaining or belonging, so to her leased to farm by indenture given under the seal of Roger Boydell, clerk, late incumbent, the fifth day of May in the first year of the reign of King Edward vj: To have and to hold to the aforesaid Elizabeth and her assigns from the feast of St. John Baptist then next following for the term of xx years from that time next following and to be fully completed. So that the aforesaid Roger Boydell and his assigns will support all charges ordinary and extraordinary to the said chapel, lands, and tenements, in whatsoever manner contingent or incumbent during the term aforesaid as in the said indenture is fully contained: Rendering therefor annually to the aforesaid Roger Boydell and his assigns at the four usual annual terms in equal portions — xxvj*s.* viij*d.*

Trent.

The Chapel within the parish church there.

John Shete, clerk, late incumbent there, holds the dwelling house of the same Chantry with a stable and garden there adjacent, and renders per ann. — ij*s.*

Somerset Chantries.

An annual rent given by the Provost and Scholars of the King's College in Oxford called Oryell College by license of King Henry vj, to the Rector of Trent aforesaid and the men of the same vill and their successors, to whom the said King gave his license to receive the said rent, for the maintenance of a chaplain there and for the Obit of John Francke, viz., for the salary of the said chaplain and the reparation of his dwelling house, and for the ornaments of the same chapel — vijli. vj$s$. viij$d$. And for the Obit of the same John Francke — xiij$s$. iiij$d$. In all per ann. — viijli.

Total — viijli. ij$s$.

Marston Magna.

Annual rent given to the use and maintenance of a priest celebrating there, called a Devotion priest, for a term of xrij years yet to come and next following.

Robert Kelwaye renders annually from the issues, profits, and revenues of his lands and tenements there during the term aforesaid. — vj$s$. viij$d$.

Total of the Deanery of Marston aforesaid, per ann. — lxiiijli. viij$s$. xd.

Deduct in. — Reprises and rents resolute in divers modes as before particulary shown. — xxxj$s$. iiij$d$.

And remains over, per annum. — lxijli. xvij$s$. vj$d$.

Deanery of Bathe.

The parish of St. Michael next the bathe within the City of Bath.

Annual rents given to the use and maintenance of a Light burning in the parish church there.

The Wardens of the parish church aforesaid render annually from the issues and revenues of a tenement lying in the street there called Walcote strete given to the said church for the fabric and reparations of the same. — vj*d.*

The parish of St. Mary within the gate of Bathe aforesaid.

Land and possessions given to the use and maintenance of divers Obits to be held within the parish church there.

Divers persons there hold certain land, tenements, burgages and cottages there, and render per ann. — iiij*li.* ij*d.*

The parish of St. Michael without the North gate of Bath aforesaid.

Land and possessions given to the use and maintenance of divers Obits to be held in the parish church there.

Divers persons there hold certain land, tenements, burgages and cottages there, and render per ann. — xljs. iijd.

The parish of Stalles within the City of Bath.

Annual rents given to the use and maintenance of an Obit and an Annivsersary to be held in the parish church there annually.

John Handelay renders annually from the issues and revenues of a tenement there situate in the street called Westgate strete in the tenure of John himself. — iiijs.

Thomas Sherston renders annually from the issues and revenues of a tenement there in the tenure of Thomas himself. —ijs. xd.

The Mayor and the Chamber of the said city render annually from the issues and revenues of lands and possessions there belonging to the said Mayor and Chamber of the said city. — xls.

The same Mayor and Commonalty of the said city render annually from the issues and revenues of a tenement there for the Obit of William Swayne, xij½d.

The same render annually from the issues and revenues of a shop there for the Obit of John Dudmerton. — ijs.

Annual rent given by the last will of Benedict Stoke for four masses there annually to be celebrated. — iiijd.

Total — ls. ij½d.

Annual rents given to the use and maintenance of a Lamp and a Light burning in the parish church aforesaid.

The aforesaid Mayor and Commonalty of the city aforesaid, render annually from the issues and revenues of their land and possessions there. — ijs.

James Huggans renders annually from the issues and revenues of land and a tenement there in the occupation of the same James. — ijs.

Evan Taylor renders annually from the issues and revenues of a tenement there in the occupation of the said Evan. — xxd.

Annual rent given by the last Will of Benedict Stoke as for the price of one lb. of wax. — vjd.

Total — vjs. ijd.

The parish of St. James within the City of Bath aforesaid.

Annual rents given to the use and maintenance of an Obit and an Annibersary to be held in the parish church there.

. . . . renders annually from the issues and revenues of land and a tenement in Bath in the occupation of . . . . — iiis. iiijd.

. . . . . . renders annually from the issues and revenues of certain land and a tenement there in the occupation of . . . . . . the gift and grant of Ralph Dyer. — iijd.

Total — iijs. vijd.

Fresheforde.

Land and possessions given to the use and maintenance of a Light burning in the parish church there.

The Wardens of the parish church aforesaid hold a piece of land there containing a virgate of land lying in Churche mede, and render per ann. — vj*d*.

Weston juxta Bath.

Land and possessions given to the use and maintenance of an Obit to be held within the parish church there.

The Wardens of the parish church aforesaid hold a tenement with a garden there, called the Churche house, and render per ann. — ij*s*.

Bathforde.

The Chapel situate in the common street of Shokerwyke within the parish there.

Robert Tyler holds the chapel aforesaid, in which oblations once were made, and renders per ann. — iij*s*. iiij*d*.

Newton Seintlowe.

Land and possessions given to the use and maintenance of a Lamp and a Light burning in the parish church there.

John Grevys, clerk, rector of the parish church there, holds iiij acres of arable land lying in the north field there, and renders per ann. — ijs. viijd.

The same holds iij acres of arable land lying in the south field there, and renders per ann. — xvjd.

Total — iiijs.

Batheston.

The Chapel situate in Hortley within the parish there.

William Lewys holds the chapel aforesaid in which an Armite once lived, and renders per ann. — ijs. viijd.

Total for the Deanery of Bathe aforesaid, per annum. — ixli. xiiijs. iiij½d.

The City of Wells With the Cathedral Church of St. Andrew there.

The parish of St. Cuthbert within the city of Wells.

The Chantry within the parish church there called Tanner's Chauntrye.

Ready money annually received and levied from the issues, profits, and revenues of lands and tenements appertaining or belonging to the Masters and Commonalty of the city of Wells aforesaid, by the hands of the Receiver of the lands aforesaid to be paid, per ann. — lxvjs. viijd.

The Service of two chaplains or stipendiary priests in the parish church aforesaid, celebrating during the good pleasure of the Masters and Commonalty of the said City, (as is presented).

Money annually received and levied from the issues, profits and revenues of lands and tenements appertaining or belonging to the said Masters and Commonalty of the aforesaid city, by the hands of the Receiver of their lands and tenements to be paid—viz.,—to each chaplain in the same service for the time being celebrating, per ann. — cxiijs. iiijd.;—in all,—xjli. vjs. viijd.

Annual rents given to the use and maintenance of divers Obits within the parish church aforesaid to be annually held.

The aforesaid Masters and Commonalty of the city aforesaid render annually from the issues and revenues of their lands and tenements there, per ann. — iiij*li*.

The Vicar of the parish church aforesaid for the time being renders annually from the issues and revenues of a tenement in the street called Chamberleyns strete within the city aforesaid, to the said Vicar appertaining, per ann. — xvj*d*.

Total —iiij*li*. xvj*d*.

The Service or stipend of a priest celebrating in the chapel situate within the Almeshouse of Wells in the parish aforesaid.

Money annually received and levied from the issues, profits and revenues of the lands and possessions appertaining or belonging to the Vicars of the Cathedral Church of St. Andrew in Wells aforesaid, per ann. —iiij*li*. xiij*s*. iiij*d*.

Prebendary of Dynder.

Land and possessions given as well to the use and maintenance of an Obit to be held annually in the parish church there, as to the use and maintenance of a Light burning in the same church.

Joan Thomas, widow, holds a tenement called Langhowse with ij acres of arable land and a virgate of meadow there, per ann. — ij*s*. viij*d*.

The Cathedral of St. Andrew in Wells.

The College or New Hall in the Mount Roye within the city of Wells ordained and erected for the maintenance of xbiij Cantarists celebrating within the Cathedral church aforesaid.

Rent of the dwelling house of the College aforesaid with a garden to the same adjacent, per ann. — xxvjs. viijd.

Rent of a free tenement there, per ann. — iiijd.

Rent of all the burgages or tenements with their appurtenances in the city of Wells aforesaid to the said College appertaining, let at will, per ann. — viijli. ijs. viijd.

Rent of an Inn called the George in the city of Wells aforesaid and all the burgages, messuages and tenements with gardens or orchards adjacent as well within the same city as without to the said College appertaining, leased to divers persons by indenture, per ann. — cxvs.

Rent of all tenements, closes, meadows, feed and pasture as well within the said city as without to the said College appertaining, leased to divers persons by indenture, per ann. — lxixs.

Annual rents to be gathered and received from the Communar of the Cathedral church aforesaid the gift of the executor of Nicholas Bubwyth sometime Bishop of Bath and Wells, as an annual remembrance (*in recompensationem*) to the said College, per ann. — xxvjs.

Annual rents to be received from the same Communar the gift of the said executor for the common table of the Fellows of the said college living there, (*ad communem mensam sociorum dicti Collegii ibidem discumbentium*), per ann. — liijs. iiijd.

Somerset Chantries.

Annual rent to be received from the same Communar the gift of John Gunthorpe, clerk, late Dean of Wells aforesaid, issuing from the manor of Alverton, per ann. — xs.

Annual rent to be gathered and levied from the issues and revenues appertaining to the house of St. John Baptist in Wells for quit rent, per ann. — xvj*d*. (*Cancelled.*)

Total — xxiij*li*. iij*s*.

Deduct in.—Rent resolute to the Bailiff of St. John Baptist in Wells for certain land called Doddysdayne. — ij*s*. viij*d*.

Rent resolute annually to the Bailiff of the Bishop of Wells as rent for iiij tenements situate in Sadler St. — xiij*s*. ij*d*.

Rent resolute to the Succentor of the Cathedral church of Wells for rent of a tenement at the Poole, per ann. — iij*s*. ij*d*.

Rent resolute annually to the Bailiff of Mynchynborough. — iiij*d*.

Rent resolute annually to the Wardens of the parish church of St. Cuthbert in Wells for the said Inn called the George. — viij*s*.

Money paid annually to the Master of the Choristers of the Cathedral church of Wells towards the maintenance of the aforesaid choristers. — xvj*s*.

Money paid annually to the Escheator of the aforesaid Cathedral church. — xxx*s*.

Total — lxxiij*s*. iiij*d*.

And remains over, per annum. — xix*li*. ix*s*. viij*d*.

Somerset Chantries.

Two Chantries there founded by Robert Burnell and Walter Hasilshewe sometime Bishops of Bath and Wells.

Ready money from the Dean and Chapter of the Cathedral Church of Wells aforesaid annually to be paid, from the issues, profits, and revenues of the rectory of Burncham to the said Dean and Chapter appropriate, viz., to each chaplain incumbent in the same Chantry five marcs, per ann. — vj*li*. xiij*s*. iiij*d*.

Two Chantries there founded by Henry Husey sometime Dean of the said Cathedral.

Ready money from the said Dean and Chapter of the same Cathedral annually to be paid, from the issues, profits, and revenues of their manor of North Cory and Knappe, viz., to each chaplain in the same Chantry incumbent five marcs, per ann. — vj*li*. xiij*s*. iiij*d*.

Two Chantries there founded by William Wellington.

Ready money from the aforesaid Dean and Chapter of the Cathedral aforesaid annually to be paid, from the issues, profits, and revenues of their manor of North Cory aforesaid, viz., to each chaplain in the same Chantry incumbent five marcs, per ann. — vj*li*. xiij*s*. iiij*d*.

Two Chantries there founded by Robert Corymailes and John Drokensford.

Ready money from the said Dean and Chapter annually to be paid, from the issues, profits, and revenues of their manor of North Cory above said, viz., to each chaplain there incumbent five marcs, per ann. — vj*li*. xiij*s*. iiij*d*.

A Chantry founded there by John Godlee.

Ready money from the aforesaid Dean and Chapter annually to be paid, from the issues, profits, and revenues above said of their Manor of North Cory, per ann. — lxvj*s*. viij*d*.

A Chantry there founded by Walter Hull.

Ready money annually gathered and levied from the issues, profits, fruits, and revenues of the lands and possessions appertaining or belonging to the aforesaid Dean and Chapter by them to be paid, per ann. — iiij*li*.

A Chantry there founded by Ralph Ergeham.

Ready money from the aforesaid Dean and Chapter annually to be paid, from the issues and fruits of the rectory of Poculchurche to the same Dean and Chapter appropriate, per ann. — iiij*li*.

Four Chantries there founded by Nicholas Bubwith.

Ready money from the said Dean and Chapter annually to be paid, as well from the issues, fruits, and revenues of the rectories of Newton and Buckelande, to the same Dean and Chapter appropriate, as from the issues, profits, and revenues of their manor of Byckenaller, viz., to each chaplain incumbent in the same Chantry—cvj*s*. viij*d*. per ann. as by the foundation. — xxj*li*. vj*s*. viij*d*.

Somerset Chantries.

One other Chantry founded there.

Ready money from the said Dean and Chapter annually to be rendered as part of a certain pension of ten pounds to the same Dean and Chapter owed and annually paid by the Archdeacon of Wells aforesaid, per ann. — lxvj*s*. viij*d*.

A Chantry founded there belonging to the Colation of the Precentor of the same Church.

Ready money annually paid by the Precentor of the Cathedral Church aforesaid as from the issues and fruits belonging to his office, per ann. — iiij*li*.

The Chantry there called Saint Martyn's Chauntrie.

Ready money lately coming from the issues of the Hospital or Priory of St. John in Wells lately dissolved, and now to be paid from the issues and revenues of the Lord the King from his Court of Augmentation, by virtue of a certain decree exemplified under the seal of the same Court, per ann. — iiij*li*.

The Chantry there founded by John Stortewatte called Stortewattes Chauntrie.

Ready money from the aforesaid Dean and Chapter of the aforesaid Cathedral Church of Wells, as part of a certain pension of x*li*. to the said Dean and Chapter owed and annually paid from the issues of the rectory of Wrexall, per ann. — vj*li*. xiij*s*. iiij*d*.

Somerset Chantries.

Money paid and expended annually for bread, wine, and wax, in divers Chantries aforesaid.

The aforesaid Dean and Chapter are held to pay annually for bread, wine, and wax, expended by the chaplains celebrating divine service in divers Chantries aforesaid as shown by the foundations of the same, viz., in the Chantry called Burnelles and Hasilshewe — iiijs.; Husyes — iijs. viijd.; Wellingtons — iiijs.; Godlees — xijs.; Ergehams — iijs. viijd.; Bubwithes — vijs. and Stortewattes — xvijs., with the maintenance of a Lamp burning there; amounting in all to, per ann. — lijs. iiijd.

Annual rents given to the use and maintenance of divers Obits and Anniversaries to be held in the same church annually.

The aforesaid Dean and Chapter pay annually from the issues, profits, revenues, and fruits of their lands and possessions by the hand of the Communar or Receiver of the same Cathedral Church, annually to be paid for the maintenance of divers Obits or Anniversaries within the church aforesaid annually to be held, viz., for the Obit or Anniversary of Helias Fellarde — vs.; Richard Bamfeld — xs.; William Cokam — xs.; John Axbridge — xs.; Robert Burnell — xxs.; Nicholas Selbrone — xs.; Henry Bathe — vjs. viijd.; Henry Bratton — xvs.; Nicholas Bubwith — lijs. iiijd.; Bishop Joceline — xiijs. iiijd.; John Roper — vjs. viijd.; William Button, bishop — xvjs. viijd.; Gilbert Sarum — xiijs. iiijd.; Walter Hasylshewe, bishop — xxs.; Thomas Bockinge — vjs. viijd.; Walter Hull — xs.; Geoffrey Ferror — vjs. viijd.; Walter Compton — xvs.; Adam Gyshe — vjs.; Thomas Bekington — lijs. iiijd.; William Wythamstede — vjs. viijd.; John de Combe — xs.; Mabelle Bonche — vs.; John Whatley — vijs.;

Somerset Chantries.

Stephen Pimpell — xiijs. iiijd.; Ralph Precos — vjs. viijd.; John Godley, dean — xxs.; Roger Crooke — vjs. viijd.; Henry Bawdyshe — xiijs. iiijd.; Henry Husye, dean — xxs.; Stephen Chichester — vjs. viijd.; Lucy Lounders — vs.; John Martell — vs.; Hugh Romynall — xvs., William Button, bishop — xxxiijs. iiijd.; Walter London, dean — vs.; Richard 1st, King — xxs.; William Wellington — xxs.; Edward iiij, King — xxxiijs. iiijd.; Ralph Ergam, bishop — xiijs. iiijd.; Isaia Martocke — vs.; John Surraye — vjs.; Richard de la bere — vjs. viijd.; Christine Barber — vs.; John Blackedon — vjs. viijd.; Robert de Lytleton — xvs.; Walter "Camerarii" — iijs.; Richard Erlye — vjs. viijd.; John Nabbe and Alice Nabbe — xvs.; John Herforde — vjs. viijd.; William Cudworth — vs.; John Gunthorpe — xxs.; John Hoo — viijs.; Robert Netilton — vjs. viijd.; John Camfeld — vjs. viijd.; Robert Bugeley — vjs. viijd.; Lucy Mambre — vs.; Richard Cobham — vjs. viijd.; Ralph de Salop, bishop — liijs. iiijd.; John de la Pole — vjs. viijd.; William Odcombe — vjs. viijd.; David de Wellington — vjs. viijd.; John Bycknell and Richard Swane — xxs.; John Button — xxs.; Mathew de Stratton — xxs.; Henry London — xs.; Lucy Mellysbury — iijs. iiijd.; Thomas Burton, bishop — xvjs. vjd.; Roger Parsones — xs.; William Archideacon — vs.; Richard Button — xs.; John Huberd — viijs.; Peter de Chester — vs.; Gilbert Byham — vjs. viijd.; John Grynfelde — xiijs. iiijd.; Walter Quintyne — xiijs. iiijd.; and Richard Teffoner — xiijs. iiijd.; amounting in all to, per ann. — xlviijli. xvjd.

Somerset Chantries.

Total of the City of Wells aforesaid with the Cathedral Church there, per ann. — clxxiiij*li.* xiiij*s.*

Deduct in.—Reprises and rents resolute in divers modes as before particularly shown — lxxiij*s.* iiij*d.*

And remains over, per annum. — clxxj*li.* viij*d.*

The total of the annual value of all the lands, hereditaments, and possessions whatsoever aforesaid, in the county aforesaid — DCCCCLXXVJ*li.* VIJ*s.* IIIJ½*d.*

Deduct in.—**Reprises and rents resolute** in divers modes as before particularly shown — XLIIIJ*li.* IX*s.* ½*d.*

And remains over, per annum — DCCCCXXXJ*li.* XVIIJ*s.* IIIJ*d.*, beyond v*s.* for perquisites of Court one year with another appertaining to the Chantry of Nettlecombe in the Deanery of Dunster aforesaid.

Examined by William Moryce, particular **Surveyor** for the Lord the King in the County of Somerset.

Index.

Index.

A.

Abbas Combe. Light, 144.
Abbot's Isle. Light, 16, 185.
Abbote, John.—Wimborne, 294.
Abdere. Chapel, 146.
Abrell, Math.—Yeovil, 317.
Abyam, W.—Bath, 148.
Adam, John.—Taunton, 198.
Adrian. Bp. Bath and Wells, 132.
Ager, John.—Wedmore, 253.
Ailston Sutton. Chapel, 78, 261. Incumbent pensioned, xix.
Aishe, W. Crukerne, 176.
Aldington.—Dorset, 166.
Alen, W.—Bridgwater, 232.
Alforde, J.—Wotton, 121, 303.
Algar, J.—Wedmore, 251, 252, 253.
Aller. St. Mary's Chantry, 105, 106, 290. Incumbent pensioned, xix.
—— Light, 106, 290.
—— Curate, 106.
—— Parsonage, 106.
—— Communicants, 106.
—— Bere manor in, 290.
Allerford. R. Horne of, 218.
Alms. Porlock, 49.
—— Greynton, 63.
—— Wedmore, 71.
—— Shepton Mallet, 134.
—— Trent, 146.
—— Wells, 163.
Almsford. Stipendiary, 121.
Almshouse. Taunton, 20, 24.
—— Glastonbury, 67.

Almshouse. Croscombe, 136, 137.
—— Yeovil, 141.
—— Wells, 154, 155, 334.
—— Bedminster, 272.
Alrington. Lord of, 257.
Alroge, Dr. Parson of Stokegurcy, 53.
Alston, T.—Chard, 173.
Altar Cloths, 3.
Amysbury, T.—Wynford, 86, 268.
Anniversaries. Ilminster, 2.
—— Porlock, 49.
—— In Wells Cath: 162.
—— Crukerne, 180.
—— Gotehurst, 225.
—— Stokegurcy, 226.
—— Bridgwater, 237.
—— Shepton Mallet, 309.
—— Stalls, Bath, 329.
—— St. James', Bath, 330.
Andersey, J. Inc: Newton Placey, 58. Pensioned, xxi.
Androse, J.—North Curry, 205.
Antill, Geo. Rent paid to, 294.
Antony, T.—Yatton, 270.
Archdeacon, W. Obit, 341.
Armstrong, N. Curate, Bradway, 12.
Arter, Dr.—Dunster, 220.
Arther, P.—Taunton, 193.
Arundell, Earl of.—Yeovil, 308, 319.
Arundell, G.—Combe Flory, 211.
Arundell, G.—Bridgwater, 232.
Arundell, J.—Taunton, 191.
Arundell, J.—Honeycote, 218.
Arundell, J.—Treryse, 224.
Arundell, Sir T. The King's Surveyor, 86.

Index.

Ashbrittle. Fraternity, 37, 213.
―― Light and Lamp, 37.
Ashton, Long. Meryat's Chapel, 93, 275.
―― Choke's Chantry, 93, 274. Incumbent pensioned, xix.
―― Obits there, 94, 276.
―― Lights, 94, 276.
―― Communicants, 94.
―― Vicarage, 94.
―― Land in, 272.
―― Church-house, 276.
Ashwick. Shepton Guild, land in, 308.
Athelney. Land in Combflory, 35.
―― Rent to the King, 232.
Atherston. Ilminster Stipends, 166.
Atkyns. J.—Chard, 174, 175.
Atwaye, L.—Milverton, 215.
Audeley, Lord de. — Wollavington, 244, 245, 246.
Augmentation, Court of, 17, 61, 62, 72, 161, 187, 211, 244, 245, 246, 258, 339.
Austen, R. Vicar, N. Curry, 27.
Avery, E.—Yatton, 270.
Axbridge. Deanery, 69, 250, 264.
―――― Obit, 81, 264.
―――― Steward of, 81.
―――― Land in, 75, 229, 259.
Axbridge, J. Obit, 340.
Ayland, R. Inc: Croscombe Guild, 136. Pensioned, xx, xxiii.

B.

Babbe, J.—Nth Petherton, 239.
Babcary.—Fodington Chapel, 123, 304.
Baber, J.—Long Ashton, 274.
Backwell. Obits, 87, 268.
Bageworth. Stipendiary, 79; Obits, 79, 262.
Bagge, J. Obit, 283.
Bagwell, J.—Chard, 173.
Baker, B.—Crukerne, 176.
Baker, J.—Wellington, 206.
Baker, R.—Abbot's Isle, 185.
Baker, T.—Crukerne, 176, 178.
Balche, G.—Ilminster, 170.
Balche, J.—Ilminster, 170.
Baldwyn, J.—Nth. Petherton, 241.

Bale, W.—Nth. Curry, 205.
Balhed, J.—Wincanton, 128, 306.
Baltesborough. Light, 65.
Bamfield, R. Obit, 340.
Banckes, H. Inc: Wellington's Chantry, 158.
―― La Mountroy. Pensioned, xxi.
Banton, R.—Yeovil, 321.
Banwell. Fraternity, 73, 258. Incumbent pensioned, xix. St. George's Chapel, 74, 259. Communicants, 74. Vicarage, 74.
Banwell, T.—Lympsham, 76.
Barber, C. Obit, 341.
Barber, W.—Marston Magna, 147.
Barfote, J.—Crikett, 168.
Barfote, J.—Ilminster, 170.
Bargen, R.—Taunton, 201.
Barkeley.—Gloucestershire, 272.
Barnes, J.—Yatton, 270.
Barnes, R.—East Chaledon, 122.
Baron, R.—Nth. Cadbury, 130.
Barons, A.—Bratton, 122.
Barons, P.—Wimborne, 294.
Barrow Farm. Long Ashton Chantry, 274.
Bartelatt, A.—Chard, 173.
Bartelott . . . .—Dunster, 220.
Bartlet, T.—Taunton, 196.
Barwick. Guild lands in, 308.
Basinge, R. Rector, Nunney, 101.
Batcombe. Fraternity, 128.
Bath, Earl of.—Hunspill, 275.
Bath and Wells. Bp., 72. Lord of Wellington, 168. Lord of Chard, 174.
Bath and Wells. Adrian, Bp. of, 307.
Bath. Deanery, 148, 328, 332.
Bath. Magdalen Hospital, 96, 279, 330.
―― St. John's Hosp., 148. St. James, 150, 330. St. Mary, within, 149, 328. St. Michael's, within, 148, 328. St. Michael's, without, 149, 329. Stalls, 149, 150, 329, 330.
Bathe, H. Obit, 340.
Batheaston. Hortley Chapel, 151, 332. St. Katherine's, 152.
Bathford, 151, 331.
Batte, S.—Nth. Petherton, 239.
Batte, T.—Shaston, 305.
Battyn, J. Inc: Ilminster, 3, 170. Pensioned, xx.
Batyn, A.—Nth. Curry, 205.

Bawdrip. Parsonage, 64. Communicants, 64. Ford Chapel, 64, 247.
Bawdyshe, H. Obit, 341.
Bawne, R.—Camerton, 96, 279.
Baylie, W. Incumbent pensioned, xxi, xxii.
Bayly, J. Inc : Dunster, 43.
Bayly, J.—Chard, 174, 175.
Bayly, J.—Crukerne, 179.
Bayly, J.—Wedmore, 252, 253.
Bayly, R.—Stipendiary, Pitminster, 31.
Bayly, W.—Frome, 285.
Baynoff, N.—Chard, 175.
Becke, W.—Curry Rivell, 11, 12.
Bedman, R.—Taunton, 201.
Bedminster. Deanery, 83, 265, 277. Hospital, 90, 272. Knolle Chapel, 91, 273. Incumbent pensioned, xx. St. Peter's, 92, 273. Chapel in Chyard, 92. Light, 92, 273. Parsonage, 92. Communicants, 92.
Beer Crocombe, 17, 187.
Bekington, T. Obit, 340.
Belde, J.—Martock, 294.
Bellamy, J.—Taunton, 197.
Bells. 3, 6, 14, 18, 34, 35, 38, 44, 47, 58, 61, 66, 67, 69, 74, 84, 90, 91, 92, 98, 101, 105, 116, 142, 145, xvii.
Bempston. Rent in, 253.
Bene, W.—Yatton, 270.
Benet, J. Inc : Heron's Chantry, 115.
Benet, J.—Crukerne, 177.
Benet, J.—Newton Placey, 301.
Benet, Ralph.—Bridgwater, 230.
Benet, Robt.—Bridgwater, 230.
Benett, J.—Nth. Petherton, 241.
Bentley, J.—Wollavington, 244, 245, 246.
Bercombe, H.—Taunton, 204.
Berde, Alex.—Crukerne, 177, 179.
Bere. In Aller, 106, 290.
Bere, Richd. de la. Obit, 341.
Bere, W.—Yeovil, 315.
Berkley. Light and Obit, 99, 100, 284.
Besye, A.—Tellisford, 95, 278.
Bevyn, J.—Crukerne, 8.
Bevyn, J.—Meriet, 180.
Bevyn, W.—Ilton, 13.
Beymaunt, H.—Lydeard St. Laurence, 32.
Bickam, T. Vicar, Pitminster, 31.
Bickcham, R.—Cannington, 227.

Bickenell. Land in, 299.
Bicknaller. Light, 45. Manor, 160, 338.
Biggegood, R.—Nth. Petherton, 240.
Billinghaye, J.—Crickett, 168.
Birge, W.—Nth. Petherton, 241.
Bishop's Lydeard. *See* Lydeard Epi.
Bishop's Chantry. St. Nicholas, Taunton, 191.
Bisport. St. Peter's Chapel, 92.
Blake, A.—Wedmore, 252.
Blake, W.—Halse, 32, 252.
Blackedon, J. Obit, 341.
Blackford. Free Chapel, 70, 254. Incumbent pensioned, xix.
Blagdon. Light, 78, 261.
Blaunchflower, T.—Kingston, 30.
Bledon. Stipendiary, 78.
Blewet, Sir Roger.—Wellington, 28.
Blewet, Roger.—Nth. Petherton, 242.
Blewett, Robt.—Chard, 173.
Bocher, T.—Ailston, Sutton, 78, 261.
Bockinge, T. Obit, 340.
Bolston, T.—Stower Eastover, 237.
Bonche, M. Obit, 340.
Bonde, J.—Bridgwater, 230.
Bonnche, T.—Sth. Brent, 75.
Bonvyle. Rent in Yeovil, 322.
Bonvyle, G.—Curry Rivel, 12.
Bonvyle, J.—Ilminster, 170.
Boode, J.—Aldington, Dorset, 166.
Boole, J.—Cheddar, 258.
Borforde, R.—Taunton, 200.
Borge, J.—Dunster, 220.
Borough. St. Michael's Chapel, 226.
Borowe, J.—Martock, 111, 296.
Boston, T.—Stower Easton, Dorset, 57.
Boucher, R.—Taunton, 195.
Bowden, J.—Kewstoke, 259.
Bowe, A.—Wells, 257.
Bowring, J.—Trull, 192.
Boydell, R. Inc : Sth. Cheryton, 145, 326. Pensioned, xx.
Boyer, R.—Taunton, 190.
Boyes, J.—Bridgwater, 233.
Boyton, L.—Taunton, 194.
Bradford. Chantry, 33, 210. Incumbent pensioned, xix. Vicarage, 33. Communicants, 33.
Bradley, Priory. Gift to Frome, 104, 287.

Index

Bradley, J. Inc : Knolle, Bedminster, 91. Pensioned, xx.
Bradley, West. Light, 124.
Bradmer, J. Yatton, 270.
Bradshawe, G.—Thornfalcon, 31, 209
Bradway. Chapel, 12.
Bragge, N.—Dowlishwake, 168.
Branchflower, T.—Kingston, 208.
Bratton. Light, 122.
Bratton, H. Obit, 340.
Brattons. Of Selworthy, 217.
Brayne, J.—Crukerne, 178.
Bread. For Chantries in the Cathedral, 162, 340.
Brekempe, E.—Bickenell, 299.
Brent, East. Stipendiary, 74.
Brent, South. Obits, 75, 259. Bequest to, 76.
Brent, J.—Westbury, 262.
Brent, R.—Moorlinch, 64, 247.
Brewer, J.—Chard, 172.
Brewer, J.—Taunton, 198.
Brewer, R. Curate, Curry Mallet, 14.
Bridge, J. E. Quantoxhead, 51.
Bridge, J.—Greynton, 63.
Bridgwater, Earl of. Founds Chantry in Sth. Petherton, 9, 182. Lord of Chelington, 169. Lord of Withycombe, 222.
Bridgwater. Deanery, 51, 225, 242.
Bridgwater. St. Mary's, 56, 232. Incumbent pensioned, xix.
——— St. George's, 56, 230. Incumbent pensioned, xix.
——— Trinity, 57, 234. Incumbent pensioned, xix.
——— Light and Obit, 57, 237.
——— Grammar School, 57.
——— Communicants, 57.
——— Parsonage, 57.
——— Land in, 229.
——— Mayor, 234, 237.
Bristol. 4, 84, 90, 265, 272.
Brodmer, J.—Yatton, 270.
Brok, K. Parson of Porlock, 50.
Broke, Sir Geo. See Cobham, Lord.
Broke, J.—Shepton Mallet, 309.
Broke, J. Inc : Husey's Chantry, 158.
——— La Mountroy. Pensioned, xxi.
Broke, M. Inc : Sth. Petherton, 9. Pensioned, xxii.

Broke, T.—Wedmore, 71, 256.
Bromfield. Light, 53.
Brompton Ralph, Lamp, 46.
Brompton Regis. Fraternity, 40.
Bromwiche, J.—Westbury, 262.
Brouscombe, A.—Taunton, 202.
Browne, N.—Taunton, 200.
Browne, N.—Dunster, 220.
Browne, R. Clerk, Taunton, 201.
Browne, R.—Netherstowey, 27.
Browne, T. Inc : Taunton, 23.
Browne, W.—Crukerne, 179.
Brownyng, J.—Wedmore, 251.
Brownyng, R.—Yeovil, 321.
Brownyng, T.—Churchill, 256.
Brushford. Light, 46, 224.
Bruton. Pension from, 28. School, 131.
Bryan. Bequest by, 76.
Bryce, R. Inc : Compton Pauncefoot, 126. Pensioned, xx.
Bubwith, Bp. Four Chantries of, 160, 162, 335, 338, 340.
——— Incumbents pensioned, xxii.
Bucher, A.—Taunton, 190.
Bucke, W.—Cannington, 228.
Buckthort, J.—Taunton, 189.
Buckland Priory.—Durston, 41, 59, 217.
Buckland, St. Mary. Rents in, 160, 215.
Buckland, West. Stipendiary 29, 207. Pensioned, xxiii.
Budde, J.—Wellington, 205.
Budde, M.—Wellington, 206.
Budde, R.—Nth. Petherton, 241.
Budleigh. Obit, 65, 248.
Bugley, R. Inc : of Chantry, Wells, 157.
Bugeley, R. Obit, 341.
Bulbecke, J.—Clevedon, 83, 265.
Bull, H. Inc : St. Andrew's, Taunton, 21. Pensioned, xxi.
Buller, T. Rent in Bickenell, 301.
Bulpan, J.—Nth. Petherton, 241.
Bulston. Hundred of, 186.
Bulting, J.—Wedmore, 251.
Buncombe, J. Trull, 192.
Burge, W. Inc : Bubwith's Chantry, 160.
——— La Mountroy, pensioned, xxii.
Burland, J.—Cannington, 228.
Burley, G. Inc : Frome, 102. Pensioned, xx.

Burman, W. Vicar, Doulting, 120.
Burne, R.—Bridgwater, 232.
Burnell, R.—Chantry, 157, 162, 337, 340.
Burnet, R.—Sth. Petherton, 181.
Burnham. Old Chapel, 80, 263.
———— Lights, 81.
———— Fraternity, 80.
———— Rectory, 337.
Burrett, R.—Walketon, 87, 268.
Burton. Chapel, in East Coker 142.
Burton, J.—South Brent, 76.
Burton, T. Bp. Obit, 341.
Bustell, J.—Churchill, 256.
Butleigh. Obit and Light, 65, 248.
Buttal, G. Inc : Stortwatte's Chantry, 162.
———— La Mountroy. Pensioned, xxii.
Button, J. Obit, 341.
Button, R. Obit, 341.
Button, W. Bp. Obit, 341.
Bybbyll, N.—Sth. Brent, 75.
Bycknell, J.—Obit, 341.
Bydforde, W.—Cannington, 228.
Bydgood, T.—Bridgwater, 236.
Byham, G. Obit, 341.
Byrde, J.—Crukerne, 7, 178.
Byrrye, W.—Wellington, 206.
Byshopes, J.—Ashbrittle, 37.
Bysse, J.—Croscombe, 312.
Bysshop, A.—Bridgwater, 230, 231, 237.

C.

Cadbery, A.—Frome, 285.
Cadbury, North. Galhampton in, 121, 304.
———— Stipendiary, 129, 306.
———— Lights, 130, 307.
———— College, 130. Incumbents pensioned, xix.
———— Earl of Huntingdon, Lord of 130.
———— Communicants, 130.
———— Parsonage, 130, 131.
Caine, J.—Nth. Petherton, 241.
Callowe, W. Inc : St. Etheldred, Taunton, 22. Pensioned, xxi.
Callow, W. Inc : W. Monkton Hosp., 34. Pensioned, xx.

Came, N.—Bridgwater, 237.
Camell, J. Obit in Butleigh, 65, 248.
Camerarii, W. Obit, 341.
Camerton. Light, 96, 279.
Camfield, J. Obit, 341.
Campion, T.—Shepton Mallet, 134.
Candlesticks.—Ilminster, 3.
———— Dunster, 43.
Canne, H.—Nth. Petherton, 242.
Canner, T. 'Parson, Stoke sub Hamdon, 117.
Cannington. Light, 55, 228. Incumbent pensioned, xix.
———— Ichstoke, 54, 227, xx.
———— Hundred, 199.
Cape, W,—Halse, 32.
Cape, W.—Wellington, 205.
Capell, Mr.—Yatton, 269, 270.
Capner, T.—Dunster, 220.
Caponer. Chapel, 85.
Capper, R.—Sth. Petherton, 181.
Capron, R.—Ashbrittle, 213.
Caraunt, Sir W. Yeovil, 316, 320.
Carde, P.—Bridgwater, 233.
Carhampton. Lights, 45.
———— Manor, 212. Hundred, 222.
———— Note, 224.
Carran, W.—Dunster, 220.
Carowe, Sir Geo. 24.
Carowe, G. Archdeacon, 291, 292.
Carrowe, G. Inc : Whitehall, 107. Pensioned, xx.
Carter, L.—Yeovil, 314.
Carter, W.—Taunton, 203.
Carver, W.—Bridgwater, 231.
Cary. Deanery, 118, 303, 313.
Cary, H.—Almsford, 121.
Castle Cary. Obit, 120, 303.
Castleman, R.—Bridgwater, 230.
Castlyn, R.—Inc : Croscombe, 136.
Castlyn, R. La Mountroy. Pensioned, xxii.
Catcote.—Chantry, 66, 248. Incumbent pensioned, xx.
Cattle. Given, 11, 13, 15, 16, 17, 30, 32, 35, 36, 40, 44, 45, 47, 50, 52, 53, 60, 63, 64, 65, 74, 75, 76, 77, 78, 80, 81, 82, 88, 96, 98, 101, 118, 121, 122, 123, 125, 127, 128, 129, 141, 143, 145.
Chaffcombe. Light, 13.

Index.

Chalices. 1, 3, 5, 6, 9, 14, 18, 19, 20, 21, 22, 23, 24, 26, 30, 31, 34, 36, 37, 43, 47, 48, 49, 52, 53, 54, 56, 57, 58, 59, 60, 62, 63, 66, 67, 69, 70, 71, 72, 74, 77, 82, 84, 88, 90, 91, 92, 93, 95, 98, 100, 101, 102, 103, 105, 108, 109, 110, 113, 115, 116, 120, 126, 127, 133, 135, 139, 140, 146, 154, 156, 157, 158, 159, 160, 161, xv.
Chalkewill. Land in, 168.
Chambour, J. Parson of Aller, 106.
Champayne, J.—Bridgwater, 235.
Champoney, J.—Wedmore, 251, 255.
Champy, E.—Wedmore, 251, 252.
Chancellor, J.—Nunney, 282.
Chanon, R.—Chard, 174.
Chantor, The. Wells Cathedral, 161.
Chantries. 1, 5, 6, 7, 9, 10, 11, 17, 19, 20, 21, 22, 24, 26, 33, 34, 38, 42, 48, 49, 56, 57, 58, 61, 62, 66, 67, 69, 72, 73, 89, 93, 95, 100, 102, 103, 105, 108, 109, 112, 113, 114, 126, 127, 128, 138, 139, 142, 146, 153, 157, 158, 159, 160, 161, 162, 165, 174, 176, 177, 178, 180, 182, 183, 187, 189, 191, 193, 195, 196, 197, 199, 204, 210, 211, 213, 219, 221, 223, 230, 232, 234, 238, 240, 244, 245, 249, 256, 258, 271, 274, 278, 285, 286, 287, 290, 292, 293, 296, 297, 299, 305, 314, 316, 319, 320, 323, 333, 337, 338, 339, 340, viii.
Chapell, J.—Chard, 173.
Chapels. See Free Chapels.
Chapels. 44, 47, 65, 72, 74, 75, 80, 88, 92, 141, 182, 212, 263, 268, 273, 275, 292, 296, 297, 303, 305, 306, 322, 326, 331, 332, ix, xiii.
Chaplyn, W.—Milverton, 214.
Chard.—Fraternity, 5, 172. Incumbent pensioned, xx.
——— St. Katherine's, 5, 174.
——— Vicarage, 5.
——— Communicants, 5.
——— The George Inn, 173.
——— Farnham Down, 173, 175.
Charde, W.—Taunton, 191, 197, 203, 204.
Charde, W.—Charforde, 200.
Charlton Adam.—Chantry, 112, 296.
——— Obit, 297.
Charlton Mackerel.—Chantry, 113, 297. Incumbent pensioned, xx.
Charlton Musgrove. Light, 124.

Chastell, T.—East Horrington, 310.
Cheddar. Trinity Chantry, 72, 256. Incumbent pensioned, xx.
——— Mary, 72, 258.
——— Westbury Park, 72.
——— Obit, 73, 258.
——— Communicants, 73.
——— Vicarage, 73.
Chedzoy. Stipendiary, 55, 229.
——— Light, 55, 229.
——— Curate, 56.
——— Parsonage, 56.
——— Communicants, 56.
Chelington. Chapel, 10.
——— Ilminster Stipends, 166.
——— Rent to E. of Bridgwater, 169.
Chelworth. Light and Obit, 85, 267. Land, 167.
Cherde, J. Abbot of Muchelney, 169.
Cheriton, North. Light and Obit, 143.
——— Fount taper, 325.
Cheriton, South. Free Chapel, 144, 145, 326. Incumbent pensioned, xx.
Cheryton, J.—Wokey, 274.
Chester, P. de. Obit, 341.
Chew Magna. Obit and Light, 87, 269.
Chewton. Light, 98, 282.
——— Communicants, 99.
——— Vicarage, 99.
——— Barrow House in, 282.
Chichester, S. Obit, 341.
Chike, J.—Horton, 170.
Chike, J.—Crikett, 168.
Chilcote, J.—Taunton, 202.
Chilthorn Domer. Land in, 321.
Choke, Sir Richd. Chantry, 93, 274.
Choke, Henry. Chantry, 93, 275.
Choke, Nichs. Chantry, 93, 275.
Churchill. Stoke in, 256.
Church-houses. 85, 112, 150, 186, 218, 220, 276, 297, 331.
Churchyard Wheat. At Martock, 111.
Chursettes. At Shepton B'champ, 298.
Chynne, J. Inc: Aller Chantry, 106. Pensioned, xix.
Clare, T. Obit, Nth. Cadbury, 129.
Clareham. Free Chapel, 88, 269.
Clementes, J.—Bridgwater, 233.
Clenche, E.—Stowell, 144.

350

Index.

Clerk, J. Gent. Inc: Blackford, 70. Pensioned, xix.
Clerke, H.—Philip's Norton, 96, 279.
Clerke, T.—Aller, 105, 290.
Clerke, T.—La Mountroy. Pensioned, xxi.
——— Inc : Corymayle's Chantry, 159.
Clerke, W.—St. Katherine's Bedminster, 91.
Cleve, Old. Light, 47.
——— Lyland Chapel, 47.
——— Note, 224.
Clevedon.—Hydall Chapel, 83, 265.
Clutton. Light, 85, 266.
Clymer, G.—Longleat, 283.
Cobham. Lord, 166, 324.
Cobham, R. Obit, 341.
Cobler, J.—Taunton, 195.
Cockes, E.—Taunton, 190.
Cockes, R.—Wimborne, 293.
Cockes, T.—East Coker, 323.
Cogan, A.—Chard, 174.
Cogen, H.—Yeovil, 316.
Cogon, D.—Bridgwater, 233.
Cogyn, R.—Crukerne, 177.
Cokam, W. Obit, 340.
Coke, J.—Milverton, 215.
Coke, J.—Bedminster, 272.
Coke, W.—Moorlinch, 248.
Coker, East. Burton Chapel, 142.
——— Chantry, 142, 323. Incumbent pensioned, xx.
——— Communicants, 142.
Coker, West.—Curfew, 143.
Cokipe, J.—Axbridge, 229.
Coklington. Light, 129.
Cole. Manor, 127.
——— Lord Zouche of, 306.
Coleford, J.—Bridgwater, 231.
Colforde, J.—Stokegurcy, 226.
Colforde, R.—Taunton, 202.
Colleges. North Cadbury, 130.
——— Mount Roy, 156, 157, 335, xxi.
Colles, L.—Sturminster Marshall, 179.
Collyn, W.—Sth. Petherton, 181.
Collyns, J.—East Coker, 324.
Collyns, W. Vicar, Frome, 104.
Collys, T. Coklington, 129.
Colman, J.—Chaffcombe, 13.
Colyns, J.—Chard, 174.

Colys, H.—Stokegumer, 45.
Combe, J.—Milverton, 213.
Combe, J. de. Obit, 340.
Combe Flory. Chantry, 34, 211. Incumbent pensioned, xx.
——— Chapel, 35, 212.
Combe St. Reigne.—J. Daubeny of, 179.
Communar. Of the Cathedral, 162, 335, 336.
Communicants. 4, 5, 8, 10, 12, 14, 25, 27, 29, 31, 33, 39, 43, 50, 53, 56, 57, 59, 61, 64, 68, 71, 73, 74, 77, 89, 90, 92, 94, 95, 99, 101, 104, 106, 107, 108, 111, 114, 116, 117, 120, 127, 128, 130, 134, 137, 140, 141, 142, 146, 147, 155, xvii.
Compton, W. Obit, 340.
Compton Dando. Light 89, 270.
Compton Martin. Obit 88.
Compton Pauncefoot. Light, 126.
——— Chantry, 126, 305. Incumbent pensioned, xx.
——— Communicants, 127.
——— Parsonage, 127.
Congresbury. Chapel in churchyard, 75.
——— Wyke Chapel, 75.
Constable, J.—Chedzoy, 229.
Cony, H.—Bridgwater, 104, 287.
Cony, M. Inc : Stafordale, 128.
Conybere, J.—Wyveliscombe, 43, 44.
Conye, M. La Mountroy. Pensioned, xxii.
Cooke, J.—Wedmore, 251.
Cooper, R.—Frome, 104, 287.
Cooper, R.—Almsford, 121.
Copes, 1, 66, xvi.
Copston, J.—Curry Mallet, 14, 185.
Coram, W.—Milverton, 36.
Coram, W.—Milverton, 212.
Corbet, J.—Portbury, 271.
Corell, T.—Wedmore, 250.
Corn. Given for a Lamp, 46.
Cornewall, J.—Taunton, 203.
Cornyshe, T.—Kingston, 208.
Cornyshe, T. Vicar, Wedmore, 255.
Corporaces, 3.
Corton. Obit, 325.
Corymales, R.—Chantry, 158, 337.
Cosyn, H.—Wedmore, 251.
Cosyn, J.—Nth. Petherton, 238.
Cosyn, W.—Dean, 69, 255.
Cosington. Light, 64, 247.

Cotherston. *See* Kingston.
Cothins, J.—Bridgwater, 231.
Cottrill, J.—Dunster, 220.
Councell, W. Rent for Smockland, 254.
Courte, S.—Nth. Petherton, 239, 240.
Courtney . . . . Of Bere, 106, 290.
Covent, S.—Milverton, 213.
Cows. *See* Cattle.
Craddock, J.—Yatton, 270.
Craddock, J.—Bridgwater, 236.
Craft, R.—Yeovil, 321.
Crampleyne, J.—Cannington, 228.
Crane, H. and W.—Dunster, 219.
Cranmore, East. Chapel, 118.
——————— Curate, 120.
——————— Note, 313.
Cranmore, West. Light, 118.
——————— Note, 313.
Crediton. Land in, 229.
Creke, H.—Crukerne, 180.
Creton, Dr. Parson of Hunspill, 61.
Cribbe, T. Inc: Nth. Curry, 26. Pensioned, xx.
Cricke, H. Land in Crukerne, 7, 178.
Crickett, 168, 169.
Criston. *See* Cryston.
Crocke, J.—Portbury, 271.
Croft, W.—East Lambrook, 320.
Croke, W.—Yatton, 270.
Cromell, P.—Yeovil, 317.
Crooke, R. Obit, 341.
Croscombe. Guild, 135, 136, 310, 311, 312. Incumbent pensioned, xx, xxiii.
——————— Light and Obit, 136, 312.
——————— Curfew, 136.
——————— Almshouses, 136, 137.
——————— Parsonage, 137.
——————— Communicants, 137.
——————— Barth: Fortescue, lord of, 309.
——————— Lake (Wilts), land in, 311.
Cross. *See* High Cross.
Cross, Silver, 3. Latten, 66.
Crosse, J.—Taunton, 198.
Crowche, W.—Tolveston, 311.
Crowde, T.—Taunton, 202.
Crowe, T.—Wellington, 210.
Cruets, 3, 43, 48.
Crukerne. Deanery, 1, 165, 188.
Crukerne. St. Mary in chyard, 6, 176.

Crukerne. St. Mary in the church, 6, 177. Incumbent pensioned, xx.
——————— Trinity, 7, 178, 180.
——————— Free School, 7.
——————— Lamp, Obit, 8, 180.
——————— Misterton Chapel, 8, 180.
——————— Communicants, 8.
——————— Parsonage, 8.
——————— Marquis of Exeter, Sir Hugh Paulet, 7, 179, 180.
——————— The King lord of, 178, 180.
——————— Anniversary, 180.
Crybbe, T. Inc: N. Cadbury. Pensioned, xix.
Cryche. Lamp, 36.
Cryston. Obits, 79, 261.
Cubbery, J.—Wedmore, 250.
Cudworth, W. Obit in Cath., 341.
Cuffe, K.—Ilminster, 165.
Culbery, A.—Wedmore, 250, 252.
Culve with Stringston. Lights, 51, 225.
Culverwell, W. Inc: W. Buckland, 29. Pensioned, xx, xxiii.
Curates, 5, 14, 29, 53, 56, 57, 61, 64, 74, 77, 89, 92, 99, 106, 111, 117, 120, 128, 134, 140, 142, 146, 155.
Curfew, 136, 143.
Curryer, W.—Bridgwater, 233.
Curry Malet. Chapel, 14, 185.
——————— Parsonage, 14.
——————— Communicants, 14.
——————— Land in, 300.
——————— The King, lord of, 301.
Curry, North. Chantry, 26, 204. Incumbents pensioned, xx.
——————— Brotherhood Priest, 26, 205. Pensioned, xx.
——————— Communicants, 27.
——————— Vicarage, 27.
——————— Rents from, 158, 159, 337, 338.
Curry Rivell. Chantry of Wykeperham, 10, 183.
——————— Light, 11, 184.
——————— Richmond's Chantry, 11, 184.
——————— Weston Chapel, 12.
——————— Bradway Chapel, 12.
——————— Spittle-house in, 12.
——————— Communicants, 12.
——————— Vicarage, 12.
——————— Free School, Wimborne, 11, 184.

Index.

Cutcombe. Light, 46.
——— Stowey of, 48.
——— Pym of, 222.
——— Note, 224.

D.

Daber, M.—Taunton, 194.
Dando, J.—Halotrow, 101, 284.
Dando, T.—Paulton, 98.
Dangerde, J. Vicar, Milverton, 39.
Danyell, J.—Bridgwater, 236.
Danyell, W.—East Coker, 324.
Darling, J.—Taunton, 48, 223.
Darvall, W.—Ditcheat, 129.
David, C.—Taunton, 190.
Davige, T.—Taunton, 191.
Davy, J.—Wimborne, 293.
Davys, T.—West Cranmore, 118.
Dawbeny, H. Lord de Dawbeny, 170, 171.
Dawbeny, J.—Combe St. Reigne, 179.
Day, J.—Bridgwater, 233, 234.
Day, K.—Taunton, 196.
Daye, T. Parson of Yeovilton, 114.
Deanery.—Axbridge, 69, 250, 264.
——— Bath, 148, 328, 332.
——— Bedminster, 83, 265, 277.
——— Bridgwater, 51, 225 242.
——— Cary, 118, 303, 313.
——— Crukerne, 1, 165, 188.
——— Dunster, 40, 217, 224.
——— Frome, 95, 278, 288.
——— Ilchester, 105, 289, 302.
——— Marston, 138, 314, 327.
——— Pawlet, 60, 243, 247.
——— Taunton, 19, 189, 216.
Decher, R.—Taunton, 194.
De la Ware, Lord.—Shepton Malet, 309.
Delegryse, W.—Yeovil, 315.
Denys, W.—Taunton, 200.
Derraunt, R.—La Mountroy. Pensioned, xxi.
Devotion Priest. At Marston Magna, 327.
Dible, J. Inc: Martyn's Chant., 161.
——— La Mountroy. Pensioned, xxi, xxii.
Dible, R.—Nth. Petherton, 241.
Dinder. Light and Obit, 156, 334.
Ditcheat. Light, 129. Stipendiary, 129.

Doble, T.—Taunton, 195.
Dodridge, R.—Stokegumer, 45.
Dole, J.—Parson, Compton Pauncefoot, 127.
Dolman, J.—Taunton, 193.
Dolman, M.—Fyffett, 185.
Donne, N.—Yeovil, 318, 321.
Donster, J.—Chard, 174.
Donyett. Chantry, 17, 187.
Dorington, J. Rent in Bickenell, 301.
Dorset, Marquis of, 108, 276, 292, 296, 298.
Dorston, W.—Sherwood, 201.
Doulting. Lights, 118.
——— Stipendiary, 118.
——— Vicarage, 120.
——— Communicants, 120.
——— Note, 313.
Dove-house. 107, 292.
Dowlish-wake. 168.
Dowlour, J.—Radstock, 281.
Downam, T.—Chelington, 166.
Downed. Light, 119.
——— Curate, 120.
Downes, T.—Croscombe, 313.
Downton, W.—Horsington, 145.
Dowrede, J.—Yeovil, 315.
Dowse, N.—Mark, 253.
Drewe, J.—Charlton Makerell, 113, 297.
Drewe, J. Inc: Charlton M'rell, 113. Pensioned, xx.
Drewe, R.—Milverton, 214.
Drokensford, J. Chantry, 158, 337.
Dudmerton, J. Obit in Bath, 329.
Due, W.—East Knoyle, 305.
Duffelde, B.—Elsworthy, 222.
Duke, A.—Lake, Wilts, 311; 312.
Dulverton, J. Sydenham of, 212, 215.
Dundry, 87. Lamp, 269.
Dune, J.—Morrewe, 60, 243.
Dunne, T.—Coklington, 129.
Dunpole, 167, 168.
Dunster. Deanery, 40, 217, 224.
Dunster. Light, 42, 221.
——— St. Laurence Chantry, 42, 219.
——— Stipendiary, 42, 221.
——— Communicants, 43.
——— Cell, 43.
——— Parsonage, 43.
——— Incumbent pensioned, xx.

Dunster. Church-house, 220.
——— Trinity or St. George, Chantry, 221.
——— Castle, 220, 222.
Duporte, T.—Ilchester, 107, 291.
Durleigh. Manor, 242.
Durcote. Croscombe Guild, 311.
Durston, 197. Buckland Priory, 41, 59, 217.
Dwale, J. Inc : Fodington, 123.
Dyble, J. Chaplain Almshouse Wells, 154. Pensioned, xxi.
Dyer, R.—Bath, 330.
Dyer, W. Inc : Sth. Petherton, 9. Pensioned, xxi.
Dyrant, R. Inc : Burnell's Chantry, 157.
——— Pensioned, xxi.

E.

Easton in Gordano. Obits, 85, 266. Church-house, 266.
Easton Major } *see* Stone Easton.
Easton Minor }
Edgeworth, R. Vicar, St. Cuthbert's, 155.
Edmonde, J.—Yeovil, 319.
Edmondes, J.—Endows Bruton School, 131, 132.
Edward IV, King. Obit, 341.
Edward VI, King. Foundations, 71, 79.
——————— Lord of Crukerne, 7.
——————— Lord of Charlton Adam, 112.
——————— Lord of Durleigh, 242.
Edwards, J. Inc : Taunton, 20.
Edys, J.—Churchill, 256.
Egill, J.—Axbridge, 264.
Einston in Ilminster, 165.
Elice, T. Inc : Norton Hawtfield, 84, 266. Pensioned, xxi.
Elleston, 308.
Elm, R.—Chelworth, 85, 267.
Elmer, J. Vicar of Wellington, 29.
Elsworthy. East and West, 222.
Elworthy. Light, 46. Note, 224.
Elyat, R. Vicar, Marston Magna, 147.
Elyott, T.—Hunspill, 167.
Elys, J.—Milborn Port, 141, 194.
Elys, J.—Chewton, 98, 282.
Emborow. Chapel, 99.
English, J.—Nettlecombe, 223.

Ergeham, R. Chantry, 159, 162, 338, 340. Obt, 341.
Erington, J. Inc : Husey's Chantry, 158.
——————— La Mountroy. Pensioned, xxi.
Erle, J.—Yatton, 270.
Eryle, R. Obit, 341.
Erlyche, T.—Yeovil, 315.
Ernesham, in North Petherton, 240.
Erneshill, Parsonage, 12.
Escheator of Wells Cathedral, 336.
Eston, J.—Limington, 108, 292.
Eston, J.—Taunton, 198.
Evered, W.—Long Ashton, 94, 276.
Evererd, A.—Yeovil, 318.
Everet, J.—Bridgwater, 231.
Everet, R.—Cannington, 228.
Evercreech.—Smaldon in, 132, 307.
Evilton, *see* Yeovilton.
Exeter, Marquis of, Lord of Crukerne, 7, 180.
Exeter. Speke's Chantry in, 15.
Exmoor. The King's Court of, 222.
Exton. Obit, 44.
Eyer, J.—Taunton, 201.

F.

Farewell, S.—Taunton, 198.
Farley Hungerford. Chantry, 95, 278.
——————— Light, 95, 278.
——————— Communicants, 95.
——————— Parsonage, 95.
Farmborough. Land in, 83, 84, 265.
Farrington Gurney.—Chapel, 98.
Farthing, R.—Kingston, 208.
Father, H.—Yeovil, 320.
Fellard, H. Obit, 340.
Fenwyke, W. Inc : Hull's Chantry, 159.
Feoffer, K.—Wedmore, 253.
Ferror, G. Obit, 340.
Fisherton Delamare. Nunney rent from, 283.
Fitz James, E.—Temple Combe, 145, 326.
Fitz James, J. Vicar of Wedmore, 71.
Fitz James, J.—Endows Bruton School, 131, 132.
Fitz Waren, Lord, 191, 194.
Fluet, R. Inc : Stokegurey, 52.
Foche, W.—Yeovil, 316.
Fodington. Chapel, 123, 304.

Ford. Chapel, 64, 247.
Ford, J.—Pitminster, 32.
Forest, S. Vicar Sth. Petherton, 10.
Forte, J.—Sth. Petherton, 181.
Fortescue, B. Lord of Croscombe, 309, 312, 313.
Fount Taper, 17, 325.
Foureaker, W.—Milverton, 214.
Fowey, T.—Frome, 286.
Fox, W.—Whitestaunton, 14.
Framborough, 83, 84, 265.
Francke, J. Obit, 146, 327.
Fraternities, 5, 23, 26, 29, 30, 37, 40, 65, 73, 81, 115, 128, 135, 141, 172, 199, 200, 205, 207, 208, 213, 258, 302, 308, 310, 322.
Frauncis, R. Priston, 86.
Frauncis, Sir W. Combe Flory, 35, 211.
Free Chapels, 8, 14, 53, 54, 58, 64, 70, 78, 83, 84, 88, 90, 91, 102, 107, 112, 116, 117, 123, 144, 181, 185, 226, 227, 238, 247, 261, 265, 266, 269, 273, 285, 291, 298, 299, 304, 310, 326.
Freke, T. Parson, Crukerne, 8.
Freshford. Light, 150, 331.
Frie, L.—Wellington, 206.
Frome. Deanery, 95, 278, 288.
——— St. John, 102, 285. Incumbent pensioned, xx.
——— St. Katherine, 102, 285. Incumbent pensioned, xx.
——— St. Mary, 103, 287.
——— St. Nicholas, 103, 286. Incumbent pensioned, xx.
——— Light, 104, 287.
——— Obit, 104, 287.
——— Vicarage, 104.
——— Communicants, 104.
——— Rent for, from Berkeley, 100.
Frye, J. Gent., Inc: Frome, 102. Pensioned, xx.
Frye, W.—Wellington, 206.
Fulford, Sir.—Watchet, 221.
Furryor, W.—Taunton, 191.
Fyffett. Speke's Chantry, 15, 185.
——— Langford Farm, 186.
——— Land in, 300.
Fyllye, L.—Milverton, 214.
Fyssher, J.—Yatton, 270.
Fyssher, J.—Yeovil, 317.
Fyssher, M.—Taunton, 189.

G.

Gadbury, A.—Frome, 104, 287.
Gale, J.—Taunton, 203.
Gale, R.—Taunton, 203.
Galgaye, J.—Wedmore, 253.
Galhampton.—N. Cadbury, 121, 321.
Galwey, M.—Bridgwater, 234.
Gamage, W.—Bathford, 151.
Gane, R. Inc: Stavordale, 128. Pensioned, xxi.
Gappers, J.—Bridgwater, 233.
Gardiner, J.—Ilchester, 298.
Garland, W.—Sevington, 16.
Garrat, A.—Taunton, 193.
Gatcombe, R.—Bridgwater, 236.
Gaye, J.—Cannington, 227.
Gaye, J.—Keynsham, 274.
Gaylarde, H.—Chiltern Domer, 321.
Gaylarde, J.—Wellington, 206.
Gedge, J. Inc: Crukerne, 7. Pensioned, xx.
Geffery, M.—Bridgwater, 235.
Gent, J. Inc: N. Curry, 27. Pensioned, xx.
Gentes, W.—Frome, 285.
Genys, J.—Martock, 294.
Getter.—Hunspill, 275.
Geyre, J.—Nth. Perrott, 289.
Gibbes, J.—Abbot's Isle, 16.
Gill, J.—Taunton, 198.
Gill, W.—Crukerne, 176.
Gilling, J.—Axbridge, 75, 259.
Gillinge, R.—Hunspill, 167, 275.
Glandfield, T.—Bridgwater, 233.
Glaston, J.—Taunton, 196.
Glastonbury. Jurisdiction of, 65, 248, 249.
Glastonbury. Chantry, 67, 249.
——— Obit land, 67, 249.
——— Almshouses, 67, 68.
——— Communicants, 68.
——— Parsonage, 68.
——— Pension from, 115.
Glose, J.—Taunton, 190.
Glover, J.—Chard, 174.
God, J.—W. Monkton, 33, 211.
Godderde, W.—Wimborne, 293.
Godfrey, W.—Middlezoy, 66, 248.
Godlee, J.—Chantry, 159, 162, 338, 340.
——— Obit, 341.
Godybarne, J.—Curry Rivell, 11, 184.

Godyn, R.—N. Petherton, 242.
Goffe, R.—Dunster, 219.
Golde, J.—Crukerne, 178.
Golde, J.—Hunspill, 243
Golde, M.—Hunspill, 246.
Golde, T.—Westbury, 262.
Golde, T.—Atherston, 166.
Golweige, J.—Berkley, 284.
Goods. Given for Obits, &c., 50, 52, 63, 65, 74, 76, 77, 125, 129, 141.
Goodson, T.—Marston Magna, 147.
Googe, W.—Corton, 144.
Goosebraden. Parsonage, 12.
Gorwey, J.—Wedmore, 253.
Gossome, W.—Dunpoll, 168.
Gotehurst. Obit, 51, 225.
Goffe, R.—Dunster, 219.
Goughe, J.—Bridgwater, 235.
Goughe, W.—Taunton, 192.
Goulde, J.—Porlock, 50, 224.
Gowlde, W.—Bridgwater, 233, 236.
Graunt, A.—Yatton, 269, 270.
Graye, R.—Incumbent Frome, 103.
Graye, S.—Sth. Petherton, 10.
Graynger, T.—Bridgwater, 236.
Gregory, J.—Chard, 174.
Gregory, R.—Bridgwater, 230.
Grendon, W.—Bridgwater, 231, 235.
Grene, H.—Taunton, 191.
Grene, J.—Portbury, 90.
Greneway, J.—Crukerne, 178.
Grevys, J.—Newton St. Loe, 151, 332.
Greynton. Light, 63. Alms, 63.
Grobyn, R.—Yeovil, 316.
Gromes, T.—Yeovil, 316.
Gryffythe, J.—East Brent, 74.
Grynfelde, J. Obit, 341
Grynslade, R.—Lowsborough, 47.
Guilds. 119, 133, 135, 225, 284, 308, 310.
Gully, J. Incumbent, Taunton, 19.
Gunfield, R.—Milverton, 214.
Gunthorpe, J. Dean, 77, 260, 295, 336.
———— Obit, 341.
Gurney, R.—Curry Mallet, 300.
Gye, J. Vicar, Chewton, 99.
Gye, J.—Bridgwater, 236.
Gye, T.—Axbridge, 264.
Gyfford, W.—Wellington, 205, 206.

Gyle, R.—Taunton, 192.
Gyshe, A. Obit, 340.

H.

Hacker, G.—Yeovil, 139, 318.
Hacker, R.—Yeovil, 314, 317, 322.
Hale, R.—Yeovil, 320.
Hall, New.—La Mountroy, 156, 157, 335.
———— Pensions, xxi, xxii.
Hall, R.—Bedminster, 272.
Hall, R. Vicar, Milborn Port, 142.
Hall, T.—Bridgwater, 235.
Halley, W. Lands of, 41.
Halowtro. 101.
Halse. Light, 32.
Ham Green.—Portbury, 271.
Hammon, J.—Kingston, 30.
Hancock, W. Inc: Langport, 115.
Handelay, J.—Bath, 329.
Hannam, W.—Milborne Port, 141, 323.
Hannham, J.—Wimborne, 293.
Harding, R.—Taunton, 196.
Harding, W.—Portbury, 271.
Hardyng, J.—Sparkford, 125.
Hare, J.—Ernesham, 240.
Hare, N.—Taunton, 198.
Hare, T.—Bromfield, 53.
Haridge. In Kilmersdon, 133.
Harris, T. Treasurer, Wells, 109, 294.
Harrys, A.—Yatton, 270.
Harrys, J.—Radstock, 281.
Harrys, R.—Ilminster, 171, 172.
Harryson, G.—E. Coker, 142.
Harryson, R.—E. Coker, 324.
Hartefelde. In Bageworth, 79.
Hartro, J.—Wellington, 167.
Harvey, C.—N. Petherton, 242.
Harvey, W. Inc: Yeovil, 139.
Harvye, J.—Galhampton, 321.
Haryes, J. Gives Light to West Cranmore, 118.
Hasarde, W.—Yeovil, 317.
Hasilshewe, W.—Chantry, 157, 337.
———— Bread, wine, wax for, 162, 340.
Hastell, H.—Culve, 51, 225.
Hatcher, J.—Cannington, 227.
Hause, J.—Taunton, 198.
Hawker, T.—Ilminster, 170.

Index.

Hawkridge. Light and Obit, 40, 217.
Hawkins, J. Stipend, Chedzoy, 55.
Hawkyns, J. Inc : Cheddar, 73.
Hawkyns, R.—Crukerne, 178.
Hawten, T.—Nettlecombe, 222.
Hayes. In Castle Cary, 120.
Hayes, C.—Taunton, 200.
Hayne, T.—Dunster, 219.
Hayne, W.—Yeovil, 315, 317, 319.
Hegens, R.—Taunton, 201.
Helyer, W.—S. Petherton, 181.
Hemmyng, J.—Curry Rivell, 183.
Hengstridge. Light, 145. Land in, 165.
Hensley, ...—Honycote, 218.
Herberd, Sir W.—Crukerne, 8.
Herforde. Bailiff of, 210.
Herforde, J. Obit, 341.
Heriots. In Lake, Wilts, 312.
Hermit.—At Batheaston, 151, 152, 332.
Heron, J.—Chantry, 114, 299.
Hethefeld, R.—Lamp in Cryche, 36.
Hewet, A.—Wellington, 206.
Hichefeld, T.—N. Petherton, 238.
Hickes, J.—Westbury, 262.
High Cross. Fraternity, 23, 199.
Hill, J.—Durcote, 311.
Hill, R. Obit, Ilminster, 4.
Hill, R. Inc : Shepton Mallet, 133. Pensioned, xxi.
Hill, R.—Founds Taunton School, 25.
Hill, T.—Kingston, 208.
Hill, T.—Curry Rivell, 183.
Hilman, J.—Yatton, 270.
Hinderhayes. In Crukerne, 176.
Hinton Bluett. Masses, 86, 267.
Hipsley, J.—Stone Easton, 98.
Hobbes, R.—Abbas Combe, 144.
Hodges, J.—Lyttleton, 83.
Hodges, J.—Milverton, 214.
Hodges, J.—Bridgwater, 231.
Hodges, J.—Wedmore, 252.
Hodges, J.—Farmborough, 265.
Hodges, W. Lord of Charlton Adam, 112.
Hodges, W. Inc : Spekington, 114, 299. Pensioned, xxi.
Hodges, W.—Taunton, 199.
Hodson, R. Inc : Murlinch, 66, 248. Pensioned, xx.

Hody, W.—Wollavington, 63, 244.
Hody, W.—Spaxton, 227.
Holcombe. Obit, 97, 280.
———— Guild land in, 308.
Holcombe, R. Gift to Chelyngton, 10.
Holcombe, T.—Dunster, 219.
Holcombe, T.—Bridgwater, 230.
Holeway, J.—Milborne Port, 141.
Holmes, T.—Taunton, 195.
Holton, ...—Wellington, 167.
Holwaye. In Corton, 144.
Holwaye, J.—King's Brompton, 40.
Holy Cross. Chantry, 139, 320.
Holy Ghost. Chantry, 112.
Holy Water Pot. Murlinch, 66.
Honycote. J. Arundell of, 218.
Hoo, J. Obit, 341.
Hooke, J.—Taunton, 194.
Hoper, R.—Dunster, 219.
Hoper, W.—Durston. 197.
Hoper, W.—Taunton, 200.
Hopkyns, T.—Bridgwater, 237.
Hopkyns, T.—Axbridge, 264.
Hore, L.—Bridgwater, 236.
Horle, J.—N. Petherton, 240.
Hornbloughton. Light, 122, 304.
Horne, J.—Bridgwater, 234.
Horne, R.—Allerford, 218.
Horner, Mr.—134.
Horrington, East. Chapel, 135, 310.
———— Incumbent pensioned, xx, xxiii.
Horsey. Chapel, 57.
Horsey, E. Inc : Crukerne, 8.
Horsey, W.—Taunton, 199, 202.
Horsington. Chapel, 144, 326.
———— Light, 145.
Horsington, J. Obit, Chew, 87.
Hosier, R.—Wimborne School, 184.
Horte, K.—Churchill, 256.
Horte, T. Inc : Stoke Lane, 120.
Horteley. Chapel, 151, 152, 332.
Horton. In Ilminster, 170.
Horton, Mr.—Wolverton, 97, 280.
Hospitals. Wells, 161.
———— Bedminster, 90, 91, 272.
———— W. Monkton, 211.
———— Bath, St. John's, 148, 279.
———— Magdalen, 96.

Hosteler, A.—Bridgwater, 235.
Hotkins, J.—Yeovil, 316.
Houghe, H. Inc: Long Ashton, 93. Pensioned, xix.
Howard, Lord T.—Radstock, 98, 281.
Howell, J.—Axbridge, 264.
Howell, J.—Yeovil, 320.
Howell, M.—Dunster, 220.
Holewaye, W.—E. Coker, 324.
Howper, J.—Wedmore, 251.
Howse, T. Obit, 16.
Howse, W.—N. Petherton, 238.
Huberd, J. Obit, 341.
Huggans, J.—Bath, 330.
Huish. Church, 116.
Hull, A.—Bridgwater, 231.
Hull, R.—Crukerne, 176.
Hull, W.—Chantry, 159, 338.
——— Obit, 340.
Hullet, W.—Crukerne, 177.
Hunshill, W.—Simon Desboro', 166.
Hunspill. St. Mary's, 60, 243.
——— St. Nicholas, 60, 243.
——— Parsonage, 61.
——— Communicants, 61.
——— Land in, 63, 167, 275.
——— Water Court in, 169.
Hunt, N.—Axbridge, 264.
Huntingdom. Earl of, 106, 130, 308.
Hurberton. Devon, 166.
Hurcombe. Milverton, 215.
Hurle, J.—Taunton, 198.
Hurman, J.—Taunton, 194.
Hurne, W. Inc: Shepton Malet, 133. Pensioned, xxi.
Hurtnell, J.—Taunton, 200.
Husey, H.—Chantry, 158, 162, 337, 340.
——— Obit, 341.
——— Incumbents pensioned, xxi.
Hussey, J.—Inc: Bradford, 33. Pensioned, xix.
Husy, B.—Wilts, 126.
Husye, R.—Wellington, 206.
Huyshe, W.—Taunton, 199.
Hydall. Chapel, 83, 265.
Hyll, R.—Brompton Ralph, 46.
Hylling, G. Parson of Ilchester, 107.
Hyndon, W.—Dunster, 220.

I.

Ichstoke. Chapel, 54, 227. Incumbent pensioned, xx.
Ilchester. Deanery, 105, 289, 302.
Ilchester. Gaol, 2.
——— Whitehall, 107, 291. Incumbent pensioned, xx.
——— Michael's. 107, 292.
——— Parsonage, 107.
——— Communicants, 107.
——— Land in, 298.
Illyn.—Penselwood, 125.
Ilminster. St. Katherine's, 1, 165. Incumbent pensioned, xx.
——— Three priests, 2, 166, 168, 169 Incumbents pensioned, xx.
——— St. Mary's and Holy Cross, xx.
——— Abbot of Muchelney, lord of, 2.
——— Duke of Somerset, lord of, 3.
——— Obit, 4.
——— Vicarage, 4.
——— Communicants, 4.
——— Cross Service, 4.
——— Light, 4, 171.
——— Winterhaye in, 170.
Ilmore. 16, 185, 186.
Ilonde, R. *See* Ayland.
Ilstone, J.—Whitestaunton, 14.
Ilton. Light, 13.
Iron, in Nunney Chantry, 100.
Irysheman, Tege.—Bridgwater, 234.
Isaake, T.—Wedmore, 250.
Ivery, T.—N. Curry, 205.

J.

James, R.—Todworth, 175.
Jane, R.—Chaffcombe, 13.
Jeffery, E.—Crukerne, 177.
Jeffray, W.—Crukerne, 176.
Jenkin, A.—Stokegumer, 45.
Jenkyns, W.—Bridgwater, 235.
Jennet, P.—E. Brent, 74.
Jennynge, J.—Ede, Exeter, 195.
Jennys, W.—N. Cheriton, 143
Jenys, J.—Yeovil, 317.

Jesus. Fraternity, 65.
——— Chantry, 20, 139, 193, 319.
——— Chapel, 127, 128, 306.
——— Mass, 71, 256.
Joceline, Bp. Obit, 340.
Johans, J.—Churchill, 256.
John, M.—Milverton, 214.
Johns, P. Inc : Dunster. Pensioned, xx.
Johns, W.—Taunton, 203.
Joyce, R., Cosington, 64, 247.
Joyner, T.—Dunster, 219.
Joyse, R.—Shepton Mallet, 134.
Jugker, J. Inc : Bridgwater, 57. Pensioned, xix.
Jyles.—E. Coker, 324.

K.

Kapc, J.—Taunton, 201.
Kaye, J.—Chard, 175.
Keche, J.—Taunton, 198.
Kele, R.—Martock, 294.
Kelley, J.—N. Petherton, 241.
Kelwaye, R.—Marston Magna, 147, 327.
Kemys, J.—Knolle, 92, 273.
Kendall, G. Inc : Mark, 77.
Keneryge, A.—Hunspill, 61.
Kent, R.—Milverton, 213.
Kerell, C.—Bridgwater, 236.
Kewstoke. 259.
Keyle, T.—Yeovil, 319.
Keyns, H.—Compton Pauncefoot, 126.
Keynsham, 274.
Kilmersdon. Light, 97, 281.
——————— Land, 129, 133, 306.
——————— Earl of Huntingdon, lord of, 308.
Kinge, J.—Wyke St. Laurence, 75.
Kinge, J.—Ditcheat, 129.
Kinge, R.—Wotton, 303.
Kingsbury. Obit, 14, 185.
Kingman, J.—S. Petherton, 9, 181.
Kingson (Taunton). Brotherhood priest, 29, 30, 208.
Kingston (Yeovil), 140, 259, 314, 319.
Kington Manfield. Light, 122.
Kirkeby, R.—Wedmore, 252.
Knappe, 337.
Knight, J.—Staplegrove, 31, 209.

Knolle. Light, 15.
Knolle. Bedminster, 91, 273. Incumbent pensioned, xx.
Knolle. Long Sutton, 113, 297.
Knolling, R.—Devon, 166.
Knoyle.—East Wilts, 305.
Kyche, W.—Bickenell, 299.
Kyes, J.—Stoke sub Hamdon, 298.
Kyle, T.—Yeovil, 319.
Kynman, A.—Doulting, 118.
Kyrys, N.—Bridgwater, 232.
Kytforde, J.—Taunton, 199.
Kytson, T.—Curate, Curry Mallet, 14.

L.

Lache, J.—Churchill, 256.
Lacy, R.—Chedzoy, 229.
Lake.—Wilts, 311.
Lambert, A.—Taunton, 195.
Lambert, J.—Wedmore, 253.
Lambert, W.—Trull, 192.
Lambroke, East, 320.
Lamps. 8, 9, 36, 37, 46, 162, 171, 180, 182, 184, 187, 217, 224, 226, 228, 229, 242, 269, 270, 273, 276, 278, 283, 312, 330, 332, 340.
Lamyat. Lights, 123.
Lancaster. Duchy of, 242.
Lancaster, W.—Milverton, 215.
Lane, J.—Trull, 192.
Langford Budvill. Light, 36, 212.
——————— Land, 210, 215.
Langdon, J. Inc : N. Petherton, 59.
Langham, in Chard. 174.
Langley, R. Inc : Hunspill, 60.
Langmend, 168.
Langport. Chantry, 114, 299.
———— Fraternity, 115, 302.
———— Bridge, 115.
———— Vicarage, 116.
———— Communicants, 116.
Lappe, W.—Wynsham, 17.
Larbeck, H. See Lyrbecke.
Larder, J.—Charlton Adam, 112, 296.
Laverton. Light, 96, 279.
Lawrence, J.—Crukerne, 176, 178.
Lawrence, J.—Bridgwater, 236.

Lawrence, R. Inc: Nunney, 100. Pensioned, xxi.
Lawrence, R. Inc: Porlock, 49.
Lawrence, J.—Taunton, 197.
Lead, 6, 26, 38, 84, 90, 93, 98, 101, 116, 135, 141, 142. xvii.
Leche, W.—Crukerne, 176.
Legatt, J.—Spaxton, 227.
Legge, R.—Chard, 172, 173.
Leighe, P.—Taunton, 191.
Letford, A.—Maperton, 123.
Leversage, R.—Frome, 286, 287.
Lewys, W.—Batheaston, 151, 152, 332.
Leye, J.—Long Ashton, 275.
Lights, 4, 8, 9, 10, 11, 13, 15, 16, 17, 31, 32, 36, 37, 38, 40, 42, 43, 45, 46, 47, 50, 51, 52, 53, 54, 55, 57, 59, 63, 64, 65, 68, 75, 78, 79, 81, 83, 85, 86, 87, 89, 92, 94, 95, 96, 97, 98, 99, 100, 101, 104, 105, 106, 108, 111, 118, 119, 121, 122, 123, 124, 125, 126, 127, 129, 130, 134, 136, 141, 143, 144, 145, 148, 150, 151, 152, 156, 180, 182, 184, 185, 186, 187, 209, 212, 216, 217, 221, 226, 227, 229, 237, 246, 247, 261, 262, 265, 266, 267, 268, 276, 279, 280, 281, 282, 283, 284, 287, 289, 290, 291, 292, 293, 303, 304, 307, 309, 312, 323, 325, 328, 330, 331, 332, 334.
Limington. Chantry, 108. Incumbent pensioned, xx.
——— Light, 108.
——— Parsonage, 108.
——— Communicants, 108.
Lloyd, J. Inc: Banwell, 74. Pensioned, xix.
Locke, J.—Yeovil, 315.
Locke, T. Vicar, Ilminster, 4.
Lockeston, J.—W. Bradley, 124.
Lokey, T.—Clutton, 85, 266.
London. Merchant Tailors' Co., 309.
London. Richard, Bp. of, 131, 132.
London, A.—Long Ashton, 275.
London, H. Obit, 341.
London, W. Dean, Obit, 341.
London, W. Inc: Wedmore, 69, 250.
Longe, A.—Wedmore, 250.
Longe, J.—Bridgwater, 235.
Longe, R.—Taunton, 202.
Longe, R.—Milborne Port, 141, 323
Longlode. Chapel, 110, 296.
Lopen. Chapel, 9, 10, 182.

Lounders, R. Obit, 341.
Loveles.—Taunton, 190.
Lovell, A.—Cannington, 227.
Lovell, J.—E. Horrington, 310.
Lovell, T.—Churchill, 257.
Loveney, J.—Greynton, 63.
Lowdon, K.—Dunster, 220.
Lowlys, W. Dunster, 220.
Lowsborough. Chapel, 46, 47.
Loxton. Light, 79, 262.
Loxton, J.—E. Horrington, 310.
Lugge, J.—Road, 282.
Lurpoole, J.—Inc: Frome, 103. Pensioned, xx.
Luttrell, Sir J. 212, 220, 221.
Lyddon, R.—Taunton, 190.
Lyde, C.—Saltcombe, 166.
Lydeard, Epi. Chapel, 35, 207.
Lydeard St. Lawrence. Chapel, 32.
Lydford, West. Obit, 122.
Lye, J.—Limington, 108, 293.
Lye, T.—Yeovil, 315.
Lyland. Chapel, 47.
Lylstock. Chapel, 52, 53.
Lymplesham. Stipendiary, 76.
Lynde, A. de la.—Ilminster, 169.
Lyne, C.—Milverton, 214.
Lynge. Chapel, 53, 226.
Lynke, T.—Wellington, 206.
Lyolle, J.—Dunster, 220.
Lyone, W.—Lymplesham, 76.
Lyons, T.—Long Ashton, 276.
Lyrbecke, H. Inc: Yeovil, 138. Pensioned, xxii.
Lyson, W. Vicar, Yatton, 89.
Lyttleton. Light, 83, 265. Land in, 101.
Lyttleton, R. de. Obit, 341.
Lyuage, J.—Bathford, 151.

M.

Maget, A. Inc: Taunton, 22. Pensioned, xxi.
Maide, J.—Churchill, 256.
Make, T.—Dunster, 220.
Makeway, D.—Bridgwater, 235.
Malet, Baldwin. 255.
Mallet F. Parson of Yatton, 89.
Mambre, L. Obit, 341.
Mante.—Taunton, 193.

Maperton. Light, 123.
Maple, W.—W. Pennard, 68.
Marchaunt, J.—Yeovil, 318.
Marchaunt, W.—Wells, 257.
Mark. St. Mary's, 76, 260.
───── Devotion priest, 77.
───── Communicants, 77.
───── Parsonage 77.
Marke, J.—Ilminster, 171, 172.
Marlent, R.—Taunton, 201.
Marler, R.—Taunton, 193.
Marney, Lord.—Radstock, 98, 281.
Marsh. Chapel, 140, 322.
Marshe, J.—Yeovil, 316.
Marshall, A. Parson of Gosebraden, 12.
Marshall, J.—See, 167.
Marshall, R.—Chard, 173.
Marshalls, R.—Hornbloton, 122.
Marston. Deanery, 138, 314, 327.
Marston Bigot. Light, 97, 280.
Marston Magna. Communicants, 147.
───────── Vicarage, 147.
───────── Stipendiary, 147, 327.
Martell, J. Obit, 341.
Marten, J.—E. Horrington, 310.
Marteyne, J.—Taunton, 200.
Martock. Stipendiary, 109, 294, 295.
───── Chantry, 109, 293.
───── Light, 111, 295.
───── Longlode Chapel, 110, 296.
───── Stapleton Chapel, 111, 296.
───── Parsonage, 111.
───── Communicants, 111.
Martocke, J. Obit, 341.
Martyn. Chantry, 161, 339.
Martyn, J.—Weston Bamfelde, 125.
Martyn, J.—Hunspill, 243.
Martyn, J.—Long Ashton, 275.
Martyn, R.—Bridgwater, 236.
Marys, J.—Stokegurcy, 226.
Marys, J.—Axbridge, 259.
Mason, J.—Crukerne, 179.
Mason, W.—Yeovil, 321.
Masses. 86, 124, 267, 329.
Master, W.—Martock, 294.
Mathewe, T.—Abbot's Isle, 16.
Mattock, J. Inc: Cheddar, 72. Pensioned, xx.
Maunsell, M.—N. Petherton, 59, 241, 242.

Mawdley, R. Lord of Nunney, 283
Mawhoude, J.—Dunster, 220.
Mayden Newton, 179.
Mayow, W. Obit in Croscombe, 313.
Meade, J.—Yeovil, 320.
Meire, W.—Milborne Port, 141.
Mellysbury, L. Obit, 341.
Merchant Tailors, 309.
Meriet. Lamp, 184.
───── Hannyng Haye, 180.
Meryatte. Chapel, 93, 275.
───── Light, 94, 276.
Meryfeld, R.—Crukerne, 177.
Meryfelde, R. Inc: Wells, 158.
Messeld, J.—See, 168.
Messolyn, J.—Taunton, 195.
Michell, J. Inc: Crukerne, 6, 176.
Michell, J.—Chelington, 166.
Michell, J.—N. Petherton, 240.
Michell, R.—Bridgwater, 231, 232.
Michell, T. Inc: Ilminster, 2, 170. Pensioned, xx.
Michell, W.—Wedmore, 253.
Michell's Bow. Chapel, 107, 292.
Middlezoy. Fraternity, 65. Land, 66.
Midsomer Norton. Guild, 101, 102, 284.
Milborne Port. Fraternity, 141, 322.
───────── Light, 141, 323.
───────── Vicarage, 142.
───────── Communicants, 142.
Milborne, P.—Wedmore, 254.
Milbourne, G.—E. Pennard, 124.
Miller, W.—Compton Martin, 88.
Milton. Light, 127.
Milverton. Chantry, 38, 213.
───── Light, 38, 216.
───── Communicants, 39.
───── Vicarage, 39.
───── Lands, 36, 212.
Misterton. Chapel, 8, 180.
Mitchell, J.—Nettlecombe, 222.
Mody, J.—Berkley, 284.
Mogridge, J.—Ashbrittle, 37.
Mogridge, R.—Wellington, 206.
Monday, H.—Chard, 174.
Mondye, J.—Wellington, 206.
Money. For Lights, 68, 119, 122, 123, 124, 125, 144, 151.

Money. For Obits, 125.
——. For Stipend, 75, 79, 118, 121, 147.
Monkton, West. St. Mary's, 33, 211.
—————— St. Margaret's, 34, 211. Incumbent pensioned, xx.
Montacute. Light, 105, 289.
More. Manor, 76, 260.
More, J. Inc: Ailston Sutton, 78. Pensioned, xix.
More, J. Incumbent, East Horrington, xxiii.
More, J.—Bridgwater, 233.
More, R.—Wedmore, 251.
Morell, M.—Bridgwater, 230.
Moreton, Mr.—E. Coker, 324.
Morfeld, J.—Yatton, 270.
Morforde, J.—Curry Rivell, 183.
Morice, R. Inc: Wedmore, 71. Pensioned, xxi.
Morice, W.—Wedmore, 250.
Morley, J.—Bridgwater, 235.
Morne, W.—Knolle, 15.
Morowe, J.—Axbridge, 264.
Morrice, N.—N. Petherton, 239.
Morrow Mass, 157, 160.
Mors, T.—Taunton, 195.
Moryce, W. King's Surveyor, 342.
Moryn, W.—Chard, 173.
Mount Roy College. 156, 157, 160, 161, 335.
—————— Pensions, xxi, xxii.
Muchelney. Abbots of, 2.
—————— John Cherde, 169.
—————— John Sherborne, 170, 171, 172.
Muddesleighe, T.—Taunton, 189.
Murlinch. Stowell in, 64.
—————— Vestments, 66.
—————— Catcote, 66, 248.
Mychell's Bow. Chapel, 107, 292.
Mylbourne, G.—E. Pennard, 305.
Mylle, J.—Taunton, 203.
Myller, J.—Shepton Mallet, 309.
Myller, . . .—Road, 282.
Mynchinborough. Rent to, 336.

N.

Nabbe, A. and J. Obits, 341.
Nabbe, J. Obit, Kingsbury, 14, 185.
Nedes, W.—Kingston, 259.
Nethercote, J.—Bridgwater, 232.

Nethewaye, J.—Bridgwater, 231.
Nethewaye. Chapel, Taunton, 22, 23.
Netilton, R. Obit, 341.
Nettlecombe. St. John's, 48, 221, 342. Incumbent pensioned, xxi.
—————— Obit, 48, 223.
Newbery, H. and R.—Taunton, 189, 195.
Newborowe, J.—Berkley, 284.
Newerton, 194.
Newes, J. Inc: Bubwith's Chantry, 160.
—————— La Mountroy. Pensioned, xxii.
New Hall. See Mount Roy.
Newman, J.—Bridgwater, 233.
Newman, W.—Frome, 285.
Newnam. Manor, 244, 245, 246.
Newport, J.—Bridgwater, 194, 231.
Newton. Rent from, 160.
Newton, J. Parson of Chedzoy, 56.
Newton, T. Lord of Swell, 301.
Newton Placey. Chantry, 58, 238. Incumbent pensioned, xxi. Land, 301.
Newton St. Loe. Light, 151, 332.
Nobbe, W. Vicar of Banwell, 74.
Noke, T.—Bridgwater, 237.
Noriche. Land in, 311.
Norman, A.—Wollavington, 244, 245, 246.
Norman, J.—Bridgwater, 237.
Northon, M.—Axbridge, 259.
Northover. Light, 106, 290.
—————— Land, 291.
Northumberland, Earl of, 119, 120.
Norton St. Philips. Light, 96, 279.
—————— Obit, 96.
Norton Hawtfield. Chapel, 84, 266. Incumbent pensioned, xxi.
Norton, W.—N. Petherton, 241.
Nosse, T.—Taunton, 193.
Nowell, R.—N. Petherton, 238.
Nunney. Chantry, 100, 282. Incumbent pensioned, xxi.
—————— Light, 101, 283.
—————— Parsonage, 101.
—————— Communicants, 101.
—————— R. Mawdley of. Lord St. John of, 283.
Nurse, S. Stipendiary, Martock, 110.
Nyneacre, H.—Taunton, 203.
Nyned Flory. Obits, 35, 36.
Nythe.—In N. Curry, 27.

O.

Obits, 4, 8, 11, 14, 15, 16, 31, 35, 36, 40, 43, 46, 48, 50, 51, 52, 57, 65, 67, 73, 75, 79, 80, 81, 84, 85, 87, 88, 90, 94, 96, 97, 99, 100, 104, 112, 120, 122, 125, 126, 128, 129, 134, 136, 143, 144, 146, 149, 150, 154, 162, 185, 209, 217, 223, 258, 259, 261, 262, 264, 265, 266, 267, 268, 269, 276, 280, 283, 284, 287, 297, 303, 306, 309, 312, 325, 327, 328, 329, 330, 334, 340, 341.
Odcombe, W. Obit, 341.
Oder, J.—Bridgwater, 232.
Okar, W.—Durston, 197.
Oke. Lord of, 192, 193.
Olyver, R. Inc: Ilminster, 3. Pensioned, xx.
Olyver, R.—Milverton, 214.
Oram, W.—Horsington, 145.
Oratories. xiii.
Orcharde, L. Inc: Pitney, 140.
Oriel College. Trent, 146, 327.
Ormonde, Earl of. Lord of Hunspill, 169.
Ornaments. 1, 3, 66. xvi.
Osborne, M. Obit, Frome, 104, 287.
Osen, J.—Blagdon, 261.
Our Lady. *See* St. Mary.
Overwere. Chapel, 78, 261.
Owkye, J.—Ditcheat, 129.
Oxford.—Oriel College, 146, 327.

P.

Page, J.—Bridgwater, 230, 235.
Pale, J.—Chard, 174.
Pale, N.—Dunpole, 167.
Pale, W.—Chelworth, 167.
Palwebbe, J.—S. Brent, 75.
Pardoner, J.—Taunton, 192.
Parker, J.—Yeovil, 316, 317.
Parker, J.—Stone Easton, 275.
Parson, J.—Pitminster, 31.
Parsones, R. Obit, 341.
Parsons, R.—Philip's Norton, 96.
Parsons, R.—Chelworth, 85, 267.
Parsons, W.—Cheddar, 258.
Partridge, J. Inc: Wedmore, 70. Pensioned, xxi.
Pascall Light, 100.

Pascall, J.—Yatton, 270.
Paul, R.—Chelworth, 167.
Paule, R.—Shepton B'cham, 16.
Paulet. Sir H., 7, 8, 170, 179, 180.
Paulet. Sir W. *See* Lord St. John.
Paulton. Light, 98.
——— Curate, 99.
Pauncefoot, Sir W. Of Compton P., 126.
Pawle, J. Inc: Bubwith's Chantry, 160.
——— La Mountroy. Pensioned, xxii.
Pawlet. Deanery, 60, 243, 247. *See* Poulet.
Pax, 24, 36, 43, 48, 66.
Payne, H.—Chard, 175.
Payne, J. Of Christon, 79, 261.
Payne, T. Of Rolston, 259.
Payton, A. Norton Hawtfield, 84, 266.
Pears, J.—Taunton, 195.
Penarde, J.—Wedmore, 251.
Pennard, East. Stone Chapel, 124, 305.
Pennard, West. Light, 68.
Penny, G.—E. Coker, 324.
Penselwood. Obit, 125.
Pensions. From Bruton Priory, 28.
——— From Glastonbury, 115.
——— List of, xix, xxii.
Percy, W.—Taunton, 189.
Perott, North. Light, 10*, 289.
——— Duke of Somerset, Lord of, 289.
Pers, G.—Taunton, 200, 201.
Pery, A. Obit, Nynhed Flory, 35.
Pery, J.—Crukerne, 177.
Perys, J.—Milverton, 215.
Petherton, North. Newton Placey, 58, 238. Incumbent pensioned, xxi.
——— Sherston, 58, 238. Incumbent pensioned, xxi.
——— St. Mary, 58, 240. Incumbent pensioned, xxi.
——— Light, 59, 242.
——— Chantry, void, 59.
——— Communicants, 59.
——— Parsonage 59.
——— Tithe from eight inhabitants, 239.
——— Warren, 239. Land in, 300.
Petherton, South. St. John's, 8, 181.
——— Chantry, 9, 182. Incumbent pensioned, xxi.
——— Light, 9, 182.

Petherton, South. Lopen Chapel, 9, 182.
―――――――― Chelington Chapel, 10.
―――――――― Communicants, 10.
―――――――― Parsonage, 10.
Petre, R.—Chard, 175.
Phelps, R.—Hunspill, 243.
Pheppyn, J.—Taunton, 198.
Philipson, R. Vicar, E. Coker, 142.
Phillippes, T. Of Montacute, 105, 289.
Pierce, A.—Compton Pauncefoot, 126.
Piers, A.—Taunton, 196.
Piers, J.—Exton, 44.
Piers, W. Inc : Chard, 5. Pensioned, xx.
Pike, T.—Martock, 295.
Pilkington, J. Vicar, Chard, 5.
Pillesdon. Dorset, 178.
Pimpell, S. Obit, 341.
Pitcombe. Rent from, 127.
Pitminster. Stipendiary, 30, 208.
――――――― Vicarage, 31.
――――――― Communictants 31.
――――――― Tenement in, 32.
Pitney. Chapel, 140.
Pittarde.—Crukerne, 177.
Pittock, J.—Bridgwater, 233.
Plate. Given for prayers, 36.
Plumer, E.—Taunton, 202.
Poculchurch. Rectory, 159, 338.
Podger, W.—Whitestaunton, 15.
Pole, J. de la. Obit, 341.
Pollarde, J. Rector, Shepton Mallet, 134.
Poole, J.—Cannington, 228.
Poole, J. Inc : Ilminster, 3, 170. Pensioned, xx.
Polsham. Chapel, 155.
Pomery, E.—Taunton, 191.
Poor. Gift to, 2, 4, 5, 23, 24, 49, 63, 87, 134, 136, 146, 154, 163.
Popham, A.—41, 240, 242.
Popwell, J. Inc : Ford, 64.
Porlock. Chantries, 49, 223.
―――――― Light and Obit, 50, 224.
―――――― Parsonage, 50.
―――――― Communicants, 50.
Portaunt, W.—Holcombe, 97, 280.
Portbury. St. Mary, 89, 271. Pension, xxi.
―――――― St. Katherine, 90, 271.
―――――― Obit and Trentalls, 90, 272.
―――――― Vicarage, 90.

Portbury. Communicants, 90.
―――――― Ham Green in, 271.
Porter, S. Inc : Yatton, 88. Pensioned, xxii.
Portman, Sir W.—240, 301.
Portshead in Gordano. Caponer Chapel, 85.
Poulet. Light, 63, 246. *See* Pawlet.
Powell, W. Inc : Portbury, 89. Pensioned, xxi.
Prate, J.—N. Petherton, 238.
Precos, C. Obit, 341.
Prior, R.—Taunton, 198.
Prior, T.—Wimborne, 293.
Priste, M.—Blagdon, 261.
Provost, The. Of Wells, 5.
Prydyll, R. Inc : Wollavington, 63. Pensioned, xxii.
Pryston. Light, 86, 267.
Pulle. Light and Obit, 125.
Pulton. Light, 121, 303.
Pulton. *See* Wotton.
Pye, J.—N. Petherton, 239.
Pye, J.—Nunney, 282.
Pyers, J.—Bridgwater, 231.
Pyers, W.—Wellington, 167.
Pykesaishe. In Martock, 111, 295.
Pyley. In Trull, 192, 193.
Pym. Of Cutcombe, 222.
Pynne, J.—Yeovil, 314.
Pyper, T.—Curry Rivel, 11.
Pysmarshe. In Chard, 174.
Pytcombe. Lord Zouche of, 306.
Pytman, J.—Yeovil, 315.
Pytman, R.—Yardley, 263.
Pyttarde, W.—Yeovil, 321.
Pytte, J. Inc : Taunton, 25. Pensioned, xxi.

Q.

Quanto, J.—Milverton, 213.
Quantoxhead, East. Light, 51.
Queen, The.—Yeovil manor, 316, 322.
Quintyne, W. Obit, 341.

R.

Radbere, T.—Ilminster, 170.
Radstock. Light, 98, 281.

Index.

dstock. Lord Marney, 281.
Randall, J.—Wedmore, 252.
Randall, W.—Taunton, 193.
Raplyn, T. Inc: Limington, 108. Pensioned, xx.
Ratclyffe, R.—Banwell, 258.
Raufe, R.—N. Petherton, 239.
Rawys, R.—Pillesdon, 178.
Rede, J.—Gotehurst, 51, 225.
Rede, W.—Taunton, 202.
Redman, Mr.—Milverton, 38.
Reede, R. Vicar, Taunton, 25.
Rendall, T.—N. Cadbury, 130.
Renyon, R. Endows Stipend, 132, 307.
Renyon, R.—Wedmore, 255.
Reynolds, M.—Milverton, 213.
Richard I, King. Obit, 341.
Richardes, E.—Milverton, 215.
Riche, N.—Hunspill, 167.
Riche, T.—Kilmersdon, 281.
Richmond and Derby. Countess of, 184.
Rimington. *See* Rymton.
Riesse, H.—Castle Cary, 120.
Rigby, T. Inc: Wells, 159.
Rippe, J. Inc: Ilminster, 169, 171.
Road. Light, 99, 282.
——— Hawkins Ham, 280.
Robertes, J.—Yeovil, 321.
Rocle, J. Obit, Nynld Flory, 36.
Rodney, J.—Barrow Farm, 274.
Rogers, Sir Edwd. 294.
Rogers, Sir John. 51, 225, 309.
Rolston. Thos. Payne of, 259.
Romynall, H. Obit, 341.
Roo, C.—Wedmore, 250.
Rose, J. Vicar, N. Petherton, 59.
Rose, J.—Durcote, 311.
Rosyter, T. Vicar, Langport, 116.
Roughe, J. Vicar, Long Ashton, 94.
Rousewell, C.—Shepton B'cham, 186.
Rousewell, R.—N. Petherton, 241.
Rousewell, T. Vicar, Bradford, 33.
Roveles-thing.—Portbury, 271.
Rowde, M.—Bridgwater, 236.
Rowe, H. *See* Houghe and Roughe.
Rowlande, R.—Crukerne, 177
Rowse, J.—Shepton Mallet, 308.
Royall, H.—Hengstridge, 145.

Royall, T.—Wellington, 206.
Roydon, R.—Taunton, 191.
Russe, H. Obit, Castle Cary, 303.
Russel, J.—Kilmersdon, 281.
Russell, R.—Wimborne, 293.
Russell, T. Inc: Charlton Adam, 112, 296.
Russell, W.—Portbury, 89.
Rydon. In N. Petherton, 59.
Rymton. Suit to the Queen, 210.
Rynon.—Croscombe, 313.
Ryse, J. Vicar, Dunster, 43.
Ryvers, J.—N. Petherton, 238.

S.

Sadler, J.—Bridgwater, 231.
Safferton, W. Inc: Curry Rivell, 12.
Safyn.—Carhampton, 45.
Saints. Dedications.
——— Andrew. Taunton, 21, 196. Frome, 102.
——— Andrie. Wells, 155.
——— Anne. Wedmore, 69, 254, 255.
——— Decumans. Watchet, 47, 224.
——— Etheldred. Taunton, 22, 199.
——— George. Bridgwater, 56, 230.
——— ——— Banwell, 74, 259.
——— ——— Dunster, 221.
———James. Curry Malet, 14, 185.
———John Baptist. Nettlecombe, 48, 221.
——— ——— Wollavington, 61, 244.
——— ——— Frome, 102, 285.
——— ——— Shepton Mallet, 133, 308.
——— John. Sth Petherton, 8, 181.
——— ——— Milborne Port, 141, 322.
——— ——— Bath, 148.
——— ——— Wells, 161, 339.
———John Jerusalem. Buckland, 41.
——— Katherine. Ilminster, 1, 165; Chard, 5, 174; Brompton Regis, 40; Wollavington, 62, 245; Bedminster, 90, 272; Portbury, 90, 271; Frome, 102, 285; Batheaston, 151, 152.
——— Laurence. Dunster, 42, 219.
——— Leonard. Farley Hungerford, 95, 278.
——— Margaret. West Monkton, 34, 211.
——— Martin. Cathedral, 161, 339.

Saint. Mary. Aller, 105, 290; Ashbrittle, 37, 213; Ashton, 93, 275; Bridgwater, 56, 232; Burnham, 80; Burton, 142; Caponer, 85; Chard, 5, 172; Cheddar, 72, 258; Crukerne, 6, 176, 177; Frome, 103, 287; Hunspill, 60, 243; Ilminster, 2, 166; Limington, 108, 292; Martock, 111; Lydeard Epi., 35, 207; Mark, 76, 260; Midsomer Norton, 101, 284; Milverton, 38, 213; Monkton, 33, 211; Petherton, Nth 58, 240; Portbury, 89, 271; Stokegurcy, 52, 225; Taunton, 19, 24, 189, 202; Trulle, 32; Wedmore, 69, 250; Weston (Glaston), 66, 248; Whitestanton, 14; Wynford, 86, 268; Wynscombe, 81; Yeovil, 138, 316.
―――― Mary Magdalen. Bath, 96, 279.
―――― Michael. Borough, 53, 226.
―――― ―――― Congresbury, 75.
―――― Nicholas. Frome, 103, 286.
―――― ―――― Hunspill, 60, 243
―――― ―――― Stoke sub Hamdon, 116, 298.
―――― ―――― Taunton, 19, 191.
―――― Peter. Bisport, 92, 273.
―――― Sepulchre. Taunton, 23, 200.
―――― Thomas Beckyt. Southwaye, 155.
St. John, Lord. 240, 283, 301.
St. Leger, Lord. 275.
St. Lowe, Sir John. Churchill, 257.
Salop, R. de. Obit, 341.
Saltcombe. Devon, 166.
Salter, E. Inc: Milverton, 38.
Sampford Brett. Light, 45. Rent, 222. Note, 224.
Sampford Parva. 210.
Sampford. Chapel, Winscombe, 82, 263.
Sampforde, H.—Combe Flory, 211.
Sampforde, N. Vicar, Bedminster, 92.
Sampson, W.—Milborne Port, 141.
Sandforde, R. Vicar, Portbury, 90.
Sandylan. Chapel, 35, 207.
Sanforde, R.—Sth Petherton, 9, 182.
Sarum, G. Obit, 340.
Satchell, J.—Stoke sub Hamdon, 165.
Sauchet, T.—Bratton, 122.
Saunderley, E.—Taunton, 201.
Saunders, J. Inc: Wykerperham, 11. Pensioned, xxii.

Saunders, J. Inc: Bridgwater, 56. Pensioned, xix.
Saunders, J. Inc: Sherston, 58. Pensioned, xxi.
Saunders, J—Taunton, 190.
Saunders, J.—Bridgwater, 237.
Saunders, R.—N. Cheriton, 143.
Savage, J.—Radstock, 281.
Saye, P.—Endows Stipend, Bagewonth, 79.
Scare J.—N. Petherton, 241.
Schools. Bridgwater, 57.
―――― Bruton, 131.
―――― Crukerne, 7, 178, 180.
―――― Taunton, "most bewtyfull," 25.
―――― Wimborne, 11, 184.
―――― Wells, 163.
Score, E.—Taunton, 197.
See. Land in, 167, 168.
Selbrone, N.—Obit, 340.
Selvey, W.—Frome, 285.
Selwoode, J.—Chard, 173, 174, 175.
Selworthy. Light, Obit, 40, 217.
―――― Church-house, 218.
Seman, J. Inc: Taunton, 20. Pensioned, xxi.
Sepulchre. Fraternity, Taunton, 23, 200.
Sergaunt, W.—Yatton, 270.
Sergaunt, W.—Wincanton, 306.
Serney. Land in, 192, 193.
Serser, H.—Coklington, 129.
Service. St. Mary, St. Nicholas, Hunspill, 60.
St. Anne, Wedmore, 69.
Sevington. Stipendiary, 16. Land in, 182.
Sewer, B.—Yeovil, 319.
Sexton, J.—Dunster, 219.
Shade, N.—Marston Magna, 147.
Shakle, T. Inc: Ichstock, 54. Pensioned, xx.
Shaldon, R.—Taunton, 200.
Shapcotte, W.—Wellington, 167.
Shaston. Dorset, 305.
Sheep. Given for Lights, 51, 118, 152.
Shelcroft, J.—Wedmore, 252.
Sheperde, J. Inc: Bubwith's Chantry, 160.
―――― ―――― La Mountroy. Pensioned, xxii.
Sheperde, W. Inc: Ergeham's Chantry, 160.
―――― ―――― La Mountroy. Pensioned, xxii.
Shepton B'cham. Light, 16, 186. Tithes, 298.
Shepton Mallet. Stipendiary, 132, 307. Pensioned, xxi.
―――― Guild, 133, 134, 308, 309. Incumbent pensioned, xxi.

Index.

Shepton Mallet. Light, 134, 309.
——— Guild money, 134.
——— Parsonage, 134.
———' Croscombe Obit, 312.
Sherborn. Almshouse, 126.
Sherborn, J. Abbot, Muchelney, 4, 170, 171.
Sheres, J.—Curry Rivell, 11, 184.
Sherelaund, W.—Milverton, 215.
Sherland, J—Ashbrittle, 37, 213.
Sherlocke, R.—Crukerne, 178.
Sherston. Chapel, 58, 238.
Sherston, T.—Bath, 329.
Sherwoode, H.—Bruton, 131.
Shete, J. Inc : Trent, 146, 326. Pensioned, xxi.
Ship. Silver, Ilminster, 3.
Shipman.—Portbury, 90.
Shokerwyke. Chapel, 151, 331.
Shorye, W.—Bridgwater, 233, 234.
Silke, R.—Cannington, 227.
Simon Desborough.—Devon, 166.
Singleton, W.—Milverton, 214.
Skelton, A.—Bridgwater, 236.
Skoryar, W.—Taunton, 194.
Skose, J.—Taunton, 202.
Skotte, J.—Taunton, 189.
Skute, J. Inc : Martock, 109.
Skynner, A.—Brushford, 46.
Slade, W. Inc : E. Coker, 142. Pensioned, xx.
Slape, W.—Yeovil, 317.
Slympe, R. Inc : Chard, 5.
Smaldon. In Evercreech, 132, 134.
Smockland. Wedmore, 254.
Smyth, J.—Chard, 172.
Smyth, J.—Bridgwater, 235.
Smyth, R.—Trull, 192.
Smythe, J. Of Long Ashton, 276.
Smythe, R.—Philip's Norton, 96.
Smythwicke, J.—Marston Bigot, 97, 280.
Sole, C.—Dunster, 220.
Solye, P.—Taunton, 202, 203.
Somer, W.—Yatton, 270.
Somerset, Duke of. 3, 4, 77, 133, 166, 228, 289.
Somerton, J.—E. Horrington, 310.
Somerton, R.—Bridgwater, 236.
Sooge, W.—Holwaye, 325.
Sooper, J.—Ilminster, 172.
Sooper, J.—Taunton, 190, 195.
Southcote.—Hawkridge, 40, 217.

Southover. Chapel of St. Andrie, 155.
Southwaye. Chapel, 155.
Southyoke. Manor, 76, 260.
Sparkford. Light, 125.
Sparrer, A.—Bedminster, 272.
Spaxton. Light, 54, 227.
——— Land, 55, 228.
Spede, J.—Yeovil, 318.
Speke, Sir John.—Chantry, Exeter, 15, 185.
Speke, Sir Thos. 168, 169, 170, 210.
Spekington. Chapel, 114, 299. Incumbent pensioned, xxi.
Spicer, J. Inc : Wellington, 28. Pension from Bruton, 28. Pensioned, xxi.
Spicer, J.—Ilminster, 170.
Spicer, J.—Bridgwater, 236.
Spiringe, J.—Taunton, 191.
Spittle House. Curry Rivell, 12.
Sprete, J.—Milverton, 215.
Spring, J.—Trull, 192.
Sprye, R. Inc : Combe Flory, 34. Pensioned, xx.
——— Inc : Godlee's Chantry, 159.
——— La Mountroy. Pensioned, xxii.
Squyre, J.—Wedmore, 253.
Stadyn, J.—Taunton, 198.
Staplegrove. Obit, 31, 209.
Stapleton. Chapel, 111, 296.
Stavordale. Chantries and Obit, 127, 128, 306. Incumbents pensioned, xxi, xxii.
Stayners, J.—Bridgwater, 234.
Sterte, W.—Hunspill, 61.
Stevens, T.—Long Ashton, 276.
Stevinges.—Honycote, 218.
Stevyn, J. E. Quantoxhead, 51.
Stewarde, A.—Chedzoy, 229.
Steympe, R.—Chard, 174.
Steyninge, E.—Stokegurcy, 226.
Steyninge.—Selworthy, 218.
Stibbe, E.—Dunster, 219.
Stipendiaries. 2, 16, 28, 42, 55, 71, 74, 75, 76, 77, 78, 79, 82, 93, 101, 109, 110, 118, 121, 129, 132, 147, 153, 154, 166, 169, 205, 2c8, 221, 229, 255, 284, 294, 295, 306, 307, 333, 334.
Stoford. 308.
Stoke, B.—Masses, Bath, 329, 330.
Stoke. In Churchill, 256.
Stokegumer. Light, 45. Note, 224.

Stokegurcy. Light, 52, 226.
——— Guild, 52, 225.
——— Curate, 53.
——— Parsonage, 53.
——— Communicants, 53.
——— Land in, 54, 227, 244, 245, 246.
Stoke St. Michael. Guild, 119, 120. Land in, 308. Note, 313.
Stoke sub Hamdon. Chapel, 116, 117, 298.
——————— Parsonage, 117.
——————— Communicants, 117.
——————— Land in, 165.
Stoke Trister. Light, 125.
Stonderd, J.—Taunton, 196.
Stone. Chapel, 124, 305.
Stone Easton. Chapels, 98.
——————— Land in, 275.
Stone, R. Inc : Woolavington, 62.
Stone, W.—Spaxton, 55, 228.
Stone, W. Endows Stipend, Wedmore, 71, 255.
Stone, W.—Yeovil, 319, 321.
Storke, T. Obit, Corton, 144, 325.
Stortewatte. J. Chantry, 161, 162, 339, 340.
Stourton, Lord, 97, 280, 286.
Stowell. Light, 144.
Stower Estover. Bridgwater lands in, 57, 237.
Stowey. Of Cutcombe, 48.
Stowyng, O. Vicar, Stokegurcy, 53.
Strange, J.—Stokegurcy, 226.
Strange, J.—E. Coker, 325.
Stratton, M. de. Obit, 341.
Street. Obit, 67, 249.
Strengston. *See* Culve.
Strete, T. Vicar, Bridgwater, 57.
Stronge, R.—Crediton, 229.
Stuckey, R.—Yeovil, 321.
Sturgyes, J. Road, 99, 282.
Sturminster Marshall, 179.
Styckelynche, J.—Yeovil, 318.
Suarpon, T. Inc : Winscombe, 82. Pensioned, xxii.
Suffolk. Duke of, 110, 111, 186, 295.
Surraye, J. Obit, 341.
Sutton, J.—Dunster, 220.
Sutton, Long. Chapels, 113, 297.
Swane, R. Obit in Cath., 341.
Swayne, J.—Alverton, 251.
Swayne, W. Obit, Bath, 329.

Swell. Light, 13. Land, 300.
Swinger, J.—N. Petherton, 242.
Swinger, W.—Taunton, 192.
Swinges. Chantry, Taunton, 21, 197.
Swyton, R.—Taunton, 202.
Sydenham, J. Of Dulverton, 36, 212, 215, 218.
Sydernym, W.—Lowsborough, 47.
Syme, W.—Sth Brent, 75.
Symes, J.—Yeovil, 140, 321.
Symys, T.—Chard, 172.

T.

Tanner. Chantry, Wells, 153, 333.
Tanner, J.—Taunton, 199, 200.
Tanner, W.—Milverton, 38, 216.
Taunton. Deanery, 19, 189, 216.
Taunton. Almshouse, 20.
——— St. Andrew's, 21, 196. Incumbent pensioned, xxi.
——— Ethelred, 22, 199. Incumbent pensioned, xxi.
——— High Cross, 23, 199.
——— Jesus, 20, 193.
——— Mary Magdalen, 19, 189.
——— Mary in St. James', 24, 202. Incumbent pensioned, xxi.
——— Nethewayes, 22, 23.
——— Nicholas, 19, 191. Incumbent pensioned, xxi.
——— Sepulchre, 23, 24, 200. Incumbent pensioned, xxi.
——— Swinges, 21, 197. Incumbent pensioned, xxi.
——— Trinity, 20, 195. Incumbent pensioned, xxi.
——— School, "most bewtyfull," 25.
——— Vicarage, 25.
——— Communicants, 25.
——— Land in, 48, 291.
Taylor, A.—Swell, 300.
Taylor, E.—Bath, 330.
Taylor, J.—Wellington, 28.
Taylor, T.—Fyffett, 185, 186, 300.
Taylor, W.—Lylstock, 52.
Teffoner, R. Obit, 341.
Tellisford, 95, 278.

Index.

Teme, J. Inc: N. Cadbury, pensioned, xix.
Temple Combe: E. Fitz James of, 145.
Terryll, R.—Bridgwater, 232, 237.
Tille, R.—Sth. Brent, 75.
Todworth. In Chard, 175.
Toogood, J.—193, 238.
Toker, R.—Stokegurcy, 226.
Toker, R.—Chard, 173, 175.
Toker, R.—Milverton, 214.
Toller, J. Inc: Bridgwater, 56. Pensioned, xix.
Tolveston. Land in, 311, 312.
Torre, P.—Porlock, 50.
Touche, J.—Chard, 175.
Thicke, R.—Stoke Trister, 125.
Thomas, J.—Dynder, 156, 334.
Thorne, T.—Ilminster, 169.
Thorne, T.—Milverton, 215.
Thornfalcon. Light, 31, 209.
Thresher, A.—Dunpole, 168.
Thresher, E.—Yeovil, 320.
Thynne, Sir John.—Longleat, 283.
Tracy, W.—Bridgwater, 230.
Traske, N.—E. Coker, 325.
Trent. Chantry, 146, 326, 327. Incumbent pensioned, xxi.
——— Parsonage, 146.
——— Communicants, 146.
Trent, S.—Yeovil, 315.
Trentals, 90, 272.
Trevylyan, W. Inc: Yeovil, 140. Pensioned, xxii.
Trinity, 7, 20, 57, 62, 72, 107, 138, 178, 180, 195, 221, 234, 245, 256, 291, 308, 314.
Trowbridge, 104, 287.
Trowbridge, J. Inc: Wells, 161.
Trowbridge, W. Inc: Taunton, 24, 201. Pensioned, xxi.
Trull. Service, 32.
——— Serney, Pyley, and Oke in, 192, 193.
Trystram.—Backwell, 87, 268.
Tubbe, H.—Sevington, 16.
Tucker, A.—Compton Dando, 89, 270.
Tucker, R.—Chard, 173.
Tucker, T.—Tellisford, 278.
Tuckefield, A.—Rector, Trent, 146.
Tuckswell. Manor, 228.
Turnor, E. Rector, Combe Flory, 35, 212.
Turnor, J. Inc: Wells, 153. Pensioned, xxi.

Turnour, J.—Yeovil, 320.
Twynhoo, E.—Frome, 286, 294.
Tychet, Sir John, Lord Audeley, 244, 245, 246.
Tydell, R.—Bridgwater, 230.
Tyke, J.—E. Horrington, 310.
Tyler, R.—Shokerwyke, 151, 331.
Tyler, T.—Chard, 173.
Tylley, J.—Spaxton, 227.
Tynkwell, R.—Wedmore, 251.
Tyrell, W.—Wyke St. Laurence, 75.
Tyse, R.—Beer Crocombe, 17, 187.

U.

Ughorowe. Devon, 223.
Upton. Chapel, 113, 297.
Upton, G.—Croscombe, 313.
Urche, W.—Winscombe, 82.
Uskavayte, J.—Wells, 311.

V.

Vant, J.—Bridgwater, 231.
Vaughan, Mr., 86.
Vauston, A.—Yeovil, 319.
Vele, T.—Yeovil, 321.
Verser, R. Inc: N. Petherton, 59. Pensioned, xxi.
Vestments, 3, 66.
Vigar, J.—Philip's Norton, 96.
Vigar, J.—Hemington, 279.
Vowles, J.—Wedmore, 252.
Voysey, A.—Dunster, 219.
Voysey, W.—Trull, 32.
Vuall, H.—Taunton, 202.
Vynpeny, J.—Yatton, 270.
Vyny, W.—Taunton, 197.
Vynycombe, J.—N. Petherton, 238.

W.

Wadham, J. 1, 2, 165.
Wadham, N. 170.
Wadham, W. 301.
Wake, J.—Bridgwater, 235.
Walden, L.—Ilminster, 4.
Walden, R.—Chalkwill and Dunpoll, 168.

Index.

Wale, T.—Yatton, 270.
Walford, A.—Taunton, 195, 199.
Walford, E.—Stokegurcy, 52, 225.
Walker, N. Rector, N. Cadbury, 130, 307.
Walketon. Lights, 87, 268.
Walle, T.—Churchill, 257.
Walles, R.—Taunton, 199.
Walshe, R.—Fyffed, 301.
Walshe, W.—Bridgwater, 234.
Walter, J.—Yeovil, 318.
Walthiane, ...—Taunton, 190.
Walton. Chapel, 67.
Walys, G.—Bridgwater, 233.
Wamperfelde, W.—Yatton, 269, 270.
Warre, G.—Downed, 119.
Warre, J.—Nyned Flory, 35, 36.
Warryn, W.—Wellington, 167.
Warshesade, A.—Old Cleve, 47.
Watchet. Land in, 42, 221.
———— Chapel, 47.
———— Sir — Fulford of, 221.
Water Court. Held at Hunspill, 169.
Watkyns, W.—South Brent, 75.
Wattes, W.—Maiden Newton, 179.
Wax. For Chantries in the Cathedral, 162, 340.
Weaver, R. *See* Verser.
Webbe, R.—Chard, 173.
Webbe, W.—Ilminster, 169.
Webber, R.—Brompton Raffe, 46.
Wedmore. St. Mary, 69, 250.
———— St. Anne, 69, 264. Incumbent pensioned, xxi.
———— Stipendiary, 71, 255. Pensioned, xxi.
———— Jesus Mass, 71, 256.
———— Vicarage, 71.
———— Communicants, 71.
———— Blackford Chapel, 70, 254.
———— King's Place in, 254.
———— Smockland in, 254.
Welche, J. Parson, Curry Malet, 14.
Welfare, I.—Yeovil, 315.
Wellington. Stipendiary, 28, 205. Pensioned, xxi.
———— Communicants, 29.
———— Parsonage, 29.
———— Land in, 167, 168, 207, 210.
Wellington, D. de. Obit, 341.
Wellington, W. Chantry, 158, 162, 337, 340.
———— Obit, 341.

Welles, R. Inc: Wells, 160.
Wells, City. Almshouse, 154, 155, 263, 334. Chaplain pensioned, xxi. Chapels —St. Andrie, St. Paul of Polsham, Southwaye or St. Thomas Bekyt, 155; Dynder, 156. St. John's Hospital, 161, 336. Grammar School, 163. Lands in, 257, 311. George Inn, 335, 336.
———— St. Cuthbert's. Tanner's Chantry, 153, 333. Incumbent pensioned, xxi. Stipendiaries, 153, 154, 333. Obits, 154, 334. Curate, 155; Parsonage, 155; Communicants, 155.
———— Cathedral. La Mountroy College, 156, 157, 160, 161, 335, 336. Pensions, xxi. A Chantry, 160, 339; Bubwith's, 160, 162, 338, 340. Burnell and Hasilshewe, 157, 162, 337, 340. Corymale and Drokensford, 158, 337. Ergham's, 157, 159, 162, 338, 340; Godlee's, 159, 162, 338, 340. Hull's, 159, 338. Husey's, 158, 162, 337, 340. Martyn's, 161, 339. Precentor's, 161, 339. Stortwates, 161, 162, 339, 340. Wellington's, 158, 162, 337, 340. A Lamp, 162, 340. Obits, 162, 340, 341. Bread, wine and wax, 162, 340.
Wells. Archdeacon, 116, 160; Adrian, Bp. of, 132; Dean and Chapter, 26, 27, 45, 69, 155, 163, 204, 253, 254, 322; Gunthorpe, 77, 295; Provost, 5; Communar, 162, 335, 336. Total, 342.
Wellysworthy, T. Inc: Glastonbury, 67.
Welshe, T.—Bridgwater, 234.
Welsheman, J.—Chard, 172.
Were Overy. *See* Overwere.
West, R.—Portbury, 271.
West, T.—Milverton, 214.
Westbury. Church, 263. Park fence, 72.
———— Obit, 80, 262.
Weston. Chapel, Curry Rivell, 12.
Weston. (Glaston).—St. Mary, 66, 248.
Weston juxta Bath. Obit, 150, 331.
Westoner, J.—Wedmore, 255.
Wether, J.—Exton, 44.

Wether, R. Inc: Wells, 160.
Wethercote, J.—Taunton, 196.
Wetheridge, J.—*See* Wyther.
Wever, P.—Curry Mallet, 300.
Wharton, R.—Taunton, 199.
Whatley, J. Obit, 340.
Wheler, J.—Keynsham, 274.
Wheler, S.—N. Petherton, 241, 242.
Whippey, T.—Keynsham, 274.
Whipping, W.—E. Coker, 323.
Whitby, J.—Yeovil, 315, 317.
White, M. Inc: Donyet, 18.
White, R.—Hunspill, 63, 246.
White, W. Inc: N. Cadbury, 130.
Whitehall. Chapel, Ilchester, 107, 291.
Whiteherte, H.—Taunton, 195.
Whitehorn, J.—Dunpoll, 168.
Whitehorne, J.—Chard, 174.
Whites, J.—Charlton Musgrove, 124.
Whitestaunton. Guild, 14.
———————— Obit, 15.
Whitewell, J. Inc: Yeovil, 139. Pensioned, xxii.
Whitinge, J.—N. Petherton, 59, 240.
Whyte, C.—Wells, 257.
Whyte, J.—See, 167.
Whyte, J.—Taunton, 203.
Whyte, T.—Vicar, Cheddar, 73.
Whyte, W.—Blagdon, 261.
Whyte, 'W.—N. Petherton, 300.
Whyteman, J.—Chard, 175.
Whytenoll, W.—Yeovil, 318.
Whyttyns, — .—Selworthy, 218.
Wiche, E.—N. Curry, 205.
Wilkins, ...—Taunton, 195, 196.
Wilkins, T.—W. Pennard, 68.
Williams, E.—E. Coker, 324.
Williams, H.—Rector, Bedminster, 92.
Williams, J.—Dunster, 220.
Williams, P.—Wedmore, 250.
Willman, J.—Ilminster, 4.
Wilmote, J.—Ilminster, 170.
Wilton. Land in, 197.
Wimborne. School, 11, 184.
Wincanton. Obit, 128, 306.
———————— Parsonage, 128.
———————— Communicants, 128.
Winchester. Bishop of, 30, 31, 190.
Wine. For Cathedral Chantries, 162, 340.

Winford. Chapel, 86, 268.
Winscombe. Fraternity, 81. Incumbent pensioned, xxii.
———————— Stipendiary, 82.
———————— Chapel, 82, 263.
Winsham. Light and Fount taper, 17, 187.
Withamstede, W. Obit, 340.
Withycombe. Light, 43. Manor, 222. Note, 224.
Withypool. *See* Hawkridge.
Wiveliscombe. Note, 224.
———————— Obit, 43.
———————— Chapel, 44.
Wocar, R.—Winscombe, 82.
Woky. Land in, 263, 274.
Wolfe, J.—Yeovil, 316.
Wollavington. St. John, 61, 244.
———————— Katherine, 62, 245. Incumbent pensioned, xxii.
———————— Trinity, 62, 245. Incumbent pensioned, xxii.
Wolverton. Light, 97, 280.
Wood, A.—Ashbrittle, 37, 213.
Woode, J. Obit, Curry Rivell, 11.
Woode, J.—Bridgwater, 232.
Woodes, H. Rector, Farley Hungerford, 95.
Woodhill, W.—Yeovil, 315, 321.
Woodward, T.—Batheaston, 152.
Workman, J.—Taunton, 196.
Worth, J.—Newton Placey, 302.
Wotes, J.—N. Cadbury, 130.
Wotton. Chapel, 121, 303.
Wraxall. Obit, 84, 265.
———————— Rectory, 162, 339.
Wyatt, J.—Yeovil, 318.
Wydecombe, R.—Kilmersdon, 281.
Wykeperham. Chantry, 10, 11. Incumbent pensioned, xxii.
Wyke St. Laurence. Light, 75.
Wykes, W.—Nyned Flory, 36.
Wylkyns, R. Inc: Taunton, 21. Pensioned, xxi.
Wylle, R.—Wellington, 167.
Wylles, T.—E. Coker, 324.
Wylley, T.—Banwell, 259.
Wylly, J.—S. Petherton, 181.
Wymbery, R. Inc: Wollavington, 62. Pensioned, xxii.
Wynesland, J.—Taunton, 202.
Wynyfred.—T. Lyons of, 276.

Index.

Wynter, E.—N. Petherton, 240.
Wysse, A.—Compton Pauncefoot, 126.
Wytham. Friary land, 72.
Wyther, J. Inc: Nettlecombe, 48. Pensioned, xxi.
Wyther, R.—Taunton, 189.

Y.

Yardley. Land in, 263.
Yarlington. Light, 121, 304.
Yatton. Chapels, 88, 269. Incumbent pensioned, xxii.
―――― Vicarage, 88, 89, 270.
―――― Communicants, 89.
Yde, R.—Taunton, 193.
Yeovil. St. Mary, 138, 316. Incumbent pensioned, xxii. Trinity, 138, 314. Incumbent pensioned, xxii. Holy Cross, 139, 320. Incumbent pensioned, xxii. Jesus, 139, 319; Pitney or Marsh Chapel, 140, 322; Parsonage, 140; Communicants, 141; Chapel in ch. yard, 141; Almshouse, 141; School, 141; Lands in, 308.
Yeovilton. Parsonage, 114; Communicants, 114. Spekington Chapel, 114, 299.
Yetton, T.—Incumbent, Stoke Lane, 120.
Yonge, A.—Yeovil, 315.
Yonge, J.—Taunton, 194.
Young, T.—King's Brompton, 40.

Z.

Zely, W.—N. Curry, 205.
Zouche, Lord —Stavordale, 127, 128, 303, 306.
Zule, R.—Milverton, 214.

www.ingramcontent.com/pod-product-compliance
Lightning Source LLC
Chambersburg PA
CBHW051242300426
44114CB00011B/862